# *FLY FISHING FOR TROUT*

# FLY FISHING FOR TROUT

## A Guide for Beginners

*by*

## Richard W. Talleur

Lyons & Burford, Publishers

Printed in the United States of America

10 9 8 7 6 5 4 3 2 1

Library of Congress Cataloging-in-Publication Data

Talleur, Richard W.
    Fly fishing for trout: a guide for beginners/
by Richard W. Talleur.
            p.        cm.
    Originally published: Piscataway, NJ:
Winchester Press, © 1987.
    Includes bibliographical references (p. 278) and index.
    ISBN 1-55821-218-3
    1. Fly fishing.  2. Trout fishing.  I. Title.
[SH456.T34 1993]
799.1'755—dc20                                    92-34993
                                                  CIP

PUBLISHER'S NOTE
*To the 1993 Edition*

A full twenty years ago, when I was editing the Sportsmen's Classics series at Crown Publishers, I got a manuscript from someone about whom I had heard nothing. It was an introduction to fly fishing—but one quite different from the handbooks common then and even more common today.

The book was *Fly Fishing for Trout*, then subtitled "A Guide for Adult Beginners," by Richard W. Talleur, and I was immediately impressed by two qualities: how truly good a teacher the author was and how frank, personal, and earthy a voice he had.

Here was no pap, no purple prose, no pretending, no peacocking. This was a fly fisherman talking to beginning adults about what he knew well; here was a man sharing a lifetime of experience, often through wonderful anecdotes that you knew had to be true. And the instruction was exactly right: practical, economical, genuinely helpful.

But I had decided to leave Crown that year and they were going to abandon my beloved little series; so I had to send the manuscript back— but with words of admiration, a bit of advice, and some warm best wishes. Happily, I was soon able to watch the good fortunes of Dick's book as it got published by Winchester Press, then—some years later—revised and cast into a larger format, the one here.

Now I have contracted to publish it under the Lyons & Burford imprint and several people have asked whether, after twenty years, the book is still valid. Re-reading it recently, I was struck by how fresh and pertinent it still is, how much I'd have liked such a book when I began to fly fish, and even after I had done so for a while. For it is, I think, as relevant today as it was then, and as valid for today's fly fishers as it was for those in the 1970s.

So it is with great pleasure that we're reprinting it for the first time in trade paperback format, for novices today and fly fishermen of the future. And I am proud, finally, to become the publisher of record for *Fly Fishing for Trout*, a book that squarely stands with the other books we have of Dick's on our list: *The Fly Tyer's Primer*, *The Versatile Fly Tyer*, and *Talleur's Dry-Fly Handbook*.

—Nick Lyons

# CONTENTS

# FOREWORD

Back in 1974, my first book, *Fly-Fishing for Trout—A Guide for Adult Beginners* was published. It brought me a lot of new friends and earned perhaps more accolades than were due me. It also created a certain amount of pressure. I was invited to speak at numerous functions, and people started walking up to me and asking all sorts of questions. As any angling author will attest, this causes one to do a lot of rethinking and redefining of his ideas and convictions about fly-fishing. It stimulates learning; there is nothing like teaching to motivate further research and refreshment of knowledge on the part of the teacher.

So it is that this book came into being. It began as a revision of *Adult Beginners* and it is that. It is also a substantially more comprehensive work, bringing into focus the intensive and delightful experiences of my last fifteen years, since the old book was submitted for publication. While still essentially a basic book which starts at the beginning and concentrates on fundamentals, it takes the reader considerably further into the subtleties and intricasies of this constantly evolving game.

Why would one write this sort of book? After all, there are lots of other ones out there, both old and new. In my case, there is a dual motivation. First, I love teaching people about fly-fishing and second, I'm dreadfully afraid that unless fly-fishing continues to grow in stature and importance, we will lose it. There are those whose attitude toward a natural resource is that its only value lies in its conversion to financial profit—for them, of course. They are relentless and insidious. They are experts at political karate and since it is within the political arena that we must confront them, we have no choice but to excel at that game also. Hence the frequent references throughout the book to conservation and environmental considerations, which are summarized in Chapter Twelve.

One of the things I've tried to avoid doing is to make the book into a quasi-catalog because catalogs get out of date very quickly. However, I do make reference to certain products because I believe them to be exemplary—in fact, archetypical—within their particular sphere of functionality. This assists me in informing readers of needs they may not yet know they will have and how to go about filling them. Certainly product evolution will continue, so please don't try to use this book as a catalog because that's not what it is.

There are several people I must thank for extraordinary assistance and contributions. Bill Hunter, the proprietor of Hunters' Angling Supplies in New Boston, N.H., somehow found time to read major portions of the manuscript and his suggestions were of great value. The inimitable Lefty Kreh was kind enough to provide insightful feedback on the casting section, which included turning me on to his videotape. Lee and Joan Wulff provided technical data on their unique Triangle Taper [Reg.TM] fly line and permitted reprinting of the line chart from their catalog. Bruce Richards of Scientific Anglers sent a most helpful care package of information on fly lines. Tom Rosenbauer and John Harder of the Orvis Company provided technical data on leader materials and knots and arranged for me to shoot some photos on premises. I certainly hope I haven't forgotten anyone.

Oh yes, the artist and the photographic people. I simply can't say enough about Ernie Lussier; I'm still in awe of his ability. What incredible luck to be able to work with such an artist! Thanks, Ernie, for letting me mess up your 1986 summer vacation. To Matt Vinciguerra, my gratitude for his personal support and excellent photography, particularly the casting sequences. To Kimberly Vigars, my heart-felt thanks for additional photography and superb photoprocessing. After serving as Kim's darkroom assistant, I fully appreciate how difficult it is to produce really great prints. It's most refreshing to work with a young person who cares about quality and has the talent and energy to excel.

And particular thanks to Poul Jorgensen, one of the world's true genius-level fly-tyers. Poul took time out from his own book project to do the color page photography, with myself acting as chief assistant and cheerleader. I must also congratulate Poul on his taste in women, he being my sister's "Significant Other". (I think that's the current term.)

Enough. Let's go fishing!

Dick Talleur

# FLY FISHING FOR TROUT

# CHAPTER I _____

# The Worm Turns

I don't know how you embarked on your fishing career—if indeed you have—but I can tell you that I began mine with a spinning rod, minnows and worms. In the early 1950s, that was the thing to do. Most of us evolved into fly-fishermen. The rest, with rare exceptions, dropped out.

As I reflect on my bait-fishing days, my only regret is the number of fish I killed. None was actually wasted, but they would have been far more valuable in the stream than in my freezer. Of course, killing your catch is primarily a matter of attitude, not method. However, it is a proven fact that natural baits and multihooked lures usually injure a trout to the extent that it cannot be released with any assurance of survival.

Today, many aspiring anglers start right out with a fly rod. This is quite feasible now because of the vast amount of information, coaching and training currently available. This was not so when I was getting started. The few experienced fly-fishermen on my home streams were generally not very nice to worm washers such as I and were very protective of their skills and crafts. In retrospect, I now realize that in many cases their reticence to share knowledge stemmed from the fact that they really didn't know what in hell they were doing.

My bait-fishing experiences served as an excellent foundation, and while untutored and ill equipped, I was still able to catch trout on flies from the first day out. This somewhat amazes me, as my woeful casting technique was exacerbated by lousy, poorly matched tackle. Perhaps the trout cooperated in an effort to get one more wormer off the river. In any case, two of their number drew short straws that day, and I was started on a journey which will not end until my final cast has been retrieved.

Whether or not you have a bait-fishing background, I believe it will be most helpful if I draw some parallels between certain common baits and the methodologies for fishing them and corresponding fly-fishing techniques. First, let's consider the worm.

A worm, while lively and wriggly, is capable of very limited self-locomotion in the water. Consequently, the presentation is generally dead-drift, on or near the bottom. As one learns to exploit the natural current patterns, it simply becomes a matter of letting the stream take the bait to the fish. Unless frightened or dormant, the trout will be deployed in spots where food is abundant and easily obtained. This being the natural situation, the angler's task is to manage the presentation with the lightest rein, exerting as little influence as is required to cause the worm to come to the fish's station in as unaffected a manner as possible.

Basic nymph fishing is very much like worm fishing. Nymphs are the larval forms of aquatic insects. With certain exceptions—and we will discuss these in a later chapter—nymphs also do a lot of wriggling without moving themselves through the water all that much. Thus, the nymph fisherman uses the dead-drift worm-fishing technique much of the time. That was about the only instruction I was armed with that first day—and it worked! I've learned other ways of presenting nymph imitations in the ensuing years, but dead-drift remains my fundamental tactic.

Minnows, another commonly used bait, were my particular favorite, and I was *deadly* with them. Larger trout become increasingly carnivorous, and that was the quarry I was after. I liked the technique of manipulating or "swimming" the minnow, emulating its natural movements—or even better, the way it might behave if crippled. This is an all too effective method for taking sizable trout, and I am relieved that it isn't nearly as widely practiced as it once was.

Fly-fishermen seek to imitate bait fish with streamer flies. While the dry fly is my preference, I must confess a great love for streamer fishing. It can be *so* exciting, as vicious strikes are provoked from huge trout which have passed up the last ten thousand dry flies that floated by. The techniques and tactics differ considerably from both nymph and dry-fly fishing. It's a marvelous weapon to have in one's angling arsenal.

There is no real bait-fishing counterpart to dry-fly fishing. I'm aware that certain terrestrial insects, such as grasshoppers and crickets, can be impaled on a light wire hook and fished on the surface with fly tackle. This is more difficult—and, I would think, less effective—than properly presenting an imitation of the particular insect.

Yes, dry-fly fishing is certainly special, to the extent that its more fanatical advocates treat it as a religion. Still, we use what is essentially the worm-fishing technique to present a dry fly, except that we do it on top. What I'm saying here is that we try to get the dry fly to float naturally and unaffectedly on the surface, just as we try to let that worm drift along the stream bed. Very rarely does a situation call for any movement to be imparted to a dry fly by the fisherman.

One of the most important things I learned from bait fishing was the effect of water temperature on the trouts' feeding habits. We were all early-season, early-morning devotees back then. The night before opening day I was like a nine-year-old on Christmas Eve. Often, I plowed through snowbanks at gray dawn for the privilege of being the first to cast my bait into a swollen, discolored river. Sometimes it paid off—there's a lot to be said for offering a trout its first mouthful of the day. However, there were many, many mornings when I would have been much better off staying in bed.

Eventually I began to realize that trout don't eat all that much when the water is extremely cold. Sometimes I would go fishless until mid-morning, then begin to get strikes as the sun warmed the water. I learned to love May far better than April. And I began to reach out for knowledge and understanding, as I became dimly aware that being competent with spinning tackle and organic baits was not the sum total of the trout-fishing experience.

As I resolutely lugged my zip gun and bait bucket around the Catskills, I began to notice a family of anglers quite different from myself. These, of course, were fly-fishermen. I enjoyed watching them cast. I did *not* enjoy having them catch fish after fish under my very nose when I couldn't prick a lip. My bait-fishing buddies sneered and made derisive comments, but I was fascinated. And as it developed, I had come together with my Karma.

Before examining the various and diverse skills and technologies fly-fishing requires, let's consider for a moment what one can realistically expect from trout fishing today. When I began fishing in the mid-1950s I often encountered older guys who loved nothing better than to tell me how poor fishing conditions were, compared to the Good Old Days. My early readings tended to confirm this. The legendary figures of the sport—men like Theodore Gordon, George LaBranche, Ed Hewitt, and Ray Bergman—wrote of great multitudes of large trout gorging themselves on blanket hatches of stream insects. They talked about trout in terms of pounds, rather than inches. Usually, they had the rivers to themselves, more or less. Unquestionably, the Golden Age of American Trout Fishing, which I define as the period from 1900 to the beginning of World War II, was a wonderful time to be alive with a fly rod in one's hand.

The realization that I had been a couple of generations too late did not cause me to love trout fishing any less. I worked hard on the development of skills, learned the streams, and did quite well. I hoped conditions would improve. Eventually, I tried to have a personal impact on such improvement, releasing my catch and working with environmental organizations.

Three decades later, I look back and ask myself whether conditions have gotten better or worse. The answer is that they have gotten better *and* worse. We have more pollution, more habitat destruction, more encroachment and more crowding. That's worse. On the other hand, we have far better resource management, much less spin and bait fishing and a host of enlightened "angling-philes" who treat our precious fish as lovers rather than adversaries. That's better—*much* better.

In the Catskills, where I currently live and fish, the magnificent rivers which comprise what was once known as the Charmed Circle of trout fishing have taken an awful beating. It began with the early settlers, who engaged in such devastating practices as clear-cut lumbering, tannery operation, indiscriminate dam building and gross overkill of trout by any means, fair or foul. After that came development, industrial pollution, and, worst of all, the New York City water-supply system, which is arguably the single largest destroyer of trout habitat in the entire Northeast.

Even with all of this, we still have some pretty fair trout fishing in these parts. Yes, there is some crowding, but at least I'm surrounded by dedicated fly-fishermen and fisherwomen who wouldn't kill a fish on a bet. The special-regulations sections on various rivers have caused the recycling of most fish caught, resulting in greater populations of larger trout. Thus, there is far less dependency on freshly stocked trout and much better quality of sport.

So, it's a mixed bag today. What I want you to realize, so that you don't become disillusioned and disappointed early on, is that things have changed. We do not have the trout Gordon enjoyed at the turn of the century. Today's fish are incredibly sophisticated—unlike humans, they learn quickly from adverse experiences. Therefore, don't be upset if you don't enjoy instantaneous success. Just hang in there. A little practice, a helping of persistence, and you'll do fine. On that note, let's get on with the learning process.

Earlier I mentioned being ill equipped as a beginner. There's no longer any reason for that, because there is a vast array of fine tackle available and lots of information on its procurement and assembly. This might be a logical starting point—the simple putting together of the basic components.

Nearly all of today's fly rods are of two-piece construction. The sections are called tip and butt. They are joined together by a ferrule, which is positioned more or less in the middle of the rod. The ferrule is a fitting which consists of two parts—an interior tube and a corresponding exterior tube—male and female, in anglers' jargon.

Our first step in assembling the rod is to join the male and female ferrules. This is simply a matter of sliding one into the other until a tight, snug fit is obtained. I emphasize that point because if the ferrules are not fully seated, two things may happen—the tip section will disengage during casting, or—and this is far more serious—the ferrule will be damaged. This is particularly true with the costly nickel silver ferrules used on fine bamboo rods.

When joining the rod sections, keep your hands close to the respective ferrules. A fair amount of force is applied in order to effect full seating, and if the hands are too far apart, the rod in between can be broken. Before the final push, hold the rod up to your eye and sight down it to see that the guides line up. Adjust if required, loosening the ferrules if necessary.

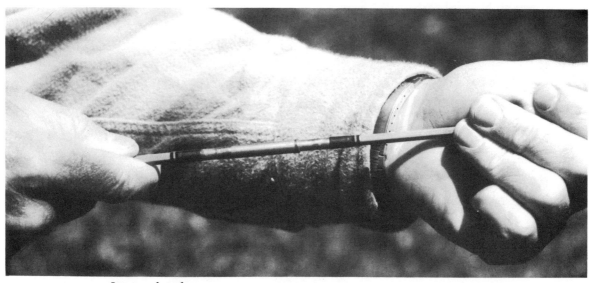

*Joining ferrules.*

A paragraph earlier I mentioned nickel silver ferrules. While it is unlikely that today's beginner will be starting with a rod having metal ferrules, I want to make the reader aware of a particularly critical factor, just in case.

It is very important that metal ferrules be fully seated. The female ferrule is nothing more than a thin-walled metal tube. When the male is not fully inserted, this tube becomes, in effect, part of the rod, and is thus subjected to the stress and strain of casting. In this situation, metal fatigue will take place, and the female will break, often very quickly.

Sometimes one encounters metal ferrules which just don't want to go together all the way. Whatever you do, don't force them. Even if you were to muscle them together, damage may result—and then you must eventually unjoin them, wherein lies even further potential for damage. In subsequent chapters dealing with rods and rod care we will examine in detail the causes and cures for poor ferrule seating.

Having put together the rod, we must now affix the reel. All reels feature a cupped metal bar which facilitates mounting the reel. It fits into a receptacle at the very butt end of the rod, which is called the reel seat, and is secured in position either by a screw-locking mechanism or a simple slip ring. In either case, see that a firm, stationary mounting is obtained. Sometimes it is necessary to wiggle the reel "foot" around a little in the reel seat, tightening the locking mechanism concurrently.

*Reel mounted for left-hand winding. Note hand position. This is the recommended grip for casting. Keep this in mind when working through Chapters II and III.*

Incidentally, many fly reels have a line guide. It consists of a piece of hardened metal or ceramic material over which the line can smoothly pass without inflicting wear on the reel itself. See to it that the line guide is facing frontward and you will never mount the reel backwards. If the reel has no line guide, be sure to mount the reel with the handle or handles on the side of the hand with which you reel. With few exceptions, fly reels can be set up for either left- or right-hand winding, in accordance with the angler's preference. More on this later.

Now we are ready to run the line through the guides. In all probability a monofilament leader is attached to the line—you should *never* cast without one, even when just practicing. Don't string up the rod by passing the tip of the leader through the guides—that's an exercise in futility. Here's the recommended procedure: Strip enough line off the reel to run the length of the rod, and then some. Let it lie loosely on the ground. Now double the line a few inches behind the butt end of the leader. Allow the rod butt to rest on the ground and simply "walk" the line out to the tip, passing the doubled end through each guide, with the leader following along. When you have passed the line through the tip guide, pull the leader through, and you're in business.

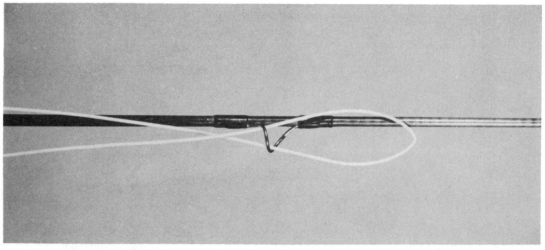

*Running doubled fly line through guides.*

Do yourself a favor and pay attention when stringing up the rod, for if you miss a guide, you must go back and pick it up. Sometimes I find myself assembling tackle at streamside, with scores of heavy trout feeding greedily close by. I string up, tie on a fly, dress it and attempt a cast above a rising fish. The line does not shoot through the guides properly, and my cast falls short. Immediately suspicious, I inspect my outfit and see that I have missed the first guide. Cursing silently—or perhaps audibly—I wade ashore, clip off the fly, disassemble and start over. I always feel like such a fool! With all my experience and discipline I still blow it now and then, and so will you, my admonition notwithstanding.

You are now prepared to begin working on the basic cast, except for one little detail—there should be something fastened to the end, or tip, of the leader. Tie on an old, beat-up dry fly with the hook cut off at the bend, or a scrap of yarn. Lack of this will cause the leader to whiplash, and the tip will fray.

Oh yes, one more thing, the unjoining of the ferrules. Normally, one simply pulls the tip and butt sections in opposite directions, again working with the hands close together. Should difficulty be encountered, there are several things you can do:

1. Grasp the ferrules with the hands very close together, put your thumbs face to face, and pull with the fingers while pushing with the thumbs.
2. If a partner is available, work together. Don't, however, have one person yanking on the tip while the other yanks on the butt. Each person places one hand on the tip and one on the butt, as though he or she were unjoining the rod individually.

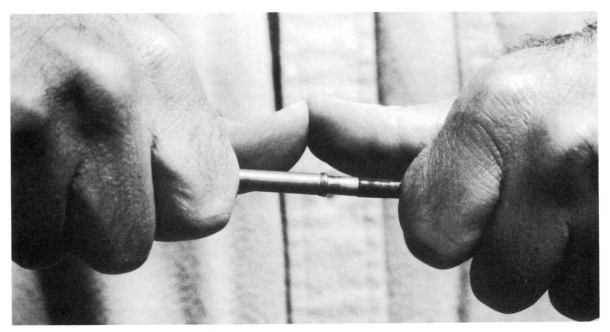

*Unjoining stuck ferrules.*

3. Use something to improve your grip. I carry two pieces of surgical tubing in my bag, which can be wrapped around the male and female ferrules. This is a great help when coming off the stream, when one's hands are wet, cold, slippery or all of those. You don't want your hands to slip while pulling a rod apart, because you can give yourself a nasty gash on a guide.

No matter what method is being used, always pull straight out in each direction. Bending the rod even slightly increases the resistance within the ferrules. In the case of graphite or fiberglass, it's okay to twist the ferrule as you pull. Not so with metal—the risk of breakage is greatly increased. A pair of chronically sticky graphite or fiberglass ferrules can be lubricated by rubbing the male with paraffin. Lubricating a metal ferrule is a bit more complicated and will be covered later.

Always unstring the rod before pulling it apart, because if the line should catch in a guide, the tip will very likely be broken. Also, be sure there's ample clearance. This is particularly critical indoors, such as when examining rods in a tackle store. A tip jammed against a wall or counter can really ruin your day.

# CHAPTER II _____

# *Learning the Basic Cast*

First, let us dispel any apprehensiveness. Fly casting is easily and quickly learned. The old curmudgeons I approached for instructions years ago liked to portray it as being difficult, simply because they wanted to be perceived as being good at something that was difficult.

Not so—nor does it require any particular physical endowment or athletic talent.

Let's begin with an appreciation of the dynamics of fly casting—that is, the interaction of the components. It is quite unlike spin casting and bait casting, because the lure—in this case, the fly—is virtually weightless. This is *the* essential difference.

In bait or spin casting, the object is to operate the equipment in such a manner as to propel the lure toward the target, pulling the line off the reel as it goes. This requires a coordinated arm-wrist movement, which (1) cocks the rod and (2) brings the lure back into the "release" position. During the forward cast, the rod uncocks, releasing the power developed by the cocking or flexing, and off sail the lure and line.

In fly casting, the lure is virtually weightless, as stated. In fact, it may cause a significant amount of aerodynamic resistance, depending on its physical characteristics. Still, weight is required in order to load the rod. It resides in the fly line.

Fly lines, even to the casual observer, look like no other type of fishing line. They have bulk and weight, in varying amounts. The weight of the line is one of the prime criteria in the fly-line rating system, but that story comes further on. For now, the important thing one should realize is that fly lines have a significant amount of weight.

A fly rod is designed to be (1) a casting machine, (2) an implement for managing the drift or presentation of the fly, and (3) an implement for playing the fish. The last two items are secondary to the first: the primary task of the rod is the cast. In effect, the rod is an extension of the angler's arm and an amplifier of its power. Ideally, it perfectly complements the caster's technique.

The reel has virtually nothing to do with casting, other than to provide a counterbalance and to store the line. The counterbalancing effect is due to the reel being mounted in back of the caster's hand, at the very butt end of the rod. It endows the outfit with a more pleasant "feel," but casting could be done perfectly well without it. The counterbalance factor was considerably more important in the pregraphite days, when rods were quite a bit heavier. I would certainly not relish the prospect of casting a heavy bamboo rod all day without a substantial reel behind my hand to balance it out.

The leader and the fly both have a significant impact on the cast, but we needn't get into detail here, as both are covered in later chapters. For now, all you need to be concerned with is that these components are present, as mentioned in Chapter I. For beginning practice sessions, I suggest a short leader, something around seven feet, of tapered design for aerodynamic effectiveness.

Continuing our study of the cast, let us consider how a bow propels an arrow. In its unflexed state, a bow is an inert object, but it *does* have potential. The archer draws the bow, activating its potential. The amount of power developed is basically a function of how far the bow is drawn. The archer releases the bowstring, and the power is discharged, sending the arrow on its swift journey.

In fly-casting classes I use a simple demonstration based on this analogy. I have someone hold one of my graphite rods in a stationary upright position while I flex the rod by walking backward with the leader and a conservative length of fly line. I release the leader, and the rod casts the line, without the holder having done a thing.

Enter the fly caster. His or her job is to impart movement—a coordinated, cohesive series of movements designed to create effective interaction between the rod and line. These movements comprise the back cast and the forward cast (not forecast—that's a prediction). They are just what the terms imply—propelling the line to the rear and to the front. Usually they are executed in a repetitive sequence: back cast–forward cast, back cast–forward cast, back cast–forward cast. These are called false casts—all, that is, except the final one, when the payload is delivered.

The main thing the caster tries to do is develop line speed on the back cast. The line shoots rearward in a tight loop, its speed counteracting the force of gravity. This sets up the forward cast. Just as the loop straightens, the caster executes the forward cast movement. The weight of the line, supplemented by its rearward momentum, flexes or loads the rod, activating its power potential. The rod straightens, discharging the power and sending the line shooting out over the water. The leader and fly go along for the ride, while the reel more or less watches the show.

I said that the development of line speed is the *main* thing the caster tries to do on the back cast, but it isn't the *only* thing. While of great importance, back cast speed can be ineffectualized if the line is in poor conformation. Two major factors affect this—the shape of the loop and the straightness of the line.

What is wanted is a tight loop—for practical purposes, the tighter the better. A tight loop is far more effective aerodynamically, because the amount of line involved in the curve of the loop itself is minimized, and the less line that has to travel through the air vertically, the less resistance. Think about a bike racer and how hunching over reduces air resistance. Also, wide or open loops have a tendency not to straighten, so the cast never actually matures. Vertically stacked line is quite impotent in causing rod flex and power buildup.

The other factor, straightness of the line, has an effect similar to the configuration of the loop. Again, we are concerned with the rod's ability to interact with the line. In order for this to happen, the line must be deployed longitudinally—in other words, it must be flat. If the line has a lot of humps or waves in it, the first thing that happens as the forward cast is executed is that these waves get flattened out. While this is taking place, very little rod flex or power buildup occurs.

I should mention that while we have been talking mainly about the back cast, all of these factors—line speed, shape of loop, smoothness of line—can affect the forward cast as well. In teaching, I concentrate on the back cast because this is usually where people have problems. Most people master the forward cast in short order, because they can see it happening in front of them—and it's a more natural movement. The super-casters, such as Steve Rajeff, Joan Wulff and Lefty Kreh, make fantastic back casts. The rest of us compensate by implementing little tricks in our forward casts. Fly casting is like golf and tennis, in that the back swing or stroke sets up the forward swing or stroke. Fortunately, fly casting is much easier—I never got far with golf or tennis.

Okay, we know what we want—line speed, tight loop, smooth line.

Now let's discuss the simple movements required of the fly caster which make it happen.

The basic casting movement is comprised of three segments: the starting movement, the power stroke and the follow-through. A simple casting sequence is made up of two of these sets, one backward and one forward. As previously stated, we usually repeat the sequence a number of times, until we feel we have it going just so. Then we release on the forward cast, and the fly is delivered.

When beginning a cast, it is very important that the line be laid out straight and neat, so that from the very inception of the pickup, the rod is working against a taut line. This embodies the "smooth-line" principle we just learned—the rod can't properly load itself against slack. In other words, you must be able to move the fly at the tip of the line/leader before you can make a cast. Of course, in actual fishing situations, the water will be moving the line around out there, and so might the wind. Thus, one seldom has a straight, taut line optimally positioned for the pickup. But here we are concerned with learning the basic cast under near-laboratory conditions, so we won't worry about wind, water and all that stuff until later.

The first thing that happens as the back cast is begun is that the line is put into motion—this is the pickup I mentioned. It is followed by a power stroke and a follow-through. Here's the sequence:

1. Position yourself as follows: casting arm extended slightly forward, elbow slightly bent, approximately a hand-shake position. The hand is slightly depressed, so that the rod and the forearm form a straight line. The feet are comfortably spread, the foot on the non-casting side slightly in front.
2. Begin the lift with a strong movement from the elbow—in other words, the straight-line relationship between the rod and forearm is maintained.
3. Quickly accelerate the elbow movement. At about the ten o'clock position, add the power stroke, which is a strong, controlled wrist movement. The power stroke must be executed by the time the twelve o'clock position is reached, otherwise the line will be driven downward and the loop will open up.
4. Follow through with the entire arm. The forearm drifts back and up, the elbow is raised, the upper arm follows. The final position is forearm slightly beyond vertical, upper arm approximately parallel to the ground, wrist cocked rearward. This establishes proper position from which to begin the forward cast.

And the forward cast is executed thusly:

*The starting position.*

*Lifting—the initial back-cast move. The rod begins to load.*

*Rearward power stroke applied here with rod well loaded.*

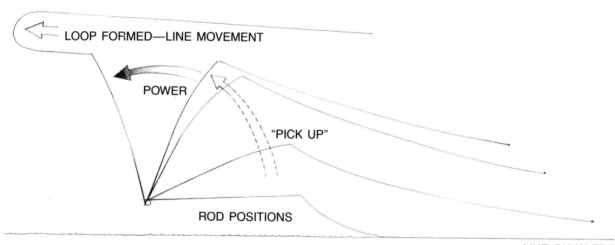

LOOP FORMED—LINE MOVEMENT

POWER

"PICK UP"

ROD POSITIONS

LINE ON WATER
STARTING POSITION

*This drawing sequentially depicts the moves shown in the preceding three photographs and also where the real impetus or power stroke is applied. Note formation of loop which travels rearward in a tight configuration. While this is happening, the rod drifts rearward, staying in contact, manicuring the line and getting into position for the forward cast.*

15

1. Begin the forward stroke when the loop is almost straight, but with the line still traveling rearward—in other words, don't let the line "die" in midair. The position is different from that of the pickup, but the function is quite similar—you are establishing unity between rod and line and starting the line's forward movement. The elbow moves downward, the forearm forward, the wrist remains cocked.

2. At the twelve o'clock position, apply the power stroke, driving the wrist forward. The power stroke must be completed by the time the rod reaches the ten-thirty or at most the ten o'clock position. Application of the power stroke as the rod is approaching horizontal will cause the line to be driven downward instead of outward, and the loop will open up. The idea is to make the line unroll completely before it drops onto the water.

FORWARD CAST—LINE MOVING "BACKWARDS"—ROD DIRECTION FORWARD

*Here we see the very beginning of the forward cast. The line is still shooting backward while the rod starts moving forward, as shown in the drawing.*

*The rod accelerates into the power stroke area.*

We have seen that the creation of a tight loop is a function of applying and stopping the power stroke at the proper positions. But what about those humps or waves in the line—where do they come from? They are caused by two things: aberrations in casting technique and rod vibrations. As your technique improves and your movements become smooth instead of jerky, the introduction of shock waves by you, the caster, will be minimized. However, rod vibrations will continue to cause them to some degree.

*The final position.*

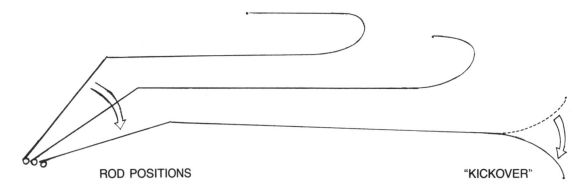

ROD POSITIONS                                                    "KICKOVER"

*This drawing sequentially depicts the rod and line positions immediately follow-
ing the forward power stroke. Remember, it is important that the loop progress
well beyond the rod tip, at least one full rod length, before the rod is lowered
toward the finishing position.*

Shock waves occur mainly on the first back cast following the pickup. We had to get the line moving from a dead stop, and that sets the rod
to vibrating. A major function of the false cast sequence is to allow the
caster to "manicure" or smooth out the waves. This is done on the
follow-through, after the power stroke is delivered. The idea is to facilitate a subtle interaction between the rod and the line while the line is
shooting rearward in that tight loop. The rod drifts back slowly while the
line is moving very fast. Thus, the waves get pulled out as the back cast
matures.

I realize this sounds contradictory—we want to maximize line speed
yet slightly retard it to get the waves smoothed out. What's important to
understand is that the front part of the line—the part that's moving
through the air—is pulling against the waves that are in that portion of
the line already suspended in midair, and not against the rod itself. The
tip of the rod merely serves as an "anchor," giving the line something to

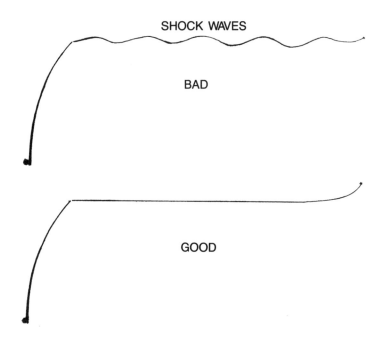

*This drawing depicts a line full of shock waves (bad) and a smooth line (good).*

straighten against. It takes very little energy to smooth out the waves, so line speed is not reduced appreciably.

Yes, this is a subtle phenomenon, and one little understood by most fly casters. As a beginner, you will be striving to get a nice tight loop moving through the air before you start working on the smooth-out technique. However, it definitely is an extremely important fundamental, which is why I explained it at this stage. Eventually, it will become automatic, and you will do it without conscious effort.

Now let's examine the grip. This is so easy you would probably do it properly with no instruction whatever. I'm writing this just after fixing lunch, and I'm thinking about how I lifted the frying pan off the stove. I simply gripped the handle with my thumb on top, pointing straight down the handle, and my index finger hooked around under the handle. That's about all there is to gripping a fly rod. Just be sure to keep that thumb on top.

While on the subject of the grip, let's also consider the wrist. It should be positioned vertically and should move in a vertical plane. Don't get into the habit of rolling the wrist when you cast. I did, and had to consciously rebuild my stroke to get away from it.

We are nearly ready for casting practice now, but first let's get you set up properly, so you're not fighting your tackle and can give full attention to the cast itself. It's important that your outfit be balanced, which essentially means that the line is the proper weight class for the rod. Less critical but still deserving of attention is the reel—we talked about counterbalancing—and the leader and pseudo-fly, which have also been covered.

I would recommend that you not begin your learning experience with a rod which runs to some extreme, meaning overly long, short, heavy or light. Something in the 8-to-8½-foot range with a 5- or 6-weight line rating is ideal. Of course, if you already own tackle, you'll probably want to use what you have, and if the outfit is balanced and not too esoteric, it should be all right.

I happen to favor weight-forward lines, particularly for teaching beginning students. The belly of the line—that is, the thickest and heaviest part—is farther forward than with the symmetrical double-taper line. Thus, one can practice with the shorter casts yet still have sufficient line weight in play to load the rod. But if you happen to have a double-taper and it matches your rod, by all means use it—don't go dashing off to buy another line just yet. Oh yes—use a floating-type line when practicing.

Rods, reels and lines are given in-depth treatment in Chapter IV, so I'll say no more here. Simply refer to that chapter as you go about assembling your basic outfit. If you already own tackle, you might check it against the data provided therein.

Now let's make some casts. First, we must find a place; fly casting requires space. In decent weather, a lawn will do beautifully; in winter, a gym will suffice. But it's best to cast onto water—after all, that's where fish live. I would consider a pond the ideal practice setting, one with gently sloped banks and lots of clearance to the rear for back casts.

It may be that you will seldom fish still water—my preference runs heavily to streams and rivers. Even so, I suggest you practice casting on a pond until you get the hang of it. Moving water introduces all sorts of line-management problems which interfere with the pure and simple execution of the cast. Also, streams usually involve wading, which makes casting more difficult, in that your height is effectively reduced by the depth of the water in which you are standing.

I've conducted many winter classes in school gyms. The only negative factor, provided space is adequate, is the slippery surface of the gym floor. We depend on resistance to help load the rod during pickup. Water surface offers considerable resistance, and the grass on a lawn provides a fair amount. In the case of a gym floor, there is virtually none, and the caster has to do all of the work. Gym floors are also rough on fly lines; parking lots and similarly paved surfaces even more so. If you have no

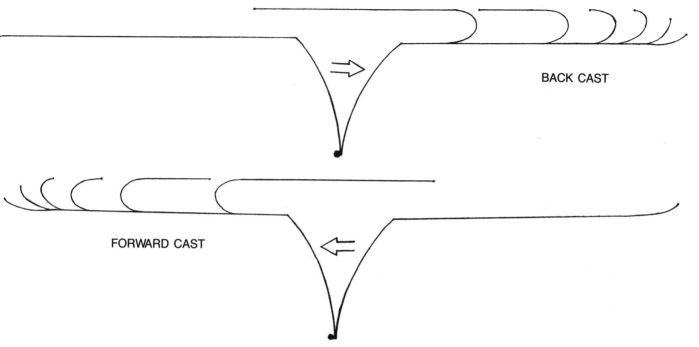

BACK CAST

FORWARD CAST

*These two drawings depict the back cast—forward cast sequence, showing typical power stroke area and loop development.*

choice but to practice on such surfaces, try to beg an old beat-up fly line from someone.

All right, here we go. Strip off about 30 feet of line and get it laid out straight in front of you any old way you can. Don't try to practice with a very short length of line; that makes it more difficult, rather than easier, because there isn't enough weight out there to load the rod.

Other than for stripping line, reeling line and other custodial operations, I recommend that you keep your left hand—or right hand, if you're a southpaw—out of action when practice casting. Simply secure the line against the rod grip with your casting hand and put the other hand in your pocket or someplace. If you prefer, wrap a few turns of line around the base of the reel. In the following chapter we'll work on techniques where the noncasting hand gets involved. For now, practice one-handed; it greatly simplifies matters. Position the feet slightly apart, with the foot on the noncasting side slightly ahead.

Now execute the back-cast–forward-cast sequence described earlier. As you become more comfortable and confident, try some false casting. Create a mental picture of the progression of the cast: the pickup, the back-cast power stroke, the tight loop speeding rearward and straightening, the waves smoothing out, the arm, wrist and rod cocked, the forward move just as the line straightens, the forward power stroke, the line rolling out in a tight loop, straightening and dropping onto the casting surface. Turns one on, doesn't it?

As you cast, think about trajectory. The power stroke propels the line rearward on a slightly upward trajectory. As the line travels backward it is also pulled downward by the force of gravity; thus, when it has almost straightened, it will be nearly level to the ground. This is as it should be, for it sets up a proper forward trajectory. Aim the forward cast on a slightly upward trajectory also. As the loop rolls out above the water, gravity is at work, forcing the line downward. The idea is to develop sufficient line speed so that the line and leader will straighten and turn over in the air, dropping the fly softly onto the water.

It is important to let the loop formed on the forward cast progress well beyond the rod tip before dropping the rod to the fishing position. As a rule of thumb, allow the loop to go at least one rod-length beyond the tip, so that the loop is not pulled apart by a downward movement of the rod.

Rather than guess, you might find it most helpful to actually watch your back cast. This is easily done—simply turn your casting-side foot outward a little (see illustration) and glance over your shoulder. Thus, you can check line trajectory, loop configuration and progression, shock wave syndrome and positioning of rod, wrist and arm. This technique may be carried over into actual fishing, where it is an aid in casting over or around obstructions to the rear.

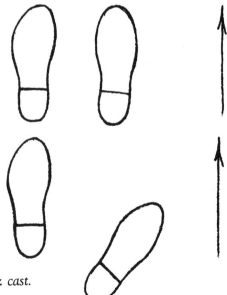

*Positioning feet to observe back cast.*

As you develop your casting style, you may find it more comfortable to cant the arm and rod slightly off vertical. Most people's bodies seem to work better that way—few baseball pitchers throw directly overhand—so you will probably fall into this naturally. Remember that the forearm, wrist and rod must still form a straight line and must travel in a straight plane. Do not describe an ellipse in the air with the tip of the rod. And don't roll your wrist—keep the thumb squarely on top.

As soon as you are laying out a neat line, I suggest you begin using targets. Aluminum-foil pie plates make good targets for a lawn or gym floor. Hula hoops (they still exist, don't they?) make excellent targets on a pond. Target casting helps form good habits which will pay dividends in actual fishing situations.

By way of reiterating and summarizing the various do's, dont's, goods and bads covered to this point, here is a brief checklist of problems and causes to aid you in the learning experience.

Problem: Wide or open loop, end of line "stacking" vertically, leader landing in pile.

Probable cause: Power stroke continued too far on the back cast and/or the forward cast, line driven downward. Remember that the size of the loop is determined by how far the wrist moves *after* the line is in motion.

Problem: Shock waves in line during back cast.

Probable cause: Slack not removed before pickup, jerky pickup and/or power stroke, no drift-back or follow-through.

Problem: Line slaps down hard following forward cast.

Probable cause: Too high a back cast and/or too low a point of aim on the forward cast.

Problem: Line fails to straighten and turn over on forward cast.

Probable cause: Open-loop syndrome, insufficient line speed, or perhaps attempting too long a cast.

Problem: Tailing loop—that is, fly catches line during progression.

Probable cause: Power stroke begun too soon, with no setup or "manicuring" move preceding. Also, driving line directly forward with the thumb. Remember to turn the thumbnail downward a bit on the forward power stroke.

Problem: All of the above, in various combinations. Little or nothing going well.

Probable causes: Poor timing. Movements jerky, rather than smooth. Lack of cohesion—various components broken up into individual movements, rather than flowing in smooth continuity. Line is allowed to "die," or stop moving in the air between power strokes. Remember, the forward cast begins while the line is still moving rearward, just prior to the loop fully straightening.

One more thing—don't become a body caster. A certain amount of bodily movement is a natural by-product, so you don't want to hold yourself rigid—but it's the arm that does the job.

How long will it take you to learn the basic fly cast? I really can't say. The amount of practice certainly has a bearing on this. Natural athletic ability does also. I meant what I said about such special endowments not being a prerequisite; however, the natural athlete will become a better caster sooner. By athlete, I don't mean the major-sports type necessarily, just someone gifted with extraordinary coordination and timing.

More than once I've seen a newcomer pick up a fly-casting outfit and within an hour be laying out a beautiful line. This strengthens my belief in reincarnation. I think about my friend Bob Dodge, whom I met salmon fishing in Iceland in 1979. The third day, we shared a beat, and he was handling that 9-weight outfit like a pro, wind and all. He being an old college friend of Ernie Schwiebert, our party leader and guru, I assumed Bob was a fly-fishing junkie, like the rest of us. Later I learned he had hardly fly-fished before—after all, where would an orthodontist from central Ohio learn to fly-fish? However, Bob is a gifted athlete.

So, I can't tell you precisely how many hours or days it will take you to master the basic cast—but master it you will, I'm quite sure. I also believe you will enjoy the process, and come to love the unique "feel" of quality fly tackle. That's part of fly-fishing's special charm—it's fun even when the fish aren't biting.

# CHAPTER III _____

# *Variant Casts and Line-Management Techniques*

Fly-fishing is like golf in certain respects. One masters the basic cast or the basic swing. Then it's off to the stream or golf course, where all sorts of subtle and not-so-subtle challenges are encountered. Streams have traps and hazards of a very special type. And of course there is the wind, which can raise just as much havoc with a fly cast as with a seven-iron to a small green.

Let's discuss wind first off, as it is perhaps the most common and frequent source of grief for the fly-fisher. Wind is sometimes a double-bladed axe, for while interfering with casting, it may actually help the fishing. I've had some banner days when the wind was skittering insects around or disturbing the surface of a quiet pool, so that the fish's vision was impaired and they could be approached and cast over without crawling on my belly.

There are several things one can do to cope with wind which are preparatory rather than technique-oriented, such as:

1. Use a weight-forward line.
2. Avoid an ultra-light outfit.
3. Shorten the leader.
4. Avoid huge, air-resistant flies, such as Variants.

There are also casting techniques which help offset the effects of wind.

One should try to cast as short a line as is practical. Where on a calm day a longer cast might be employed to reach a certain spot, some discreet wading is perhaps a better choice in the presence of wind. Also, try to cast as tight a loop as possible, and maintain line speed. The wind will tend to defeat line speed on either the back or forward cast, depending on whether it's blowing from the rear or face-on. In either case, be particularly firm with the power stroke into the wind.

If the situation allows, try to keep your cast a bit lower than you normally would, in order to take advantage of whatever protection the shore may offer. As casting proficiency develops, you will learn to cast from various positions and bodily attitudes: hunched-over, side-arm, even cross-body. In certain situations, you can even cast with the rod almost parallel to the water. These techniques often enable you to cast virtually beneath the wind.

If the wind is blowing hard enough to "stack" your back cast or forward cast—that is, to prevent the loop from completing its normal course—you will want to adjust your timing. As we learned, a casting stroke is begun while the line is still traveling in an outward direction, as propelled by the previous stroke. If the wind is stopping the line, there's no point in waiting the normal interval—things will only worsen very quickly. You will have to accelerate the subsequent casting movement and allow the wind, which is then favoring the cast, to compensate for the damage it did on the upwind stroke.

Let's run that by again, for purposes of clarification. Suppose the wind is from the rear and it's stacking your back cast. First, use your best Sunday technique to generate maximum line speed on the back cast, creating a low, tight loop. Use a shorter back cast than normal, but have sufficient line in play to fully load the rod. In your noncasting hand, hold some loose coils of line, enough to allow the fly to reach the target. Just as the back cast dies, execute the forward cast. As the loop begins to straighten over the water, release the coils and "shoot" the slack, aided by the tail wind.

Let's be sure we understand what is meant by "shooting" line. It involves holding an amount of extra line—that is, line not involved in the back-cast–forward-cast sequence—in the noncasting hand, then releasing it as the forward cast straightens. Neatness counts here—we can't afford any knots or snarls, so hold the line in a smooth loop or bunch of loops. The act of shooting line not only contributes to distance casting; it also makes for a more delicate delivery, with the line falling lightly, rather than slapping on the water. I often shoot a little line on short casts for just that reason.

It is possible to do the same thing in reverse, after a fashion, but that is trickier, because one must actually deliver the fly into the wind on the forward cast. Shooting line to the rear may affect a great back cast, but then what? You can't recapture the excess line in a few milliseconds, thereby shortening the upwind forward cast. What may be possible is to generate so much power by taking advantage of the very strong back cast that the line, leader and fly are virtually driven into the teeth of the wind.

One often encounters winds from the side, especially in deep ravines and canyons, where the contours of the landscape actually redirect the wind. This can be troublesome, particularly when the wind is coming from the casting side, thus blowing the line, leader and fly across the caster's body. If the wind isn't too strong, you may compensate by casting with the rod tilted or canted in a windward attitude, so that the line travels farther from the body while it's in the air. If the wind is blowing really hard, you can execute the back cast with the rod tilted windward, then tip it the other way on the forward cast, causing the fly to pass on the downwind side. This is a departure from classic technique, for, as stated earlier, we normally cast on a flat plane and avoid describing an elliptical path with the tip of the rod. However, in this case the wind is moving the line out of that flat plane, and by adjusting the position of the rod to compensate, we restore the dynamics which facilitate casting.

These aberrations in casting techniques take practice, so don't become discouraged if your first windy day astream is somewhat of an exercise in frustration. Those golf pros we see making a mockery of par on television didn't learn to fade an approach shot into a crossing wind their first day on the course. Work on the development of effective wind casting, and take the weather as it comes. Trout country is generally windy, and those who only go out on calm days don't get to fish very much.

Earlier I mentioned the cross-body cast. While not a natural casting stroke, it is a useful one to have in one's arsenal. I use it more than most people, because I have a partially disabled left hand from an old automobile injury and can't switch hands when circumstances dictate. Otherwise, I would simply have learned to cast left-handed long ago, in order to adapt to wind, current direction and so forth. As with basketball players, anglers who can use either hand have a distinct advantage.

The cross-body cast is executed with the rod tilted across the caster's body, as the name implies. Therefore, the back cast is made over the "wrong" shoulder, and the ensuing forward cast likewise, as shown in the illustrations. The effect simulates casting with what is normally the non-casting hand.

*The rearward and forward movements for the cross-body cast.*

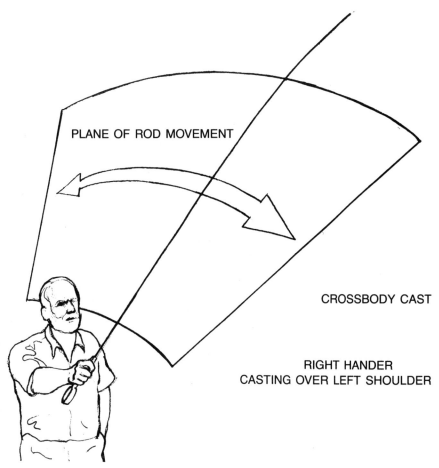

PLANE OF ROD MOVEMENT

CROSSBODY CAST

RIGHT HANDER
CASTING OVER LEFT SHOULDER

*Actual plane the rod follows during the cross-body cast, shown in a drawing for clarity.*

There are other important applications of the cross-body cast besides compensating for a crossing wind. Envision the following situation: you are wading a short distance out from a brushy bank, with trout rising in center stream in front of you. Wading into better position is inadvisable, because of either water depth or the need to stay out of sight. You are a right-handed caster, and the current is flowing from right to left. A classic back cast puts the fly in the bushes. However, a cross-body cast, where the line travels over the wrong shoulder at more of a downstream angle, may solve the problem.

The cross-body cast is also helpful in adapting to current direction. Usually, it is easier to present a fly—particularly a dry fly—when the current is flowing from the noncasting side. Being a right-hander, I always like a stretch of water that allows me to fish from the left side, facing upstream—I call that a right-handed pool. However, we must be able to effectively deal with left-handed pools as well. Therefore, I sometimes emulate left-handedness by adapting my casting technique.

Why is it easier to fish water which is flowing from the noncasting side? There are several reasons. Since an up-and-across presentation is used much of the time, it is an advantage to be positioned with the casting arm out from the bank—this helps keep the back cast clear of shoreline obstructions. Also, I find it easier to execute a curve cast from that position. I call this the slack-curve cast.

The slack curve is not a classic-curve cast of the type highly skilled casters demonstrate in clinics. Actually, it is nothing more than a moderate adjustment of the basic cast, whereby the forward cast is allowed to drop to the surface just before it straightens completely. In other words, we retard the energy of the cast slightly, so that instead of kicking over, the fly remains behind the line and leader.

This cast is performed with a tilted rod, so that the loop develops along a plane which is off vertical. In effect, the loop then becomes an upstream curve. When properly managed by the caster, the line and leader fall to the water in that position, and the fly begins its drift with an

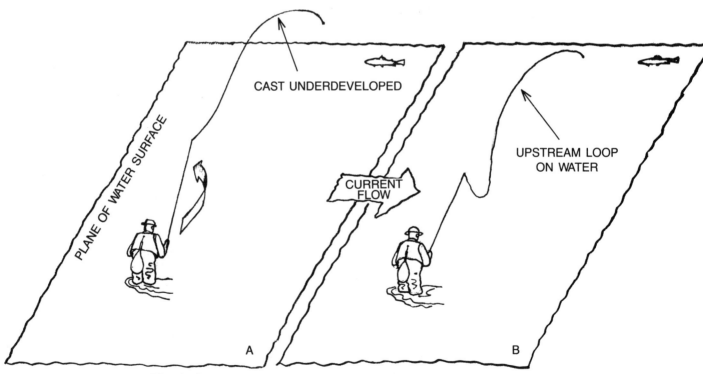

*The slack curve cast.*

upstream belly behind it, so that current-induced drag does not immediately occur.

Several techniques facilitate the upstream slack-curve cast, and they may be used in combination. First, one simply makes a less forceful forward cast. Secondly, some slack line may be released or shot, as the forward loop rolls out, so that the line cannot use the "anchoring" effect of the rod to straighten against. Also, the rod is employed to control the development of the loop and to influence the line and leader to drop on the water at the desired time, in the curved deployment. This is accomplished by reaching upstream with the rod—in effect, following the line as it rolls out over the water. Here again, we are defeating the anchoring effect by repositioning the rod during the course of the line's forward movement.

Of course, we can't always choose a pool which sets up exactly as we would like, so we must be able to manage our casts effectively when the current is flowing from the casting-hand side. Frequently, this involves getting the line to curve a bit in the other direction. In this case, we want just the opposite of the slack-curve dynamic—we want a powerful forward cast where the loop straightens with such force that the fly kicks over and precedes the leader and line as the drift begins.

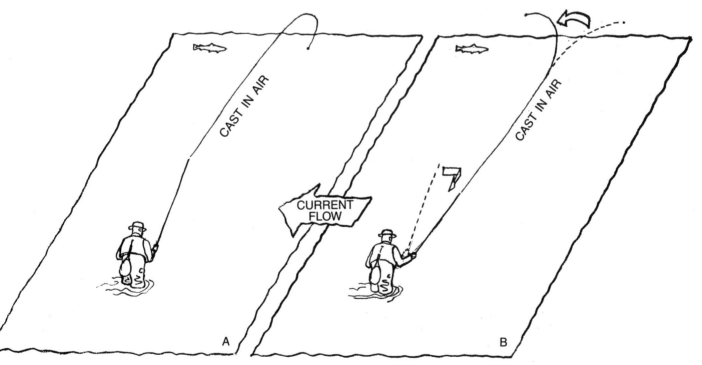

*The kick-over curve cast.*

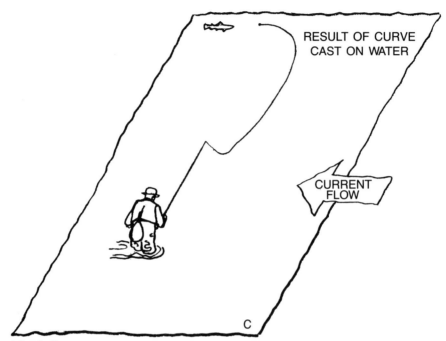

*The kick-over curve cast.*

This cast is also executed with a tilted rod. False casts are used to develop line speed. Then, as the line shoots outward and the loop straightens, the caster again employs a "reach" move to effect the desired result. However, this differs from the slack curve in that the rod is pulled sharply backward while reaching upstream. This has the effect of accentuating the kickover by working against the forward thrust of the line and leader.

Effective as these casting variations may be, we generally need to utilize additional methods to obtain a drag-free float or drift throughout the course of a presentation. Drag is the eternal enemy of natural-appearing presentation. Remember, no natural insect has an attached leader pulling it this way and that. Often we must cast across faster currents to present a fly to trout lying in slower water on the other side of the stream. Thus, we must do whatever is required to offset the workings of the current against the line and leader.

The most frequently used and, I believe, important drag-offsetting technique is called mending the cast. It is a very simple maneuver in both concept and execution. One merely flips a portion of the line which is drifting on the surface into an upstream belly, which acts as a buffer against the tendency of the current to create a downstream belly in the line, causing drag.

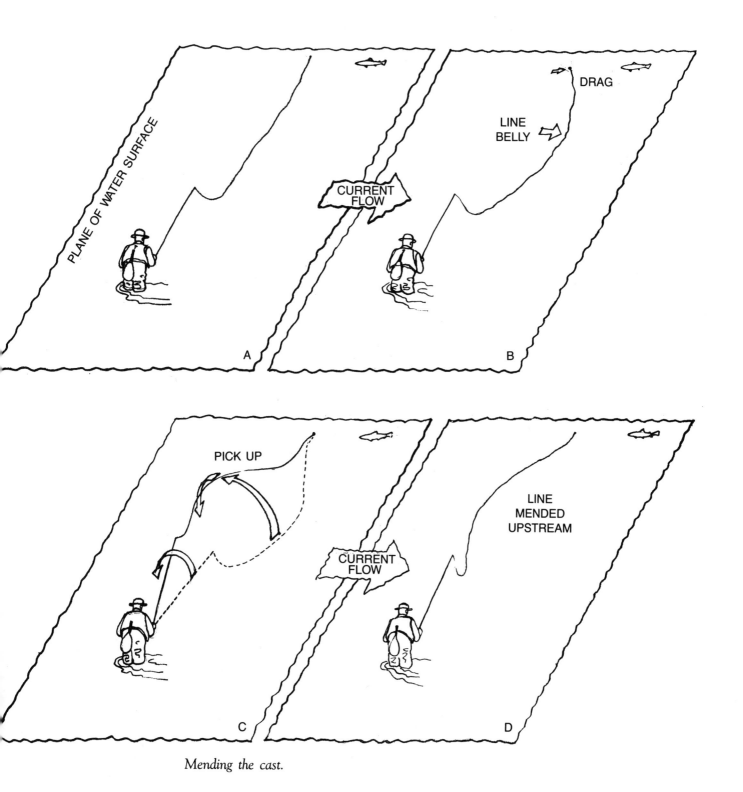

*Mending the cast.*

Everyone recalls skipping rope as a child, or watching other kids do so. The mending move is somewhat reminiscent of that, though not an exact replica. The idea is to lift the line between you and the butt end of the leader with the rod tip and roll it or loop it upstream. In skipping rope, the far end is secured by someone holding on to it. In mending a cast, the leader is held in position by the surface tension of the water. Sometimes a portion of the leader is involved in the mend. Other times it remains on the water, along with the front portion of the line. It all depends on the circumstances.

It is not at all uncommon to mend a cast as soon as it falls on the water, or shortly thereafter, in order to correct any undesirable configurations which may have been created by wind or initial contact with the current. Additional mends can be made throughout the duration of the drift as required; however, one must take care not to alarm the trout in the vicinity. It's best to try to make whatever mends are necessary well upstream, out of the target area, especially when fishing dry-fly.

There are other ways to fight drag and effect an illusion of detachment regarding the drifting fly. One of the easiest and most effective is the S cast, sometimes called the wiggle cast or snake cast. The execution is as follows: on the forward cast, just as the line straightens, waggle the

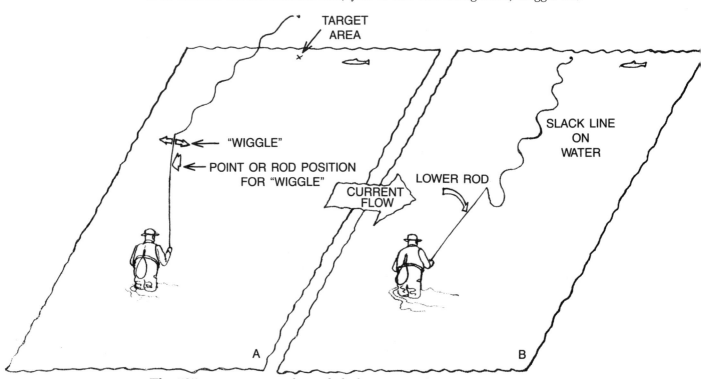

*The "S" cast, a commonly used slack-casting technique.*

rod tip laterally a few times. This causes the line to fall onto the surface with a series of distinct S's throughout. Of course, you must use a few extra feet of line to allow for the S's and still get the fly to the target area.

As you've probably deduced, the phenomenon that makes the S cast effective is the interaction of the current and the S's. Before it can cause drag on the fly, the current has to cope with straightening out those curves. When a cast lies dead straight on the water, the current can create a downstream belly and cause drag immediately.

I know what you're thinking: how does one strike a fish with all those slack S's between oneself and the fly? Well, first of all, those curves are introduced at the very beginning of the presentation and may be pretty well straightened out by the time the fly is taken. Also, the surface tension of the water can be used in hooking fish. The idea is to use a backward or sideward rather than upward motion in striking, so that the line isn't immediately tossed into the air. Quite often, a fish will hook itself against a slack line, for which I am always thankful. In such cases, the resistance created by the water is sufficient to cause hook engagement.

The S cast is also an effective technique when one must make a downstream or down-and-across presentation. Here, we are concerned with effecting a drag-free float of sufficient duration to put a fly to a waiting fish. The S cast often is the answer. Execution is the same as for the cross-current version.

While on the subject, let's examine another variant cast which abets the downstream technique. It's known by other names, including the slack-line cast, and it definitely is that. I call it the stop cast, as this is what one does to the momentum of the forward cast to achieve the desired result.

Again, this is easy. One drives the forward cast out over the water, perhaps a bit higher and faster than normal. Just as the forward cast straightens, the rod is pulled back and upward to approximately an eleven o'clock or twelve o'clock position. This sharply arrests the progression of the line and leader, the result being a pronounced kickover, with the line and leader dropping to the water in a slack attitude.

With practice, it is possible to produce some extremely effective leader configurations on the water using this type of cast. There are many times when we want the leader to fall in a set of loops or swirls, even more curvy than the S cast produces. One might consider this a "controlled bird's-nest." The purpose, of course, is to effect a drag-free float in swirly, whirlpoolish currents. Quite often, a trout will take a feeding position just off the main current, where food drifts within easy reach. This trout has the best of both worlds—protection from the current and a catered banquet. Also, the fish is somewhat protected from outside-world threats, such as birds of prey and us, by the swirling currents, which make

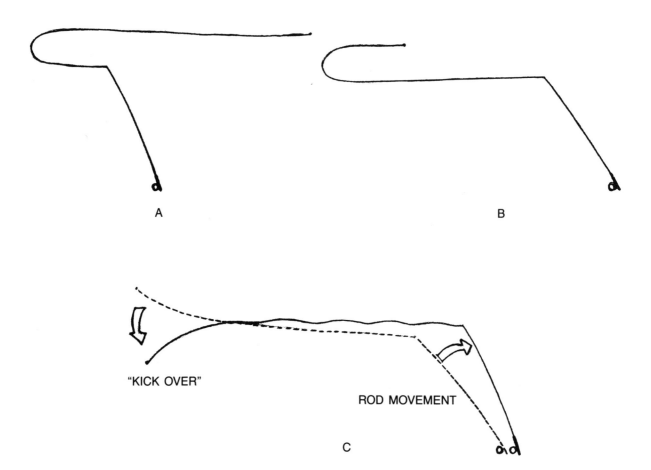

*The "stop-cast".*

it more difficult to see and get at the creature. These are frequently larger trout, ones which have learned the ropes.

I can't overemphasize the importance of the slack-leader technique. Drag is the great rise killer; it not only can influence a trout against taking your fly but may actually put the fish down. And it doesn't take much. On slower pools, drag often occurs which is imperceptible to the angler but alarming to the trout. There are situations when a tiny bit of drag can actually prevent a taking fish from drawing the fly into its mouth. We shall examine this in more detail in a later chapter.

Not infrequently we find ourselves with obstructions to the rear which limit back-casting space. Picture yourself wading the perimeter of a pond, with lots of trees and bushes around the shoreline. You can't move out very far, because of depth. Fish are cruising within what would be easy casting range, if only a back cast were possible. What to do?

This is a made-to-order setup for the roll cast. Envision a large hoop made out of fly line rolling out across the water. That's what an evolving roll cast looks like. It's not difficult to execute once the mental picture is in place. Refer to the pictures and captions.

The secret of successful roll casting is using the resistance of the water to load the rod. You start by skidding the line toward yourself across the surface, getting it moving. This movement is stopped for an instant before the forward cast is made, which causes the water to "grab" the line. This causes the rod to load as the forward cast is begun. The power thus developed is released on the power stroke, and the line and leader roll out across the water, delivering the fly.

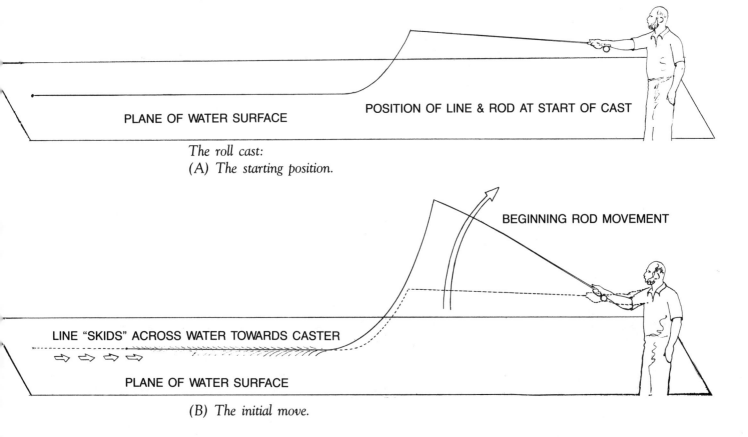

PLANE OF WATER SURFACE  POSITION OF LINE & ROD AT START OF CAST

*The roll cast:*
*(A) The starting position.*

BEGINNING ROD MOVEMENT

LINE "SKIDS" ACROSS WATER TOWARDS CASTER

PLANE OF WATER SURFACE

*(B) The initial move.*

The roll cast is effective in streams as well as ponds and lakes, provided the current is not too fast or diffused. It is also of value as a "pickup" move, getting the line positioned for a normal back-cast–forward-cast sequence. In any case, it is important to bring the line to the surface and get it skidding across the water. It is very difficult to roll cast a

*(C) Continuation of rearward move.*

*(D) Position for starting forward cast. Line stops for an instant.*

*(E) Forward cast. Line rolls out across water.*

line when the front end is submerged. The brief pause prior to the forward cast is the key to good roll casting.

Another technique for coping with limited back-casting room is the change-of-direction cast. Here, you do your false casting in a more upstream-downstream direction, utilizing the greater space thus obtained. Then, on the final forward cast, the line is redirected cross-stream, in order to deliver the fly to the desired target. Remember that the line follows the direction in which the rod tip was going when it stopped *at the end of the forward power stroke.*

This isn't really a difficult technique, but it is a bit tricky to execute and still maintain accuracy. The degree of difficulty increases with the amount of deflection, or change. You will find that moving the rod tip to redirect the cast will create some loops or curves in the final forward cast. Some practice is required to develop techniques for "manicuring" the forward cast in its outward flight, thus countering this effect. I suggest you become a reasonably good fundamental caster before trying to do much change-of-direction casting.

Now let's learn a power-casting technique which will help you develop more line speed and make longer casts when required to do so. It is called the double haul. Here, we get the so-called noncasting hand

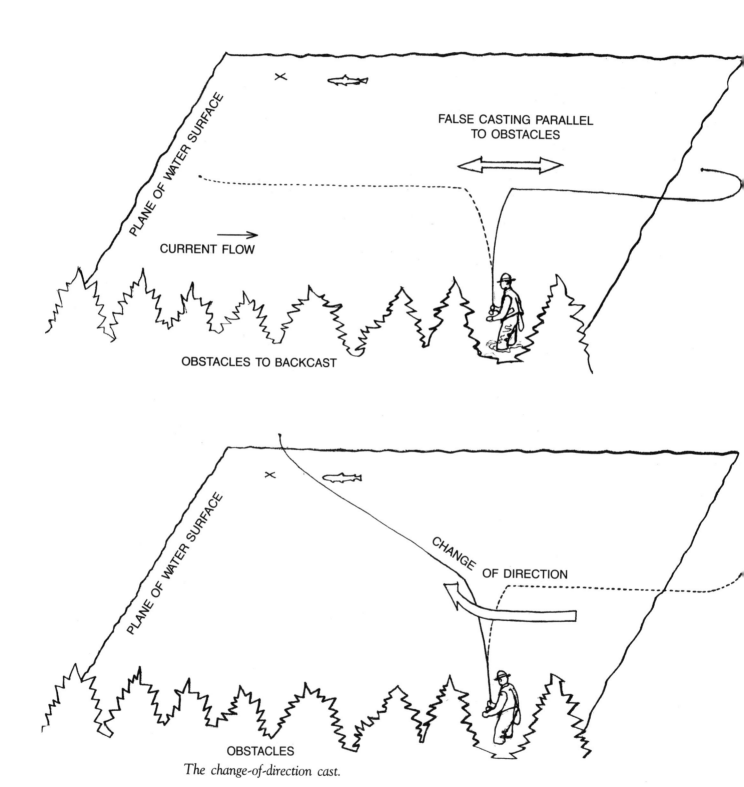

The change-of-direction cast.

actively involved. It is, in fact, the enabler—the critical source of supplemental power which makes the double haul work.

First, let's define what is meant by the term *haul* in this context. A haul is either a back cast or a forward cast in which the noncasting hand is employed to effect greater line speed. The movement is simply that of pulling or "hauling" the line back through the guides, toward oneself. This is coordinated with the basic casting movements—the starting move and the power stroke. They accelerate in a complementary manner, thus moving the line more effectively.

A double haul is a casting sequence whereby a haul is employed on both the back and forward casts. These may be combined in a series of false casts to further increase line speed. Of the various techniques covered in this chapter, the double haul is perhaps the most athletically challenging. However, it is well within the average caster's capabilities. It's a bit like patting your head and rubbing your stomach at the same time. It's also like swimming; once learned, it's never forgotten. The double haul is best understood visually, so we will allow the pictures and captions to tell the story.

*The double haul:*
*(A) Starting position.*

(B) *Lifting and hauling. Left hand is moving downwards.*

(C) *More lifting and hauling. Note rod loading.*

*(D) Position for beginning forward haul. Note that left or "line" hand has followed line rearward.*

*(E) Forward cast and haul in progress.*

43

(F) Haul complete, ready for "release" move. Again, note rod loading.

(G) The release.

There is a natural tendency when practicing the double haul to become a body caster. Please resist this. It is the hands, wrists and arms that do the work. Body movement is strictly supplemental, for purposes of balance and comfort. This is not to imply that the body is held rigid— simply relax and allow your moving parts to coordinate. Early on, be conservative. Don't overaccentuate the haul movements or try to cast too far.

*Artist's rendition of final moves of double haul:*

(A) *Forward haul completed, loop shooting forward. Left hand still holds line, for control.*

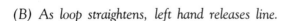

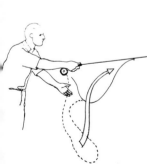

(B) *As loop straightens, left hand releases line.*

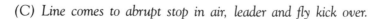

(C) *Line comes to abrupt stop in air, leader and fly kick over.*

The haul, like the roll cast, is often employed as a pickup move. Often, we actually haul against the friction introduced by the water. This is called a water haul, and it can generate a great deal of potential power very quickly, as the rod is heavily loaded by the combined effect of the water's resistance, the haul and the back-cast movements. However, I would caution you not to try to pick up too much line with the water haul. It's not conducive to casting efficiency and can also overload a rod to the extent that breakage may occur.

There is also an inclination to try to aerialize too much line via the double haul. Yes, one can effectively false cast more line using this technique, but there is a point at which maximum efficiency is reached. Beyond that, efficiency drops off sharply. Each rod has a point of optimization, where it functions at peak efficiency with a given line. This can be extended by better technique, but not infinitely. It is advisable to determine the length of line your rod false casts best, in your hands. If more distance is required, it is generally best to shoot whatever additional length of line is required to reach the target area.

In practicing the double haul, you will find that a greater range of movement naturally occurs. There is more extension and drift-back. With that comes a requirement for a better manicuring job on the line traveling through the air. The increased pressure on the rod introduces more and bigger shock waves, which need to be smoothed out. A suggestion: practice the double haul using only the tip section of the rod—this makes you learn proper technique.

The variations in casts and line-management techniques are practically infinite. Each situation and each type of angling presents a problem which we attempt to solve by using one or more of these coping mechanisms. To a large degree, this is what "makes" a fly-fisher: the ability to get the job done under less than ideal circumstances. Everyone gets to beat up on the easy fish in the accessible spots. The angler who is willing and able to go for the more difficult fish in the tougher places in effect expands the available resource and greatly enhances his or her angling pleasure.

# CHAPTER IV _____

# *The Three Partners—Rod, Reel and Line*

In this chapter we will study the three integrated components that comprise the nucleus of a balanced fly-casting outfit. We will explore the various characteristics of some of the more common types of rods, reels and lines, with an eye toward developing a working knowledge of their functions and interrelationships. The intent is to provide sufficient orientation that even a relative newcomer is prepared to select fly-casting tackle suitable to his or her physique, casting style, bank account and, most importantly, the angling environment in which it will be used.

Today it is far easier to match up an outfit than when I was getting started, because the manufacturers have become much more enlightened. Rod designs are greatly improved. The system for rating fly lines by weight has been developed and standardized. Many good reels are available. Reputable dealers and their personnel understand their products. Unless you shop in a discount department store, you almost can't go too far wrong. Still, it is the purchaser's responsibility to make the optimum choice.

A wide price range exists in the case of all three basic components, more so in rods and reels than lines. On one end are the bargain-basement items, on the other elitist merchandise. I'm not against bargains—however, you have to know what you're doing, or you may end up with tackle worth even less than the small amount paid for it. I also have no problem with premium-priced tackle, provided the products have excellent functional characteristics, as well as cosmetic appeal and prestige labels. Within those two extremes there exists a vast array of quality merchandise, from which most of us will make our selections.

## RODS

First, let's discuss fly rods. The early rods of the modern fly-fishing era were made of bamboo or, more properly, cane. Throughout the late 1800s and well into this century, cane rod design and construction evolved, under the careful nurturing of people like Hiram Leonard, Edward and Jim Payne, the Hawses, Wes Jordan, George Halstead, Pinky Gillum, Paul Young and Everett Garrison. These were master craftsmen, and their rods were marvels of beauty and a joy to cast. These rods are valuable collector's items now, and are rarely fished, a fact which would dismay their makers.

Rod-making bamboo grows only in a small mountain province about a hundred miles northwest of Canton in mainland China. It is commonly called Tonkin cane, but the proper name is Arundinaria Amabilis, or "the lovely bamboo." It was so named in 1931 by Dr. F. A. McLure, a botanist who at that time was associated with Lingnan University in Hong Kong.

Efforts to transplant Tonkin cane were never successful, for some mysterious reason. After 1949, when the cold-war trade embargo against China went into effect, quality cane began to get scarce. Without the large American market, many of the provincial Chinese who cultivated Arundinaria Amabilis became disinterested in the crop, and the British and French rod makers began to encounter problems in obtaining top-quality cane, even though no trade barriers existed. Fortunately, bamboo keeps almost indefinitely when properly stored, so the American rod makers were able to at least stay in business until ping-pong diplomacy thawed U.S.-China relations and trade was resumed, circa 1972.

At the same time bamboo became scarce, the demand for rods began to increase. Enter fiberglass, a synthetic substance which came into its own in the years following World War II. Very inexpensive and available in limitless quantities, fiberglass took over. By the mid-1950s, the public was marching streamward armed with an array of low-price-tag synthetic rods.

The earlier models of fiberglass fly rods came in for much criticism from knowledgeable casters, and rightfully so. There were two problems— the material itself and the rod designs, or tapers. Some unfortunate compromises were made, due to either lack of competence or a desire to produce rods which would cast virtually any weight of line. Thus, fiberglass was branded a secondary or inferior material, a reputation it has never entirely lived down.

The attempt to develop a "universal" taper was a most interesting misadventure in rod design from which much can be learned. In the 1950s, the fly-line business was in chaos. With the advent of synthetic lines, the traditional system of classification by diameter became inappropriate and misleading. Rod companies received complaints that their products weren't accurately designated with regard to what line a particular rod was designed to cast. This was quite true, but the poor rod designer was in a quandary because of the tremendous variances between lines which were rated the same.

In an effort to cope with this situation, several companies produced rods designed with what was called a "progressive" taper. The idea was that the rod would cast various weights of line, working progressively down into the thicker, more powerful butt section. It was a brilliant concept that degenerated into a product, the result being that these rods didn't cast *any* weight line very effectively. Light lines only worked the tip section, and the power in the butt was never tapped. Heavier lines got the butt working but overtaxed the tip, which simply broke down. The design exceeded the limitations of the material.

Throughout the 1960s, fiberglass rods went through dramatic improvement. They became much lighter and thinner-walled, and the glass more dense, which increased power while reducing undesirable vibration. Fiberglass thus evolved into a very good fly-rod material which, coupled with much-improved taper designs, produced rods which were highly functional and a pleasure to cast. But just about the time the fiberglass folks really got their act together, a tough new kid walked onto the block. His name was Graphite.

As I was putting the finishing touches on *Fly-Fishing for Trout—A Guide for Adult Beginners* in 1972, someone handed me an early-model graphite rod—a prototype, actually. I didn't much like it. It was very stiff, and I couldn't get the feel of the line and rod interacting. Still, the potential was obvious. My statement in the book read, "Don't be the first kid on the block to own one," a policy I adhere to tenaciously in this world of high-tech hype.

Development of graphite accelerated rapidly, and by the late 1970s it had become firmly established as *the* rod-building material. Concurrently, some work was done with boron, a material similar in some respects to graphite. Several companies experimented with graphite-boron mixes, seeking to combine the strength of boron with the casting properties of graphite. Results were only moderately successful, at least to this point in time. I had a graphite-boron rod rated for a 9- or 10-weight line. It would tip a big salmon or bluefish right over on its dorsal fin, but the casting qualities were mediocre. The boron composites I have tried to date run to two extremes: soft and slow or strong and stiff.

I wouldn't rule out boron or boron-graphite, any more than I would have done with graphite in 1972. At any time a technological advancement could come about which would leapfrog boron ahead of graphite. With my luck, that will happen the day this book comes off the presses. But at this writing, graphite is numero uno.

Graphite has some marvelous attributes: great strength without weight, quickness of recovery and a particularly beneficial characteristic which the rod builders call "low damping action." What that means is that the rod stops oscillating very quickly after a casting movement is completed. This means less shock waves in the line—remember those shock waves we discussed in Chapter II? This plus its strength, lightness and quick recovery make graphite a superior rod-building material.

Another term often heard in discussions of graphite is "modulus." Within the context of rod building, this simply refers to relative stiffness—high modulus means lots of stiffness, low modulus means much less stiffness, and so on. Modulus can be controlled in the manufacturing process, so that graphite of a desired modulus can be produced. Most fly rods today use comparatively low-modulus graphite. Incidentally, I'm aware that stiffness does not directly correspond to the dictionary definition of modulus and is not a true synonym. For purposes of this discussion, however, it will do.

And what of bamboo and fiberglass? These two materials are still viable, at different ends of the pricing spectrum. Bamboo rods are still preferred by many collectors, traditionalists and various others who are willing to pay the price. There is a very active collector's market in vintage rods—Paynes, Leonards, Gillums and particularly Garrisons. The owners generally don't fish them, for fear of breakage. I can't really blame them. At this writing, a vintage rod of proper lineage in excellent condition will bring three thousand dollars or more. There are a number of excellent contemporary rod craftsmen active today, so the worshipper of Arundinaria Amabilis need not risk his Jim Payne onstream.

What is it about bamboo that would compel a person to spend a small fortune when a serviceable rod can be had for a fraction of the going price for cane? Certainly, aesthetics and tradition play a part, but make no mistake; a top-quality cane rod is a marvelous casting machine. It has a certain sweetness, a feel that synthetics may never quite duplicate. And it is remarkably durable. Properly cared for, a cane rod will last indefinitely. Many pre–World War II rods are as sound as the day they left the shop.

Fiberglass today fills the need for good-quality, low-priced rods to fit limited budgets. While not quite as quick and powerful as the graphites, today's glass rods are very good indeed. For the young beginner or the occasional fisherman, glass offers a fair bargain.

Since graphite now dominates the fly-rod market, we shall talk about actions, tapers and designs essentially as they relate to this material. In my fledgling days, a number of terms were commonly used in describing fly-rod action: fast, slow, medium, fast-tip, parabolic, progressive and others even less specific. I recall hearing the term "fast action" used synonymously with "dry-fly" action and "slow" correlated with "wet-fly" or bass-bug action. All rather arbitrary.

TIP ACTION                    PARABOLIC                    TYPICAL

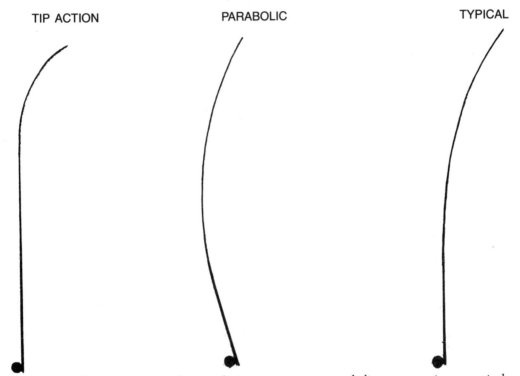

*Three common rod taper designs: tip action, parabolic, compromise or typical.*

Fast-tip action basically meant, in effect, that the tip did most of the work, traveling in a short arc. An old bamboo term, it was borrowed by the fiberglass manufacturers as a buzz word to sell their compromise tapers. Parabolic was a more meaningful term in that it described the shape of the bend or arc of the rod when loaded. These rods were designed to work well down into the butt section when taxed. This resulted in a slower overall response and greater damping action, but given quality materials and efficient taper design, it also resulted in more power. I always have liked this type of action, as it suits my casting style.

If you are interested in determining the taper design of a given rod, it is easily done. Simply mount a reel and run the line out through the guides. Then tie the end of the line to an immobile object or have someone hold on to it, while someone else raises the rod, flexing it into the "loaded" position. Now observe the arc formed by the rod. Is most of the bend out near the tip? That's like the old fast-tip design. Does the rod describe almost a uniform arc? That's similar to the parabolic taper. Most likely, you will see a compromise somewhere between the two.

The most important thing is how a rod behaves when actually being cast. However, much can be learned from the stationary-loading exercise just described. With a little practice, you can soon learn to detect nonlinearities in taper which may cause the rod to function—or malfunction— in certain ways during casting. For instance, if there is a point where the rod bends sharply, particularly in the tip section, this may indicate a weak spot which prevents the potential power of the lower portion of the rod from being exploited. My old friend Dudley Soper, a rod builder par excellence, used to call that a "button-hook."

Graphite has given the rod designer a greatly expanded set of parameters. For example, with bamboo and fiberglass, it is not practical to build a very long rod for a relatively light line—a 9-footer for a 4- or 5-weight, for example. Many have tried. The result is either a very slow, soft rod with the damping action of a cooked noodle or an iteration of the fast-tip design, where only the upper portion of the rod actually does the work.

With graphite, these rods have become not only practical but highly popular. Longer rods have many advantages. Casting is easier. Management of line on the water is done with more efficiency. A greater variety of flies can be cast and fished effectively. It's amazing what you can do with a 9-foot graphite for a 5- or 6-weight line.

Graphite has also made possible the design of extremely light rods for specialized types of fishing. Several producers now offer rods for 3-weight and even 2-weight lines. Within the scope of angling for which they were designed, these rods are quite functional and a lot of fun to use. Even a modest-sized trout feels like a trophy on these light outfits, and larger fish assume tarponlike proportions.

These rods have their limitations, of course. Casting distance is reduced, as is the size of fly you can effectively deliver. Casting in wind can be a real problem, especially when a long leader is needed. Striking a fish requires some adroit technique, as the tip tends to dip when the butt is brought upward in the typical "hook-setting" movement. This is true of all rods, more or less, but critical in the super-lights.

I was going to state that ultra-light rods were quite limited in length, due to the practicalities involved in designing rods for such light lines. However, while I was working on this chapter, someone handed me an 8½-footer for a 2-weight line. I could not believe how well it performed. The refinement of graphite continues to expand the parameters of rod design, and where it will end, no one knows.

Graphite has also benefited the users of heavy tackle, perhaps even more so than the ultra-light clan. In the days of bamboo, the design and construction of big fly rods posed certain problems. Top-quality bamboo has an extremely dense layer around the outer portion of the culm called power fiber. This is the material that imbues cane with its tremendous strength and resilience. But the layer of power fiber is not very thick, making it most difficult to build a long rod for a heavy line—a 9½-footer for a 10-weight, for example. Some of the earlier rod makers employed a process called double-building, in which two layers of power fibers were used—a rod within a rod, so to speak. It worked, after a fashion, but the rods were almost as hard on the fisherman as they were on the fish. They were extremely heavy, and real wrist killers. That's why the great power casters of that era were big men, like Marvin Hedge.

Fiberglass revolutionized large-rod construction, and graphite has moved it ahead yet another quantum step. Today's big-game-fish rods are light, powerful and easy to cast with. That 9½-foot 10-weight now weighs a mere 6 ounces, compared to at least 10 ounces for a comparable cane rod. This, coupled with equally dramatic advancements in fly reels, has opened up a whole new world for the saltwater fly-rodder. It is now possible to catch giant tarpon, permit, jack crevalle, striped bass and even sailfish on fly tackle.

Very well, what does all of this mean to you, the aspiring fly-fisher, who wants to purchase a serviceable rod, matched to your physical characteristics and appropriate for the type of fishing you want to do? Simply this—the more you know about rod design and performance characteristics, the better a selection you are likely to make. Also—and this is critical—ability to judge rods increases exponentially with casting skills. Someone who can't cast, or has very limited experience, is at a severe disadvantage when choosing a rod. Therefore, it is better if you can develop a reasonable level of casting competence before making any major investments in rods. If you have an acquaintance who will lend you some tackle to cut your teeth on, you'll be far ahead of the game. And when you do make that initial purchase, don't buy the cheapest—you are almost certain to be disappointed.

Many rods are purchased by mail today, and while this is not the best practice, it's quite practical, provided you know just what you want.

Good-quality rods are fairly consistent; top-quality rods are extremely so. Therefore, if you have cast with a particular model and liked it, you can probably obtain a virtually exact replica simply by ordering that model number. Additionally, better stores are more than pleased to provide consultation by phone. A meaningful ten-minute conversation with a knowledgable supplier can work miracles in producing a good match-up between rod and customer.

There are a lot of great fly rods out there today. Are there any bad ones? That's a strong word, but this I can tell you—there are those which I feel could and should be much better. As long as mass production and price competition exist, compromises will be made. Which is not to say that all mass-produced rods are poor—some are very good indeed. Neither does it guarantee that all of the products of the smaller producers are super-perfect. I've seen some that are pricey, highly cosmetic and quite mediocre as casting machines.

There are several areas where one might look for, shall we say, expedient practices in rod construction, particularly in mass-produced rods, and especially in those sold at heavy discount. One is the matter of spining. Every rod blank, regardless of material, has a spine—that is to say, a side that is stiffer and stronger than the others. In bamboo, the old rod makers called it the "high flat." This simply meant that one of the triangular strips of bamboo that was glued together with the others was a bit stiffer than its companions. In glass and graphite, the spine is a by-product of production methodology and minor variations in material.

Graphite rods tend to have pronounced spines because the material is so sensitive that slight differences in thickness or density are detectable. This is not a serious problem unless it is extreme. However, it is a factor that needs to be compensated for in the rod-making process.

The manner in which the builder deals with the spine is to locate it by flexing and rotating the blank, so that the guides may be wrapped on along the spine. This maximizes the power of the rod and also ensures that it will work in a flat plane during casting. Rods with pronounced spines that do not have the guides properly located tend to "orbit" a little—that is, the tip follows a slightly elliptical path, with commensurate decrease in casting efficiency.

Over the past couple of years I have asked various rod makers and manufacturer's representatives whether or not they spined their rods. Some didn't know what that meant. Others were evasive. A couple told me it really didn't matter. Still others were pleased to inform me that they certainly did spine their rods. I can't understand why one wouldn't; it's that simple to do. And as for it not making a difference, I can only say this. When my old friend Dud Soper was alive, I spent countless hours in his shop working on rods. One of the first things he taught me was spining. Further, he proved to me that it did make a difference, more so on some blanks than others. So there.

What then? Should you ask some mail-order clerk at the other end of an 800 number whether or not the rod you want to order has been spined? You might as well ask your local bartender if the hops used to make your favorite beer were organically grown. What I'm saying is that this is one of the things you give up when going strictly for price and economies of scale. The unspined rod may still cast quite satisfactorily, even though the potential of the blank was not optimized.

Another area of concern is the guides. There are several considerations here—windings, finish, metallurgy and placement. The guides should line up precisely, so that when you eyeball the rod they are in a perfect row. Also—and this is the province of the rod designer—the guides must be spaced along the rod so as to properly match up with the taper of the blank. This is something the new customer could never question—even the sophisticated purchaser with lots of experience in rod work would have trouble with this one. We have to take it on faith that the rod is properly engineered. If it is not, this will affect both casting and fish-fighting capabilities.

Guides are fastened to a rod by thread windings which are then coated with a protective substance. The aesthetics of the windings are a function of the skill and dedication of the craftsperson. You may or may not care much about this—I happen to care a lot. The bottom line is that the windings must hold the guides absolutely in place. As for the protective finish, most builders are now using single-coat polymers, which are both tough and good-looking. Years ago, we used to see a lot of production rods with poor-grade varnish or lacquer finishes on the windings. These dried out, chipped, cracked and came off, exposing the thread, which shortly followed suit.

As for metallurgy and general guide quality, I also see improvements here. The smaller wire guides, which are called snake guides, need to be of hardened material, so that they will hold up under the friction of the line passing through them. This is *very* critical. If a guide becomes worn or grooved, it will destroy a fly line in short order. You should check your guides frequently for wear and have them replaced at the first sign of deterioration.

Most manufacturers are using chrome or stainless-steel snake guides today, which ensures hardness and protection against rusting. A few builders use black stainless steel, which I think is classy. The traditional bronze guides are now more or less relegated to bamboo. They are okay but will rust quickly if the rod is put away wet.

The larger guides usually located on the butt section of a rod are called stripper guides, or sometimes shooting guides. Today, they are generally made of a Teflon or ceramic material, for reduced friction. Previously they were made of Carbaloy and, before that, glass. Their main job is to gather and pass the line coming through during the casting sequence with as little resistance as possible. This is particularly critical when one is double-hauling and shooting line. Thus, in addition to being made of low-friction material, these guides should have sufficient inside diameter to accept the line readily, with no constriction. All rods should have at least one stripper guide—the lowermost one. I prefer at least two, except on the lightest of rods, and three on large, heavy-duty rods, each slightly smaller than the one before.

There is also the matter of ferrules. Not much need be said in this regard, as there are only two types being used currently. The spigot type utilizes a graphite plug which connects the sections. The slide-over type is simply a matter of the tip section sliding over the top butt section a couple of inches or so. It is generally agreed that the slide-over is a little stronger, but I have no big problem with the spigot type. In either case, it is important to keep the ferrules waxed—this keeps them from sticking

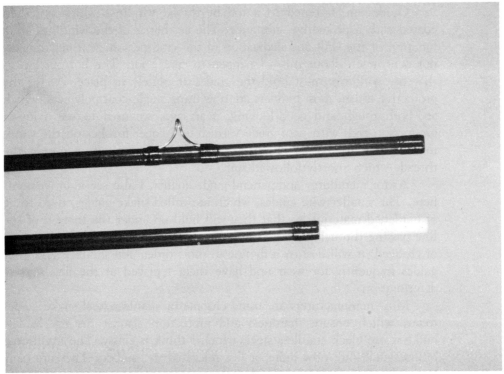

FIGURE 1

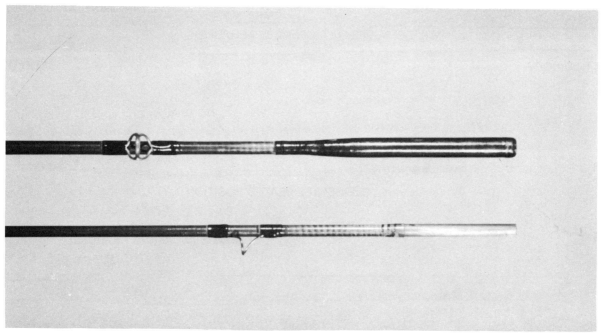

FIGURE 2

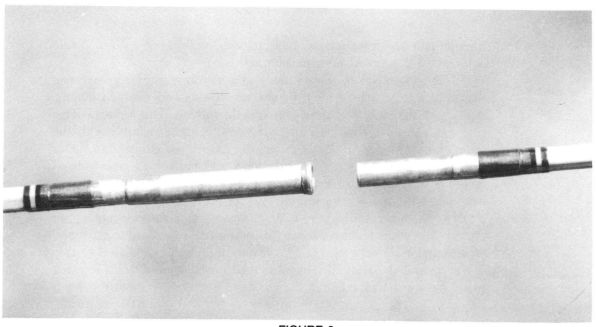

FIGURE 3

*Three types of ferrules: (1) spigot type, with "male" on butt section, (2) spigot type with "male" on tip section, (3) traditional nickel silver ferrules, still used on cane rods.*

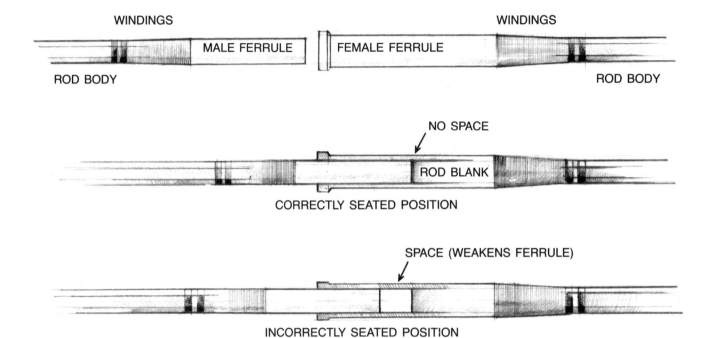

*Illustration of correctly and incorrectly joined ferrules. Failure to fully seat can cause trouble with any type of rod or ferrule.*

together and also reduces wear. Plain paraffin is okay, but a storm candle is better, as it contains both paraffin and oil.

The grip or rod handle is made of cork rings glued together and shaped in a lathe. There are a number of styles, most of which may be satisfactory if the individual is comfortable with it. This is, to a large extent, a matter of the diameter of the cork being compatible with the caster's hand. There is a degree of ambiance here, but either too large or too small a diameter produces discomfort and fatigue. A good rule of thumb is that the fingers should not make contact with the heel of the hand when the rod is gripped.

The diameter and design of the front part of the grip are rather critical. Some manufacturers slim this portion down in a distinct taper, apparently for cosmetic effect. This leaves nothing for the caster to grip or rest the thumb against. (Remember the thumb position?) This is a case where beauty should definitely be sacrificed for comfort, beauty being a matter of individual perception anyway.

Reel seats also vary in design, the screw-locking type being the most popular. The reel is fixed in place by pressure from a threaded ring which forces a knurled ring over the reel foot. I have seen reel seats on bargain-

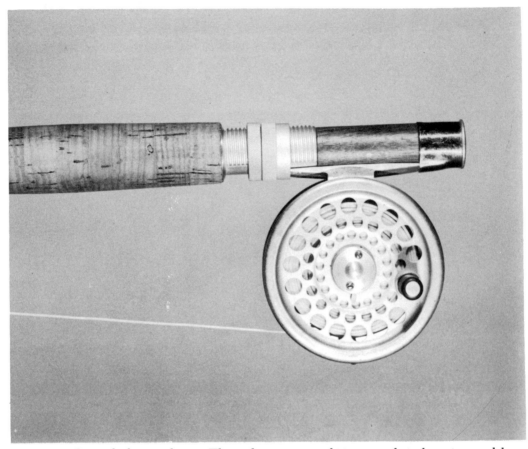

*Screw-locking reel seat. The reel is an external-rim-control single-action model.*

basement rods where the knurled ring was omitted. This is poor practice, as that mechanism is likely to jam.

Screw-locking reel seats are either up-locking or down-locking, meaning that the ring mechanism may force the reel foot into a receptacle either at the very butt end of the rod (down-locking) or at the bottom end of the grip (up-locking). If well made, either is satisfactory, although there is general agreement that the up-locking type is a little more resistant to jamming.

On ultra-light rods we often see the simple slip-ring type of mount, a concession to weight reduction. This is a less stable system but workable, if the slip rings and the diameter of the arbor on which the reel is mounted match up with the reel foot. This can be a bit problematical, as there are inconsistencies among manufacturers.

When it comes time to make the final selection, it is very important

*Slip-ring reel seat.*

to consider the type of fly-fishing for which the rod will be used. You would not be well advised to go to an extreme for your first, and perhaps for quite a while, your only rod. For typical stream and pond fishing, a 5- or 6-weight outfit in the 8- to-9-foot range would be suitable. The shorter the rod and the heavier the line, the stiffer the action, so if delicacy is a strong consideration, an 8-foot for a 6-weight line might be a bit strong. By the same token, if power is the prime consideration, a 9-foot for a 5-weight might be a little soft. It depends very much on the particular rod. I do most of my fishing with a 9 for a 5-weight, and can cast some pretty big flies a fair distance. However, that rod is actually a very light 6-weight, and besides, I've been at this for three decades.

Which brings to mind another point. Some rod manufacturers—larger ones in particular—are producing rods which they say will handle a range of lines. To a degree, that's true—graphite is an extremely versatile material. However, every rod is optimized at a particular line weight, and that should be the one printed on the butt section. If it's not, I would question the design integrity of that rod.

Part of the problem has to do with all the shows and expositions that have become a major part of the fly-fishing scene. They are lots of fun and quite useful, for you can see and often try out a large selection of rods, reels, lines and practically everything imaginable. The trouble is that we are becoming a generation of lawn and plastic-tank casters. Many of the manufacturers are designing their rods to throw line in that sort of environment, rather than for actual fishing.

We all love the feel of laying out a long line, and also watching the world-class people lay out even longer ones with little apparent effort. But that's not fishing. It bothers me to watch a representative from some rod company working with a relative newcomer at the casting pool, hyping the fact that a particular rod will cast everything from a 5-weight to a 9-weight, then demonstrating such. Sure, I can get a modern graphite rod to do that, but what's the point? The idea is to design a rod for a specific line, and to manufacture the rod in such a manner that it casts that line superbly.

What bothers me even more is that I see design compromises sneaking back into rod design and production. I thought we had seen the last of the fast-tip compromise tapers back in the 1960s, when the line-rating system was still in a state of chaos. Now all of a sudden I'm seeing some "tippy" rods again, with stiff butt sections. They tend to button-hook in the middle of the tip section and do not have a smooth action throughout. Wonderful as graphite is, it still can't compensate for such aberrations in design.

For most specialized fly casting, one may need a heavier rod. I do most of my bass bugging with a 6-weight, but when really large, air-resistant bugs are called for, a 7- or 8-weight is a more efficient tool. When I'm in Alaska, Iceland, Canada or some other wonderful place where huge flies and powerful fish are the order of the day, I'll want a selection of rods ranging from 7-weight to 10-weight, 8½ to 9½ feet in length. These also enable me to do battle with the bluefish and weakfish we encounter around the Atlantic coast, and the occasional striped bass.

When one branches out into salmon fishing, saltwater fly rodding and such, the second major function of the fly rod—that of fighting the fish—comes to the fore. Nowhere was this more dramatically brought home to me than in Iceland in 1979, my first Atlantic salmon trip. I took four rods—two 9-weights, a light 7-weight and a 6-weight. One day, when the wind wasn't too awfully strong, I made the mistake of using the 7-weight in a run of fast, surging water—"Strengur," the Icelanders called it, for "strong currents." The first fish was small, a 6-pounder, and did not pose a problem. The second went 14 pounds—my largest, as it developed. I got the fish eventually, but no thanks to the rod. I simply could

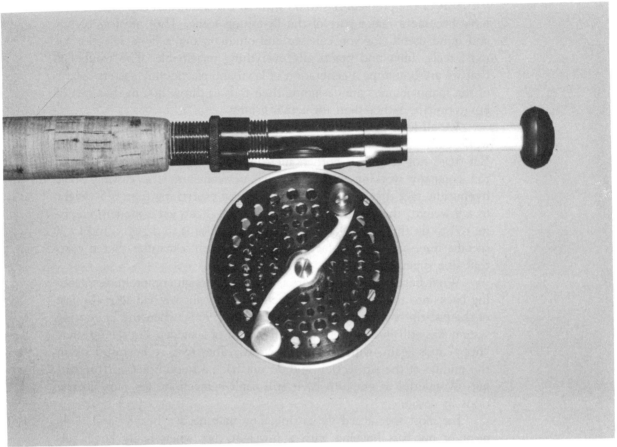

*A typical extension butt for fighting larger fish. The reel is a multiplying type.*

not put sufficient pressure on the fish to tire it, and it took me far downstream. After that, I went back to the 9-weight.

If and when you do get into heavy-game fishing with fly tackle, seek out the best advice available. All of the components are subjected to tremendous stress and pressure, orders of magnitude beyond those imposed by everyday stream fishing. There is also the matter of salt water and its corrosive effect. In short, it's a whole new ball game.

One closing note. Rod manufacturers are prone to use a lot of buzz words and high-tech, gee-whiz terminology. Some of these terms, such as "IM-6," are somewhat meaningful in that they describe a certain type or generation of material. IM-6 is acrospace graphite, but there are variations within IM-6. Other terms are simply ad-man hype. I can't list them here, much as I would like to, because they are brand-specific. I really wish the rod people would refrain from using such noninformative, confusing terminology. As a matter of fact, I deplore the manner in which media and advertising people are causing the wholesale destruction of the English language by such practices.

## REELS

As we learned in Chapter II, the fly reel is not actively involved in casting. However, it is definitely involved in fishing, sometimes to the extreme. Thus, its various characteristics need to be understood.

Basically, the reel is a place to store the line and backing. Backing is supplementary line used to fill the spool and to provide additional line for playing large fish which take out all of the fly line.

The fundamental reel is of single-action design, which means that one full turn of the handle cranks the spool 360 degrees. There are also multiplying reels which have a gear system whereby one full turn of the reel handle cranks the spool more than 360 degrees. Various ratios are available, such as 2:1, 2.5:1, and so on. This feature is very useful in big-game fishing where long lengths of line must often be retrieved quickly. However, it can be a mixed blessing, because the higher gear ratio makes it harder to reel against a large fish. It's just like a car's transmission in that respect. Also, it allows one to unknowingly overpressure a fish, causing the leader to break.

All fly reels have some sort of drag system which allows the angler to adjust the amount of pull required to take line from the spool. In average trout fishing, a terribly sophisticated, heavy-duty drag system isn't needed, because the fish can't put that much pressure on it. Actually, the drag serves more as a protection against overwinding or backlash when the angler strips line from the reel than as an implement in fighting the fish. But with large game fish, capable of long runs at high speeds, it is all-important. Many a great salmon, bonefish or tarpon has been lost when a drag system blew apart or locked up from overheating, a little puff of blue smoke signifying disaster.

Essentially, drag systems involve some sort of mechanism for applying a controlled amount of friction, thus retarding the spool's inclination to spin. The key word here is "controlled"—you need to be able to adjust the drag to suit the situation. Unless you're after large game fish, the control or adjustment mechanism is, in my opinion, more important than the technology of the drag system proper.

Let's say you're fishing a cold-water lake where large trout abound. A big fly is called for, and a substantial leader tippet—6 pounds perhaps, maybe even more. Under such circumstances, you would tighten up on the drag a bit, so as to avoid overwinds and have more control over a large, fast-running fish.

Now we switch the scenario to a placid spring creek. The trout are taking small dry flies, and you must go to a 7X tippet, testing perhaps a pound and a half. In this situation, you will adjust for minimal drag, only enough to prevent overwinds or backlashes. This protects the critical link—that fine tippet and the knots that connect it to the fly and the heavier portion of the leader.

Most fly reels feature detachable spools, which are easily interchangeable, so that one may readily switch lines. Some incorporate an exposed-rim design, making it easy to thumb the spool when a large fish is running. It takes a little practice to learn to avoid getting whacked by the reel handle, but even so, the exposed-rim feature is a good one, especially on larger reels.

With the exception of complex models with sophisticated drag systems and/or multiplying actions, nearly all fly reels available today can be set up for either left-handed or right-handed winding. I am right-handed and therefore prefer to crank with my left hand, rather than having to switch hands, as was required with bait-casting reels of yesteryear. To convert from right- to left-hand wind, or vice versa, two operations are required: the chrome or hardened metal line guide must be moved to the front, and the drag mechanism must be reversed. Neither operation is at all difficult if you have proper-sized screwdrivers to fit the small screws inevitably found in reels. Most manufacturers provide an instruction sheet showing how the conversion is done. Lacking that, I suggest you get some assistance from the dealer.

I mentioned the line guide. Its purpose is to provide a very hard, smooth surface over which the fly line may pass. Fly lines tend to have a rough texture, which can cause wear rather quickly on softer metal. Eventually, after much use, wear may also occur on the hard metal of the line guide. When that happens, the line guide should be replaced, in order to avoid damaging the line. In most cases, the line guide is attached with one or two screws. Better manufacturers can be expected to offer line guides as a low-cost replacement part.

Although fly reels are relatively simple devices, a fair amount of precision in manufacture is required. I prefer a reel with close tolerances—that is, not a lot of spaces or gaps where the line can get caught or gravel can lodge. When examining a reel, I turn the handle and observe the precision with which the spool revolves, noticing how well the tolerances are maintained. I test the drag at all settings to determine the range and integrity of the adjustment mechanism. If the

*A fly reel showing typical line guide.*

reel is to be used for very light-tippet fishing, I want to see that the drag is sufficiently sensitive to protect the finest of tippets.

We must also concern ourselves with capacity. While all reels have a rated capacity, usually expressed in terms of line weight plus backing, I find that some are overstated. The idea is to allow for an adequate amount of backing plus the weight line intended to be used on that reel. Backing should not be too thin, as it is hard to handle and tends to bury itself on the spool, creating snarls. Also, very light backing may be of insufficient strength to hold a large fish and an entire fly line, with additional pressure exerted by the current. Twenty-pound test is a good all-around thickness, or perhaps a little heavier on large reels. Backing should consist of a nonstretch braided material, such as Dacron. Never use monofilament line for backing. It is so stretchy that pressure can actually build up to a point where the spool can be sprung.

How much backing do you need? For typical trout fishing, 100 yards should be more than adequate. On light reels, ones where the intended use is small stream and spring creek fishing, 50 yards is generally sufficient. A salmon reel ought to have 200 yards of backing, and a heavy game-fish reel 300.

As mentioned, backing complements the fly line, as well as serving as supplementary running line. It is not good practice to attach a fly line directly to the arbor or core of a reel, particularly if it is a double-taper line, where both ends can be used. Backing supplements the diameter of the arbor, so that the fly line isn't all curled up in tiny ringlets. This also makes for more efficient reeling when playing a fish, especially with a nonmultiplying reel. But care must be taken not to overfill a spool. This causes tangles, and also may result in the fly line being damaged from contact with the frame of the reel.

When selecting a reel, I urge you to choose one which is of good-quality metal—aluminum perhaps, or one of the tough, light alloys used today. Certain modern synthetics, such as Delrin and Teflon, are great as parts in drag mechanisms, but for the frame, spool and reel foot, there's no substitute for metal. Several reels are or have been manufactured predominantly out of synthetics, including graphite. I do not recommend them. Graphite is a wonderful material for rods but not for reels. Perhaps some day a synthetic will be developed that will lend itself to reel construction, but at this writing that time has not arrived.

## FLY LINES

As we have learned, fly lines are quite different from other types of fishing lines, in that they have weight and bulk. This is an essential ingredient in successful fly casting. Of the three major components, fly lines have gone through the most dramatic evolution, what with the advent of synthetics and improved manufacturing techniques. In order for you to appreciate the significance of this, a brief history is in order.

There was a time—not that long ago, actually—when all fly lines were made of braided silk. The better-quality silk lines were a pleasure to cast (they still are), but there were several negative aspects. In order to get them to float, frequent dressing was required, meaning several times in the course of a long day astream. And at day's end, one did not merely reel up the line and head for the nearest tavern. The line was removed from the reel, dried with a cloth or paper towel and either laid in coils or wound onto a line drier. A line put away wet was difficult to dress for the next day's fishing. Worse, rotting occurred if a wet line was reeled up tightly and put away for any length of time.

In order to protect silk lines and minimize absorption of water, an oil impregnation process was used. Here again, the angler had to take some precautions, because impregnated lines had no tolerance for heat. A line left in a car on a hot, sunny day would start bleeding oil in a very short time. This created a mess and damaged the line.

Despite their problems, silk lines were a joy in some respects. They were supple and pleasant to handle. The weight-to-diameter ratio was just about optimal for smooth, effortless casting. The tapers were nicely graduated, at least in the more expensive ones. And given lots of TLC, these lines would last for years, even when used frequently.

When all lines were silk, the weight-to-diameter ratio did not vary appreciably among manufacturers. Thus, the old alphabetic rating system was quite viable. Letter designations were used to express the diameter, and thereby the weight, of a line. The closer the letter was to the beginning of the alphabet, the heavier the weight of the line—in other words, an A was heavier than a B. The heaviest I ever encountered was rated triple-A. Tapered lines were rated with a three-letter code which expressed the diameter of the front end, the belly or middle section and the rear end. A double-tapered line, which is symmetrical, was coded something like HDH or GAG, depending on its diametric range. A weight-forward line, which is nonsymmetrical, might be designated GAF, HCF and so on.

Shortly after World War II, fly lines made of synthetics began to appear on dealers' shelves. The early versions were not very good and were justifiably shunned by the rank and file of the angling fraternity. They were, however, accepted by inexperienced fishermen who had nothing else to relate to, and so the revolution was begun. By the mid-to-late 1950s it was in full swing. New materials and technology generated rapid improvements, and synthetic lines were accepted by all except the most crusty traditionalists.

Perhaps the central figure in the development of the synthetic fly line was Leon Martuch of Midland, Michigan. Leon and two friends started Scientific Anglers, Inc., in 1946, initially to produce silicone-based floatants for lines and flies. Throughout the late forties and early fifties, Leon experimented with various synthetics and coating techniques. Meanwhile, the Cortland Line Company came out with a synthetic floating fly line. It worked reasonably well, except that the plastic coating was prone to cracking, at which point the line would absorb water and sink.

In the mid-1950s, Martuch and his partner, Clare Harris, developed two processes which radically altered the way fly lines were manufactured. One was a mechanical method for extruding a tapered plastic coating over a level nylon core—in other words, the taper was in the coating itself. This was different from the new Cortland line, which built the taper into the braided core—a much more complex process—then coated it with a uniform plastic layer.

The second innovation was the incorporation of tiny bubbles—microballoons is the proper name—into the plastic coating. These extremely tiny hollow balls performed a miracle—the lines became lighter than water and floated! This gave birth to the trade name Aircel®, which is still used by Scientific Anglers. The two processes were patented and proved so successful that until quite recently virtually all synthetic fly lines were manufactured under a licensing arrangement with Scientific Anglers.

With the advent of synthetic lines, the ancient letter-designation rating system became worse than useless. The problem was that weight-to-diameter ratios were no longer constant—they varied among manufacturers, technologies, designs and substances. Sinking lines and sink-tip lines of various densities appeared, further exacerbating the situation. People were angry, because they could not reliably purchase a line that was the proper weight for a given rod. Clearly, it was time for a new rating system, and sure enough, it wasn't long before one emerged.

The new system is known as the AFTMA (American Fishing Tackle Manufacturer's Association) standard. It utilizes numeric and alphabetic designations to identify weight and design, respectively. Weights are expressed in grains, with 480 grains in an ounce. As the chart indicates, a high-low range of tolerance is allowed. In extremely light lines—weights 2, 3 and even 4—the tolerance is such that if a line is on the edge, so to speak, it may become noticeable. I own a 3-weight rod that doesn't care for lines on the light edge of the range.

Here's how the new system works. The numeric designator identifies the actual rated-weight classification of the line, which is determined by weighing the front 30 feet, exclusive of any level tip, if such are present. Alphabetic prefixes and suffixes describe the design characteristics—for instance, a DT6F is a double-tapered, weight-6 line that floats. A WF7S is a weight-forward, weight-7 line that sinks. Here is a list of commonly used letter designations:

| | |
|---|---|
| L | level |
| DT | double-taper |
| WF | weight-forward |
| WFL | weight-forward long-belly |
| ST | shooting-taper |
| S | sinking |
| F/S | floating/sinking |
| I | intermediate, or slow-sinking |

We have been referring to various taper designs, so let's become familiar with their characteristics. A level line is one which has no taper—it's the same diameter throughout. While still available, level lines are not very popular because of the superior casting properties of tapered lines. They have the advantage of a low price tag but the disadvantage of being less pleasant to cast. The absence of a taper causes these lines to behave in a tip-heavy manner, slapping the line onto the water. A nice, tight loop is difficult to obtain—thus, distance casting is more difficult.

The double-taper has been around for a while and is still a favorite. It has a level center section which tapers to a fine tip at either end. It is noted for delicacy of delivery. Double-taper lines are symmetrical—that is, both ends are the same. Thus, the line may be reversed when one end gets worn out, which means one actually gets two lines for the price of one, compared to asymmetrical designs.

The weight-forward taper, sometimes called the torpedo taper, makes longer casting easier, because most of the weight resides in the forward portion of the line. Interestingly, this design also facilitates very short casts, because the abbreviated front taper causes more line weight to be exposed sooner, enabling the caster to load the rod with a shorter length of line. Some delicacy is sacrificed, and the lines do not roll cast as well as double-tapers. This is an asymmetrical design—the belly quickly tapers into a fine-running line which shoots well.

LEVEL

DOUBLE TAPER

FORWARD TAPER

LONG BELLY

TRIANGLE TAPER

SHOOTING HEAD

*Common line taper designs.*

The long-belly version of the weight-forward line is exactly what the name implies. Approximately 20 feet is added to the belly and a comparable amount to the overall line, which allows an experienced caster to carry more line in the air for easier distance casting.

The shooting taper is designed for extremely long-distance casting. It is a very short line, only about 30 feet in length, and corresponds to the front end of a weight-forward taper. It is attached to a special shooting line, which is actually nothing more or less than fine level fly line or monofilament. The idea is to get the shooting head moving very fast in the air with a series of power strokes, then shoot a great amount of the level line. This is a very valuable technique in certain angling situations. However, it requires a fair amount of skill and is not something I would recommend to the rank beginner.

Recently, a new taper was introduced which has enjoyed wide acceptance within the angling clan. This is the triangle taper, brainchild of Lee Wulff, whose innovations have already benefited several generations of fly-fishers. The triangle taper is simply that—a long, continuously graduated taper involving the first 40 feet of the line, at which point it drops off sharply to a fine running line. This taper is a joy to cast and fish. Presentations of great delicacy are facilitated, and the line roll casts better than any I've ever used. Score one for Lee. This is, of course, an asymmetrical design. Some anglers find that casting characteristics are improved by cutting back the tip a little—2 to 4 feet or so. I agree, but advise great caution here, especially for a beginner whose casting technique is still under development. If you want to try this, do so in small steps, and get an experienced hand to assist you.

Designations such as F, S and F/S define the floating or sinking characteristics of lines. Used alone, F simply stands for floating and S for sinking. F/S identifies a line which sinks at the front and floats further back. There are a number of variations in sinking fly-line designs, both in density and length of the sinking portion. In a sinking-tip line, only the front 10 feet sinks. In a sinking-head line, the first 20 feet sinks, and in a sinking-belly line, the first 30 feet sinks. How fast and deep these tips, heads and bellies sink depends on the density of material used in their construction.

What about these floating/sinking designs anyway? They are widely misunderstood, I believe, in terms of where and how they should be used. Obviously, the idea is to get the fly down to where the fish are, hence the heavier front end. For this, one pays a considerable price in casting characteristics. A sinking fly line does not have the same aerodynamics as a floating fly line. The longer and more dense the sinking portion, the greater the effect on casting. When coupled with floating line in the designs just described, a certain nonlinearity is effected. I notice this particularly in sinking tips and heads. It is difficult to maintain a nice loop, because it feels as though there is a hinge in the line where the sinking portion joins the floating portion.

Despite the casting drawbacks, a sinking-type line can be a great asset to an angler in appropriate circumstances. They are particularly useful in lake and pond fishing, or in large, slow-moving pools in rivers. I do not particularly favor them in faster water, especially broken water where there are a lot of rocks, because they tend to get tangled around obstructions. In that sort of setting, I prefer a floating line, possibly with a strike indicator, and a weighted fly or leader.

As you become familiar with the great array of fly lines available today—at this writing, Scientific Anglers alone makes over 250 different models—you will notice that they come in a wide range of colors. There is controversy here. I just read in a catalog that while color does not scare fish, line flash does. On the very next page, where they recommend their bright fluorescent orange line, they state that line flash does *not* scare fish. I hope that is a misprint. The truth is that line movement in the air *does* scare fish, particularly when accompanied by line flash, or reflections off the line when it is being cast.

The question then becomes, does color contribute to this? I can assure you that it does. How much it matters depends on the angling environment. In rough pocket water, it matters little, as the fish doesn't get a good look at things in the outside world. On calmer waters, light-colored lines with shiny finishes have a significantly higher reflection factor than duller, darker lines. When floating in the surface film outside the fish's "window," the light-colored line is *much* more visible—an argument in favor of subdued colors in fly lines and, also, for longer leaders.

While they may seem a bit pricey, modern fly lines are actually a pretty good bargain. If properly cared for, they last a remarkably long time—I refer you to the section on tackle maintenance for detailed information on line care. I would not advise resorting to any brand-X purchases, because the modest saving may be more than offset by short line life and poor casting characteristics. Production of a quality fly line takes a high level of process control—the line must meet weight, diameter and design criteria. The braided core must be centered within the plastic coating. So stick to proven brand names—it's worth it.

If economy is a consideration, try one of the special beginner's lines offered by several major producers. Scientific Anglers currently offers one of these, called the Concept®. The entire line is about 57 feet long, quite enough for most fishing situations. The taper is a little shorter, which helps the beginning caster. This is a particularly good line for a younger person to start out with.

## BALANCING

In my first book, I emphasized the importance of the balance relationship between the reel and the rod. While I no longer consider this as critical as I did back then, it is still a matter worthy of consideration, as it affects your comfort over a long day on the stream.

To check the balance of an outfit, simply mount the reel with line and backing in place, then determine the point at which the outfit balances horizontally on your finger. If this point is anywhere within a couple of inches on either side of the front of the grip, you're in good shape. Graphite is lighter than other materials; therefore, a long rod will balance with a lighter reel. I own a 9½-foot 6-weight that balances perfectly with a Hardy Princess.

If you have an outfit that falls a bit outside the parameters just stated, I wouldn't be too concerned. I have salmon fished with heavy reels that slightly overbalanced the rod and have not suffered for it. About the only adverse effect I've noticed is that when I begin to tire, I have a tendency to adjust by moving my hand up or down the grip. This is not really good practice, as most grips have a point of optimum comfort and effectiveness, and that's where the hand should stay. This is particularly true of grips which are designed for specific thumb placement.

# CHAPTER V _____

# *Leaders, Knots and Attachment Methods*

As you probably know, the leader is the link between the fly line and the fly. It, along with the knots employed to make the connections, is *the* critical factor in effective fly-fishing. A strong statement, perhaps, but a supportable one. More fish are lost because of the leader and its knots than any other factor, including the ineptitude of the angler.

Leaders are generally made of synthetic monofilament material similar to that used in the manufacture of spinning line. Formulas are varied to produce degrees of stiffness or limpness, but essentially they are all nylon-based. Diameters vary from the gossamer .003 (three-thousandths of an inch) to .025, or even more, in large game-fish applications. Breaking strengths, of course, vary proportionately.

First, let's become familiar with the rating system and designations which describe the smaller diameters of material commonly used to form end sections on leaders, which are called tippets. The breaking strengths are approximate and slightly on the optimistic side, as I used a particularly strong brand as a guide. Also, this reflects the unknotted breaking strength only.

| Diameter   | Rating | Breaking strength |
|------------|--------|-------------------|
| .011 inch  | 0X     | 14  pounds        |
| .010       | 1X     | 12                |
| .009       | 2X     | 10                |
| .008       | 3X     | 7                 |
| .007       | 4X     | 5                 |
| .006       | 5X     | 4                 |
| .005       | 6X     | 2.8               |
| .004       | 7X     | 1.9               |
| .003       | 8X     | 1.1               |

The X rating system is perhaps a bit archaic, but it is still widely used in describing leader material. As you can see, the graduations are in thousandths. This helps relate the X system to measured diameter, because if you can remember just one—5X is .006, for example—you can obtain the others by counting backward or forward and adding or subtracting .001 for each step.

The question then becomes, how true are the labeled diameters on the package? Frankly, they could be more accurate. There is significant variance among brands. In smaller diameters, this becomes critical. I don't mind being a thousandth over at lX or even 2X, but I very much mind at 7X, where .001 represents a 25 percent error.

The only way to be sure of diameter is to carry an accurate micrometer. I invested in a very good one years ago, when I became aware of the credibility gap between the numbers on the package and the true diameter of the material inside. It gets a lot of use. A pain in the neck but very necessary.

While writing this chapter, I picked out a number of spools at random and "miked" them. The marked diameters ranged from .010 to .003. Here are the results:

| Brand     | Marked diameter | Actual diameter |
|-----------|-----------------|-----------------|
| Maxima    | .010            | .012            |
| Maxima    | .009            | .011            |
| Dai-Riki  | .010            | .0102           |
| Dai-Riki  | .009            | .0097           |
| Dai-Riki  | .008            | .0083           |
| Dai-Riki  | .007            | .007            |
| Dai-Riki  | .006            | .006            |
| Dai-Riki  | .005            | .0054           |
| Kroic GT  | .004            | .0041           |
| Kroic GT  | .003            | .0035           |

This is about what I expected. Dai-Riki and Kroic GT, two leading contemporary brands, ran quite true, as they consistently do. Maxima, as usual, was .002 over. Why, then, do I bother with Maxima? Because it's great stuff, despite the diameter problem. I use it for making the main portion of my leaders, miking each spool and remarking accurately.

Now let's examine the tapered-leader concept and its relationship to diameters. A leader tapers from a thick butt section to a relatively fine tippet, in graduated steps. For purposes of this exercise, I will confine my remarks to hand-tied knotted leaders rather than extruded tapered leaders—we will touch on those later. The idea is to step down about .002 with each succeeding section, making it somewhat shorter than the preceding one.

That last statement incorporates what is perhaps the most critical factor in leader design. I have found that if one begins with a reasonably thick butt section, drops approximately .002 at each step and makes each succeeding section a little shorter than the one before (tippet excepted), the leader will cast effectively. I've reached a point where I can sit beside a stream and tie up a leader without even measuring the sections, and it will cast beautifully. If I know the length of the butt section, I can estimate the rest. The overall length of the leader is determined by the relative lengths of the sections, which can be varied, as long as the "slightly shorter" rule is adhered to.

To further understand taper, let's look at a typical leader formula, one I use frequently for general dry-fly, wet-fly and nymph fishing:

|                  | Length     | Diameter   |
|------------------|------------|------------|
| Section 1 (butt) | 36 inches  | .020 inch  |
| Section 2        | 30         | .017       |
| Section 3        | 21         | .014       |
| Section 4        | 12         | .012       |
| Section 5        | 10         | .010       |
| Section 6        | 8          | .008       |

This leader measures 9 feet 9 inches. Add a 27-inch tippet, which could be either .007 or .006, and we have a 12-foot leader. You have probably noticed that in the heavier sections I stepped down .003 instead of .002. That's perfectly okay. When I get below .015, I adhere to the .002 rule. In finer diameters, a step-down of only .001 is frequently used.

There is flexibility in this design. For instance, if I'm on-stream with the leader previously described, with a 5X tippet, and find that I have to drop to 7X for some reason, I simply cut back the 5X so that it's slightly shorter than the previous section and knot on the 7X, thus observing the

.002 rule. In doing this, one must allow for the amount of material required to form the knot, especially in the 5X section, which ends up too short unless a compensation is made.

At one time I believed in the premise that leader butts and thicker sections should be made of the stiffest material available, for casting efficiency. I have abandoned this, and joyfully so, as that hard nylon was terrible stuff to work with. I now use Maxima for the butt and all succeeding sections down to around .010, after which I go to one of the newer materials, such as Dai-Riki, which is more limp and has greater strength for diameter. Why Maxima for the heavier sections? It straightens beautifully, knots easily and has what I feel is an ideal consistency for effective casting. I realize the mention of brand names somewhat dates this information, as new materials and changes in existing ones will continue. Still, I feel it is the best way to clearly explain the various points, these brands being prime examples of their respective properties.

For tippets, I want a more limp material with excellent knot strength and accurate diameters. The two mentioned earlier are excellent in both respects, Dai-Riki being the strongest I've yet encountered. There are other good ones, Aeon and Climax, to name a couple, and certainly more will come. As a matter of fact, I was given a sample of the new Orvis Super-Strong by John Harder of that company just as this book was going into production. It is fantastic. The three spools—4X, 5X and 6X—miked right on the numbers, and the strength is incredible. I tied a surgeon's knot in the 6X and tried to break it. Nearly cut my hands. Yes, ladies and gentlemen, high-tech fishing has arrived in force. Incidentally, John Harder's analysis and testing work is the most accurate, sophisticated and meaningful of any I've yet encountered.

As new brands appear, they must pass the knot-strength test, for some materials have a tendency to retain their breaking strength better than others when knotted. The simple test I use is not accurate to the fraction of an ounce, due to the limitations of my equipment, but it does give me a good idea of the relative knot strengths of various materials. I tie one of the few knots I use in fishing, hook the material to a fish-weighing scale and exert pressure until breakage occurs. The breaking point is a function of the properties of the material, plus the type of knot and how proficiently it is tied. I wouldn't recommend a knot that reduced the breaking strength of the material by more than 10 percent. There are a few complicated but very important knots used in saltwater fishing that actually test at 100 percent.

With knotless tapered leaders available, you might wonder why I continue to make up my own knotted leaders. The answer is that I have yet to find an extruded leader that casts as well as my knotted ones. I may have to eat that statement some day, as commercial leaders are showing improvement. However, it would take a clear superiority to get me to switch, because I can tie up a leader for pennies, and I have to make do on an angling writer's earnings.

Probably, you will want to use store-bought leaders, at least for a while. That's fine—as I've stated, they are much better these days. I would suggest you buy them somewhat shorter than you want the overall leader to be, to allow for a tippet of around 30 inches. Also, select those which taper to within .002 of the diameter of the tippet you intend to tie on. For example, a leader tapered to 3X will accommodate a 4X or 5X tippet.

My philosophy on leader length is simply this: use the shortest one you can get away with. Of course, if you are fishing a glassy pool on the Battenkill, that might mean 16 feet. Even with optimal taper design, that's a lot of leader for a fledgling angler to throw. I recommend that you not use a longer leader than you can cast effectively—you are better off making a good presentation with an 8-foot leader than a bad one with a 16-footer. Something in the 7-to-10-foot range would be appropriate for the beginner, exact length depending on skill level, tackle and angling situation. As you gain experience, you will develop a sense for knowing when a really long leader is required, and you will also develop the casting skills to deliver it efficiently.

Apart from deceiving fish, there are other factors which discipline the length and type of leader you might choose. As I mentioned, you can probably resort to a shorter leader in the wind, because of the riffles created on the surface. By the same token, a heavier tippet may suffice. For example, a pool which demands a 10-foot leader tapered to 5X on a calm day may be fished with an 8-footer tapered to 3X on a breezy one.

The size of the fly also has a direct bearing on the choice of leader and particularly the thickness of the tippet. A large Variant or Green Drake imitation is virtually impossible to cast with a long leader and fine tippet—nor is there a need to do so. A large fly will drift properly with a fairly heavy tippet, and that's what's important. When fishing a very large dry fly, I'm usually using 3X or 4X, maybe 5X if the water is very still, although 5X is really pushing it when casting a big, bushy fly. With a size 14 dry fly, I'll probably be fishing 5X most of the time, perhaps 6X in demanding circumstances or 4X when wind or rougher water serves to aid my efforts at deception. I use the ultra-fine tippets—7X and 8X—only in the most critical situations where tiny flies and great delicacy are mandated.

So far we've been discussing leaders essentially from a standpoint of the dry fly. Of course, there's no reason why you can't fish a subsurface fly with the same leader; however, there are reasons why you might not want to, particularly if a sinking line of some type is involved. This relates to the "use the shortest leader you can get away with" philosophy. A sunken leader is much less noticeable. Thus, camouflage is achieved with a shorter leader and perhaps a heavier tippet.

There are other reasons for altering the leader when going subsurface. A heavier tippet makes it easier to handle weighted flies or weight added to the leader. It also is helpful when you are extricating a sunken fly from some snag. It helps absorb the force of those unexpected strikes encountered in this type of fishing. And a shorter leader is more compatible with a sinking line, when the situation calls for one. Leader material tends to be buoyant; thus, an overly long leader begins to counter the sinking effect of the front end of the line.

In an average-sized wadeable river, I would bottom-fish a nymph or wet fly with a leader of about 7 or 8 feet—if I'm staying with a floating line, which is usually the case. I try to sink the fly and leader, while the tip of the line floats, in effect becoming a strike indicator. When using a sink-tip line in a slow pool or lake, I might shorten up even further, depending on the circumstances. For example, I fished Alaska for silver salmon with a leader only a few feet long. This helped when casting a heavy fly in the wind and permitted the full effect of the sink-tip line to be obtained.

A shorter leader is also recommended for fishing streamer flies. Here again, we have a larger fly which is usually fished weighted, to some degree. Any time a fly is weighted or weight is added to the leader, the dynamics of casting are affected. A short leader and substantial tippet help generate sufficient force to deliver the fly, weight and all.

Earlier I used the term "strike indicator," so let's see what that's all about. When fishing a subsurface fly deep, the strike is usually invisible and sometimes remarkably subtle. This is understandable. You are dead-drifting a bug to an unsuspecting trout which is finning away unalarmed in a bottom lie, and the fish has to do little more than open its mouth. Sometimes you feel nothing, and the only indication of a take is a hesitation of the line's drift.

If only a moderate amount of weight is required, the front end of a floating line can effectively serve as a strike indicator. For increased visibility, a couple of inches of bright-colored plastic sleeve can be slipped over the leader butt—these are available in shops everywhere. If even greater visibility and perhaps a little supplementary flotation are wanted, you can resort to a polyfoam-type strike indicator, which is really in essence a tiny bobber. I'm not crazy about them, because they further encumber the terminal tackle, and besides, bobber fishing begins to get a lot like bait fishing. These gimmicks do work, however; I've used them when fishing heavily weighted flies in rough water.

Let's talk about weighted flies and supplementary weight, having raised the issue. I consider weight of any sort a necessary evil, for it detracts from the pleasures of fly casting and introduces negative dynamics which can cause all sorts of tangles and snafus. However, catching fish on a weighted fly beats hell out of sitting forlornly on the bank, or flogging the water, praying for one upward-oriented fish. It can, in fact, be quite exciting.

The key is to limit the amount of weight to what is absolutely needed. Weighted flies are available, particularly out west, where large nymphs bottom-fished in heavy currents are often very productive. That's fine in such situations, because the power and turbulence of the water causes even a heavily weighted fly to behave in a lifelike manner. In calmer waters, weighted flies tend to drift in an unnatural manner. Even a bottom-fished fly needs some buoyancy—after all, what does a natural nymph weigh? Thus, when fishing quiet waters, I prefer to use an un-weighted fly and add a bit of weight to the leader.

In my prehistoric bait-fishing days, I used wraparound sinkers, which are small strips of lead that one twists around the leader. I've long since abandoned them for small, soft-lead split shot, preferably the type with the little lips on the back, to facilitate easy removal. Generally it is best to attach the split shot just above the first leader knot—that is, the one that connects the tippet to the leader proper. This prevents the sinker from slipping. A shorter tippet is recommended, so that the tendency of monofilament to float is reduced and the effect of the sinker is optimized. Something like 14 to 16 inches works quite nicely.

Today there is some experimentation taking place with another method for weighting leaders, using braided leader material. Envision a Chinese finger trap which expands and contracts—that's what the braided material resembles. As it is hollow, a section of thin lead wire can be inserted, creating a hunk of leader that sinks like baling wire. The problem is, the weight is at the wrong end, as the braided material is invariably used as a butt—one wouldn't want it for a tip section. In effect, this converts whatever line is being used into a high-density sink tip. This is okay, if that's what the situation calls for. I can see where steel headers and Alaskan fishermen would find such a rig ideal, after adding a section or two of regular monofilament to build out the leader. For general stream fishing, I have the same objection as I do to sinking lines—they drag the bottom and tangle. In addition, the casting properties of such a leader are abysmal. Wear a motorcycle helmet.

What about braided material in a dry-fly leader? Here also, much experimentation is taking place with braided-butt leaders. I've tried them and am not inclined toward immediate conversion. The modest increase in delicacy is more than offset by their mediocre casting characteristics with larger dry flies, where even a mild breeze creates miseries. Also, the braided material tends to wick up water, causing the fly to be dragged under during the pickup.

Here again, we are seeing technological advancements at a very rapid pace. For example, the latest Orvis braided leaders incorporate vastly improved taper designs and cast extremely well, given relative absence of wind and not too bushy a fly. The Sue Burgess braided tapered leader, a British import, is also excellent. I can see the day when I will be using this type of leader for my delicate, spring-creek-type fishing.

There is a great deal of controversy these days over leader material as related to leader design and casting efficiency. As I mentioned, we've gotten away from the old stiff-butt principle. Now we have disciples of a totally opposite school who advocate extremely soft materials for the butt. A few years ago, flat oval monofilament butts were all the rage, but they weren't a panacea, although they were easier to straighten. Now we have braided, woven and twisted material demanding attention.

Okay, what is it we are asking the butt section of the leader to do? Essentially, the idea is to effect continuity of energy of the cast. The problem with extremely stiff material is that it resists forming a nice, tight loop, which is what we are trying to do when casting. Also, it is hard to stretch out all the kinks, which in effect become little built-in shock waves. On the other hand, too soft a material isn't a totally effective transmitter of energy either. So at this point, I still prefer my home-tied leaders, as described.

There are other considerations, apart from sheer strength, which might—in fact, should—influence selection of leader material, and I speak primarily of tippet material. I consider lack of shininess to be very important, so that the sun doesn't glint off the tippet. I also look for texture as it relates to knottability. Some material is so slippery the knots actually pull out. Also, I've encountered several brands that develop curlycues or pigtails when knots are tightened. This is one of my pet peeves, and I recommend avoiding material which behaves in this manner.

Leaders and leader material come in small envelopes or on spools. In either event, it must be straightened before use. This also applies to a leader wound up onto a reel. The heavier the material, the more it resists straightening; thus, the butt section presents the biggest problem.

Some leader materials straighten more easily than others. For example, Maxima only needs to be pulled through the fingers a few times under moderate tension, even in butt-diameter calibrations. You should be careful not to apply too much pressure when rubbing the kinks out of leader material, because too much heat build-up can weaken it, especially in lighter sizes. For harder-to-straighten materials, I suggest this method: grasp the material with the hands 2 to 3 feet apart and stretch it. Hold it in this position for a few seconds, then slowly release the tension. Avoid the use of rubber or leather leader straighteners—they invite the use of too much friction, with resultant damage.

Before moving on to knots and connections, I want to briefly mention a recently introduced material which shows promise. It is a stretchy monofilament, currently being marketed under several names, including Powergum and Shockgum. It is used to form a short butt section between the fly line and leader. The elasticity creates a shock-absorption effect, protecting the tippet against breakage on sudden strikes or lunges by a strong fish. The steelheaders are in love with it, as it allows the use of finer tippets, steelhead being somewhat leader-shy. How it affects casting I can't report at present, not having personally tried the material. The concept is certainly a valid one.

One more thought. Monofilament has a certain life span, which averages 12 to 18 months. This is drastically affected by exposure to direct sunlight, fluorescent light and heat, so do not store leader material in those environments. A cool, dark place is ideal, preferably one with a fair amount of humidity, as monofilament is somewhat weakened when it loses its moisture content. Don't stockpile tippet material; the loss in strength is critical. With heavier material, it doesn't much matter, because even though it loses some strength, it is still stronger than fresh tippet material.

Very well, how does one tie all of this stuff together? There are a few knots and connection techniques which will suffice for most types of fishing. Do yourself a favor and learn to tie these knots properly—it will save you a lot of disappointment and frustration. Here is a list of the knots for which instruction is provided, and their applications:

| **Knot** | **Applications** |
| --- | --- |
| Backing knot | Tying backing to spool of reel |
| Blood knot | Joining sections of monofilament, also for making droppers |
| Surgeon's knot | Same as blood knot |
| Needle knot | Attaching leader butt to fly line |
| Nail knot | Same as needle knot, also may used to attach backing to fly line |
| Perfection loop | Making loop in monofilament |
| Whipped loop | Making loop in end of fly line |

Improved clinch knot     Fly attachment, also attachment of backing to fly line which has a loop

Figure-eight turle knot     Fly attachment

Duncan loop     Fly attachment

Learning to tie knots requires visualization, so we will dispense with further narrative in favor of detailed illustrations and captions. Note that in the drawings, scissors are shown for trimming. This was done for graphic effect. Actually, nail clippers or the equivalent are recommended.

For those who move on to heavy game fishing, there are additional knots and tackle-rigging techniques to be learned. This information is available in book form and also from experienced dealers who specialize in equipping anglers for saltwater fly-fishing. A book I particularly recommend is *Practical Fishing Knots*, by Lefty Kreh and Mark Sosin.

## THE BLOOD KNOT

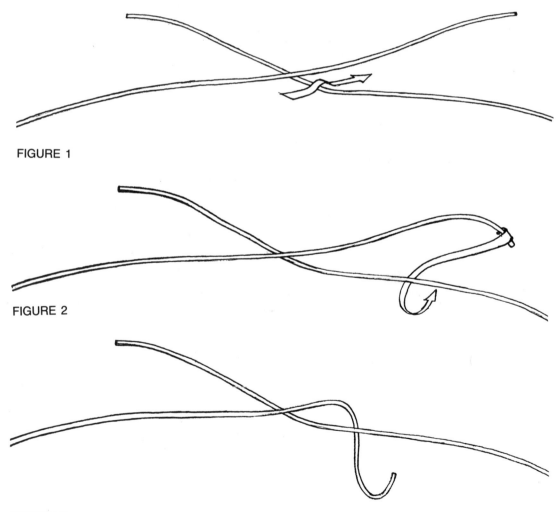

FIGURE 1

FIGURE 2

FIGURE 3

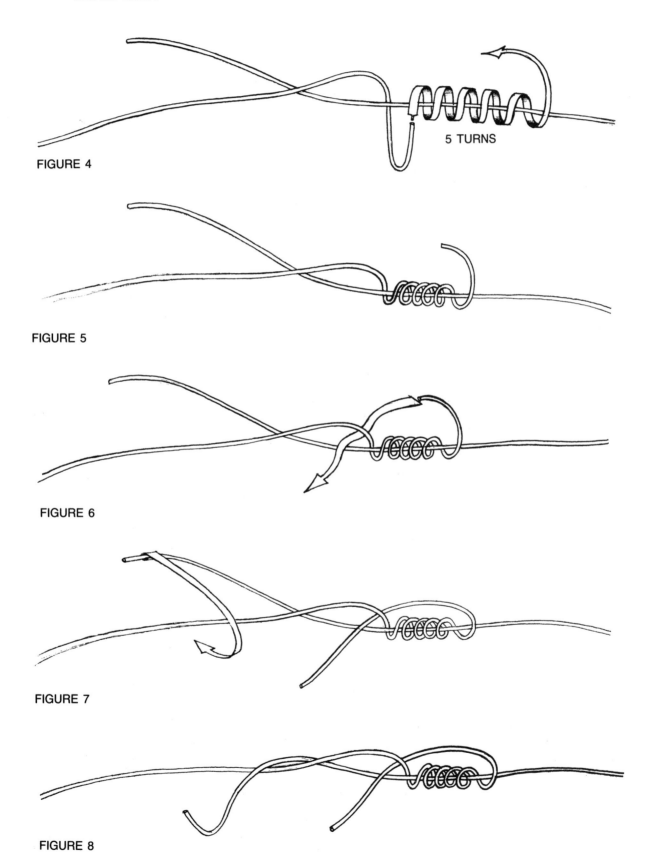

FIGURE 4

5 TURNS

FIGURE 5

FIGURE 6

FIGURE 7

FIGURE 8

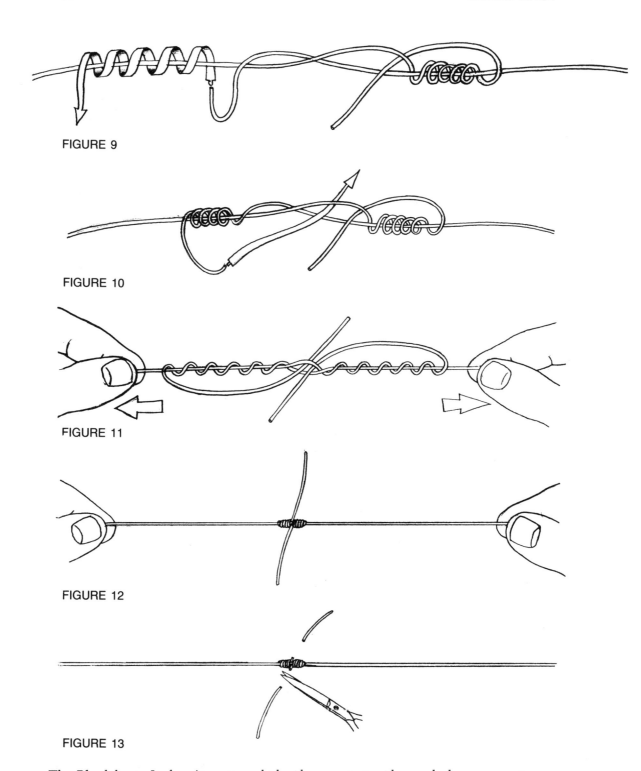

FIGURE 9

FIGURE 10

FIGURE 11

FIGURE 12

FIGURE 13

*The Blood knot. It doesn't matter which side you start with or whether you wrap over or under—the knot will come out the same. The most critical factor is that the two ends are passed back through the opening in opposing directions (Fig. 10 and 11). Five turns is recommended. Moisten with saliva before tightening. This knot tests approximately 90% or slightly more, depending on the diameter of the material.*

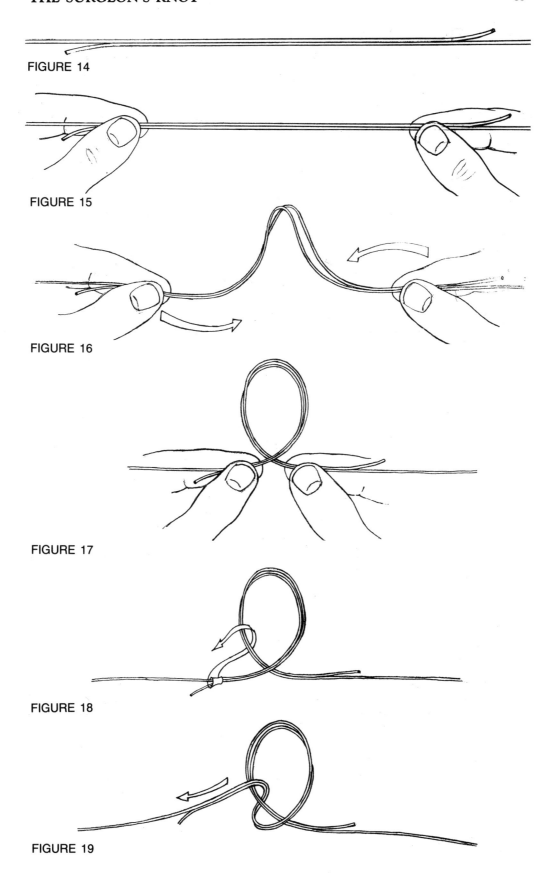

FIGURE 14

FIGURE 15

FIGURE 16

FIGURE 17

FIGURE 18

FIGURE 19

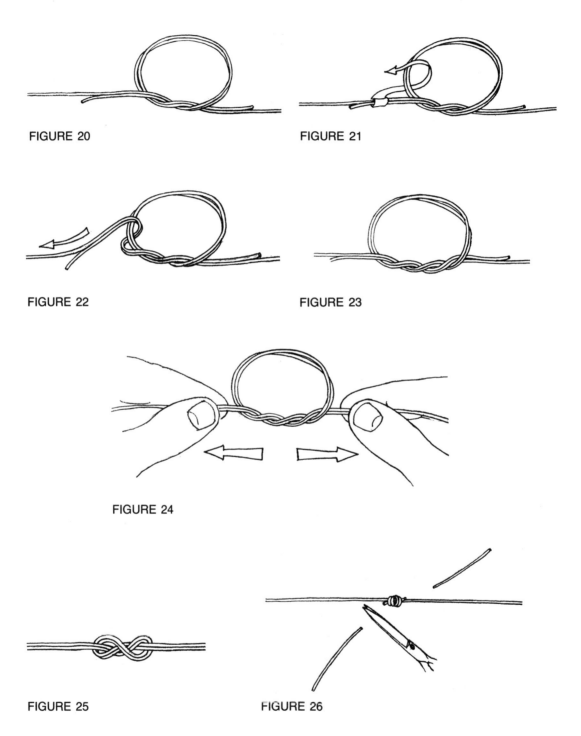

FIGURE 20

FIGURE 21

FIGURE 22

FIGURE 23

FIGURE 24

FIGURE 25

FIGURE 26

*The Surgeon's knot. It may be used in place of the blood knot for joining pieces of leader material. It is suggested that this knot be used only with finer diameter material, as it is more bulky and cumbersome than the blood knot. Example: joining last two sections of a leader. The critical factor is to pull evenly on all four strands when tightening, so that the configuration of the knot is maintained. Lubricate with saliva. This knot tests approximately 95%.*

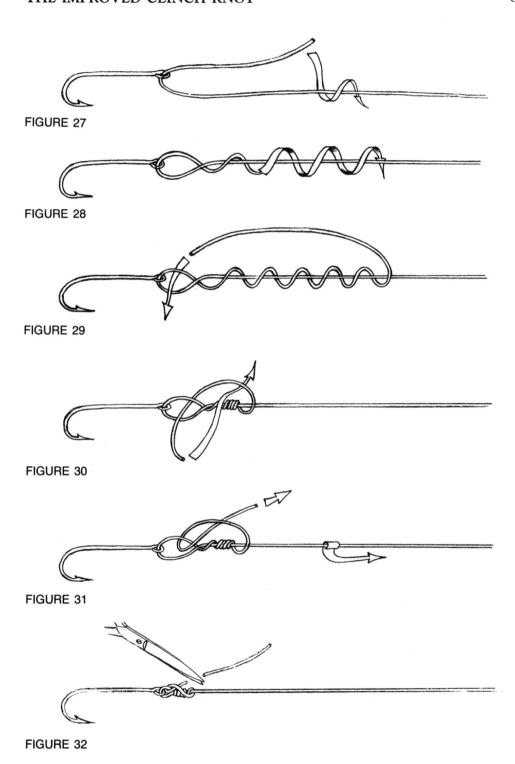

FIGURE 27

FIGURE 28

FIGURE 29

FIGURE 30

FIGURE 31

FIGURE 32

*The Improved Clinch knot. This knot is recommended for straight-eye hooks, as it rides in front of the eye. It may also be used on up-eye and down-eye hooks, provided the bend of the eye is not too severe. Again, five wraps is the recommendation. When tightening, keep a little tension on the tip end, so that the knot configuration is not altered. This knot tests approximately 95%.*

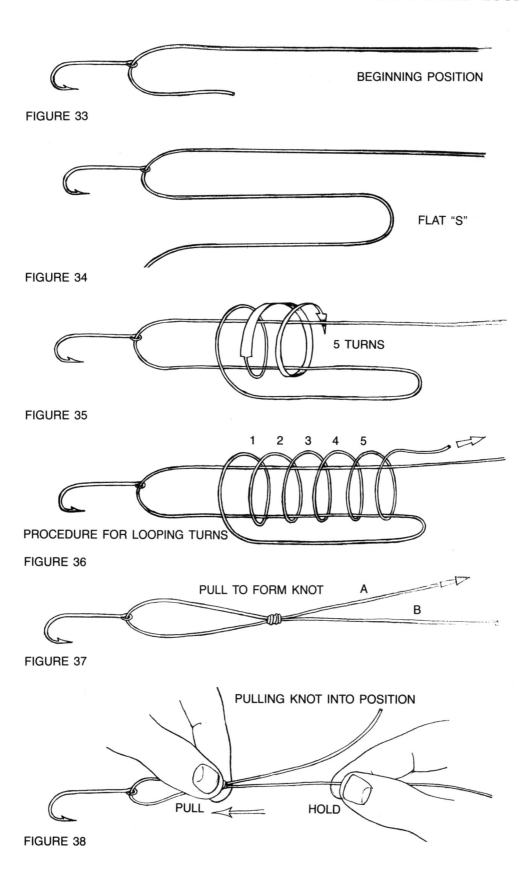

FIGURE 33

BEGINNING POSITION

FLAT "S"

FIGURE 34

5 TURNS

FIGURE 35

1  2  3  4  5

PROCEDURE FOR LOOPING TURNS

FIGURE 36

PULL TO FORM KNOT          A
                           B

FIGURE 37

PULLING KNOT INTO POSITION

PULL          HOLD

FIGURE 38

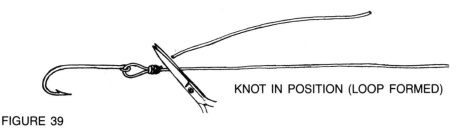

KNOT IN POSITION (LOOP FORMED)

FIGURE 39

*The Duncan Loop. This knot is also recommended for straight-eyed or moderate-deflection hooks. It is particularly good with large nymphs and streamer flies where a heavier tippet is used, as it allows the fly to swing more freely in the water, thus enhancing its action. This knot is in effect a noose, which remains slightly loose as the fly is fished (Fig. 39). When a fish strikes, the noose tightens around the hook eye. After the fish is released, the knot can be opened up again with the thumb nail. Precise statistic on test strength is not available. I estimate at least 90%.*

## THE FIGURE 8 TURLE

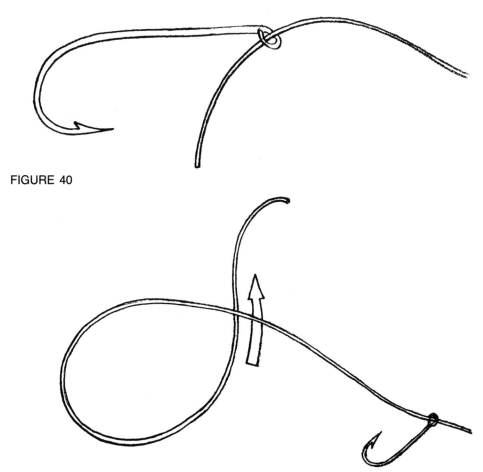

FIGURE 40

FIGURE 41

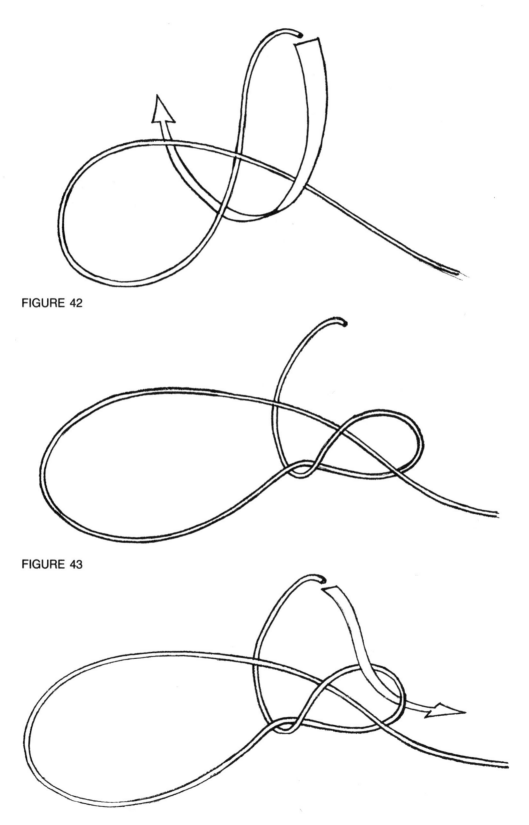

FIGURE 42

FIGURE 43

FIGURE 44

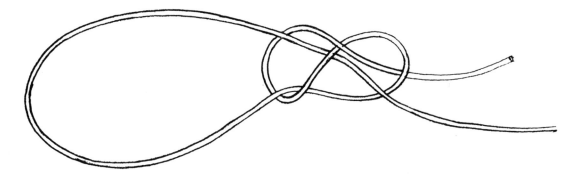

FIGURE 45

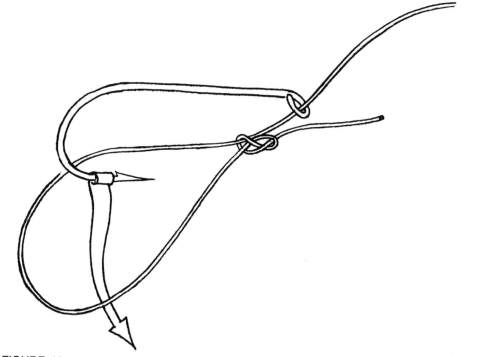

FIGURE 46

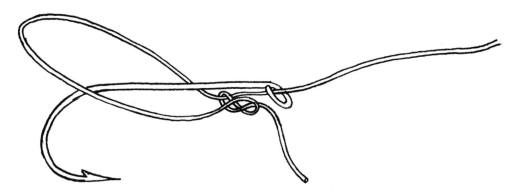

FIGURE 47

FIGURE 48

*The Figure 8 Turle knot. It is recommended for down-eyed or up-eyed hooks, as the knot itself seats behind the eye. The leader then passes through the eye, affecting a straight pull. While this knot is being tied, the fly (hook) is slid down the leader, and perhaps held in the palm of the hand. It is critical that the tip end be passed through the upper loop as shown in figs. 44 and 45, thus forming the figure 8. The fly (hook) is then brought into play and is passed through the main loop (Figs. 46 and 47). When tightening, be sure the loop remains in position around the "neck" of the fly (Fig. 48), and doesn't slip forward around the leader, as this weakens the knot considerably. No test statistic is available. However, I estimate this knot tests at least 90% and has less tendency to slip than the commonly used improved Turle.*

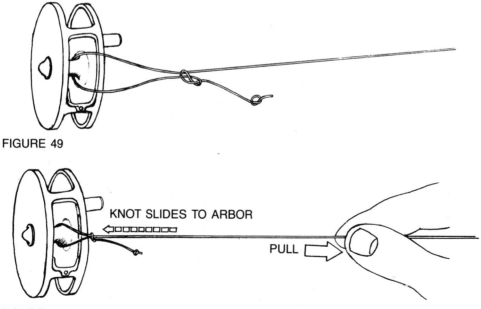

FIGURE 49

FIGURE 49A

*The Figure 8 Turle is also a good knot for attaching backing to a reel. It is tied exactly the same as described except that the line is passed around the arbor of the reel preparatory to forming the knot. Some reel manufacturers have incorporated a little protuberance of some sort, in which case the line is tied around that rather than the arbor. It is suggested that a simple overhand knot be tied in the tag end, as a fail-safe.*

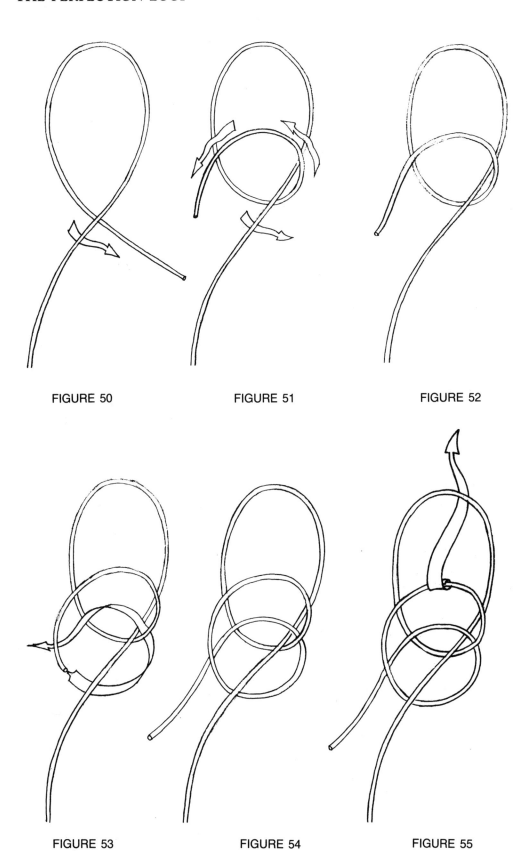

FIGURE 50          FIGURE 51          FIGURE 52

FIGURE 53          FIGURE 54          FIGURE 55

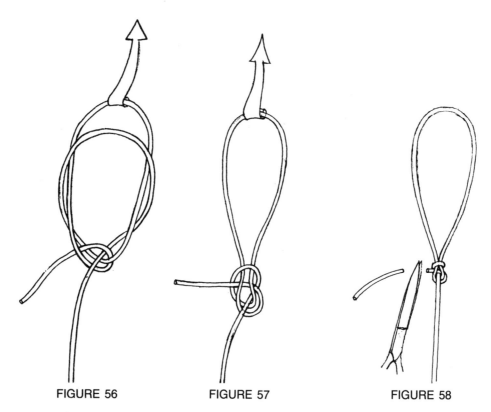

FIGURE 56                    FIGURE 57                    FIGURE 58

*The Perfection Loop. This knot is used primarily to form a loop in the butt end of a leader. It is a slightly complicated knot to learn but easy once mastered. The main thing to remember is that the loop you actually end up with is formed by the second loop created during the tying process. The first one is tightened to form the knot. Refer to Figs. 55, 56 and 57. An important attribute of this knot is that the leader butt comes straight out of the loop, which facilitates accurate casting.*

*An end loop can also be formed using the Surgeon's knot by doubling the material instead of using two pieces. This knot tests slightly stronger than the Perfection loop, however, it doesn't come out straight, as the Perfection loop does. It is recommended for limp material, such as backing, where this is not a factor. Both knots test at least 90% so the slight difference in strength doesn't matter.*

## THE WHIPPED LOOP

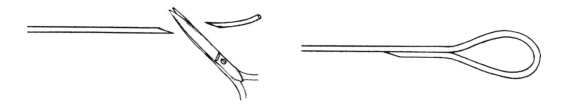

FIGURE 59                                              FIGURE 60

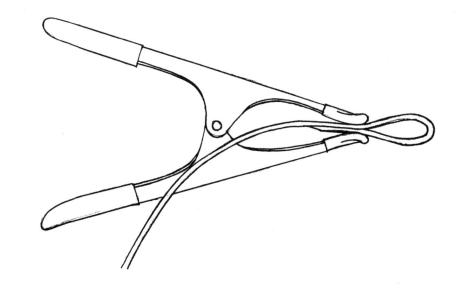

FIGURE 61

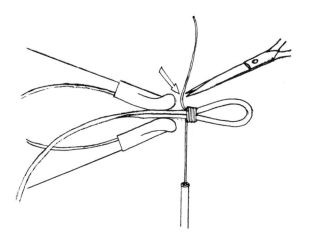

FIGURE 62

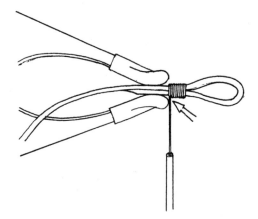

FIGURE 63

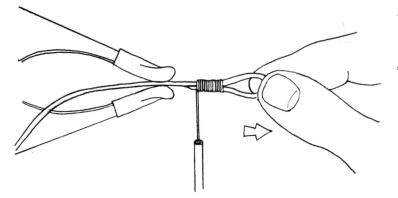

FIGURE 64

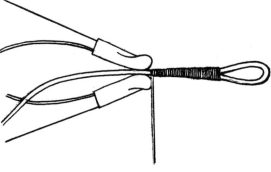

FIGURE 65

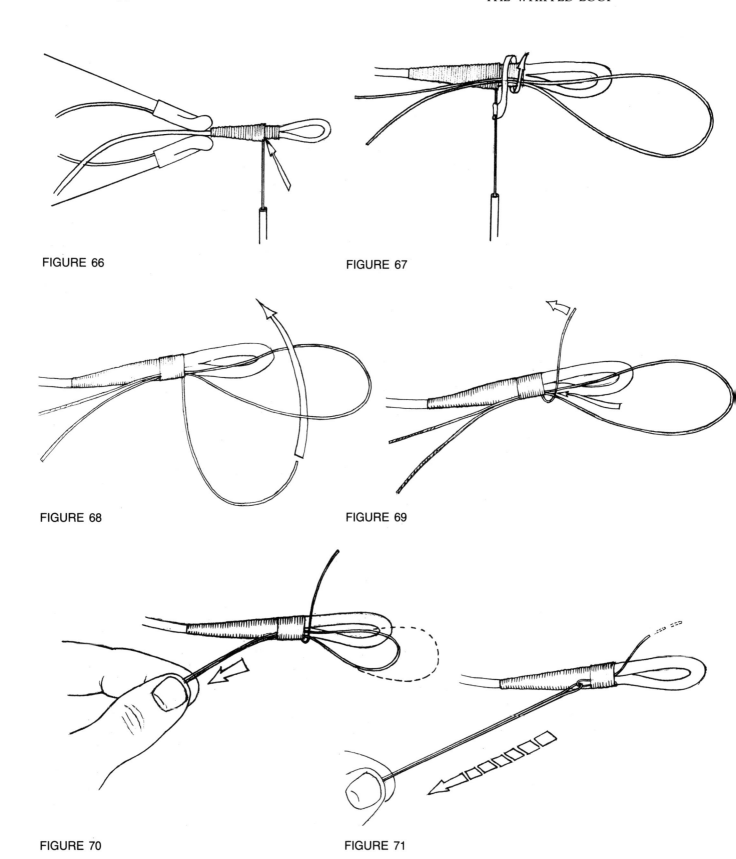

FIGURE 66

FIGURE 67

FIGURE 68

FIGURE 69

FIGURE 70

FIGURE 71

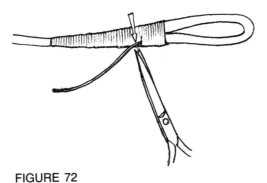

FIGURE 72

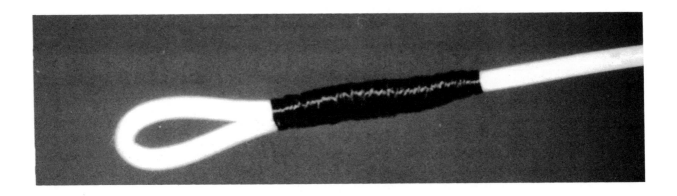

*Whipping a loop in the end of a fly line. This sort of loop may be used to connect the tail end of the line to the backing. It may also be employed at the front end of the line to facilitate an "interlocked—loops" connection of line to leader, which some people prefer for ease of changing leaders. In either case, the loop must be a small one, so it will pass through the guides readily.*

*The tools utilized in whipping a loop include a fly-tyer's bobbin and a spring clamp which can be obtained in a hardware store. Begin by cutting the tip of the line on a taper, then form a small, tight loop and mount the line in the spring clamp, as shown (Figs. 59–61). Mount a spool of fine-diameter rod-winding thread in the bobbin and tie on by wrapping the thread over itself, working towards the clamp. Clip off the tag end. When the thread reaches the clamp, expose a bit more line and wrap some more. Repeat until the tapered end is bound down (Figs. 62–65). Then wrap the thread back over itself, working out towards the end of the loop (Fig. 66). Form a loop out of a 6-inch piece of thread and bind it to the wrappings, as shown in Fig. 67. Pass the tag end of the wrapping thread through the thread loop (Figs. 68 and 69), then pull the tag end back under the wrappings and clip it off (Figs. 70, 71 and 72). Finished loop should resemble the photograph (Fig. 73). Coat with epoxy or something of that type.*

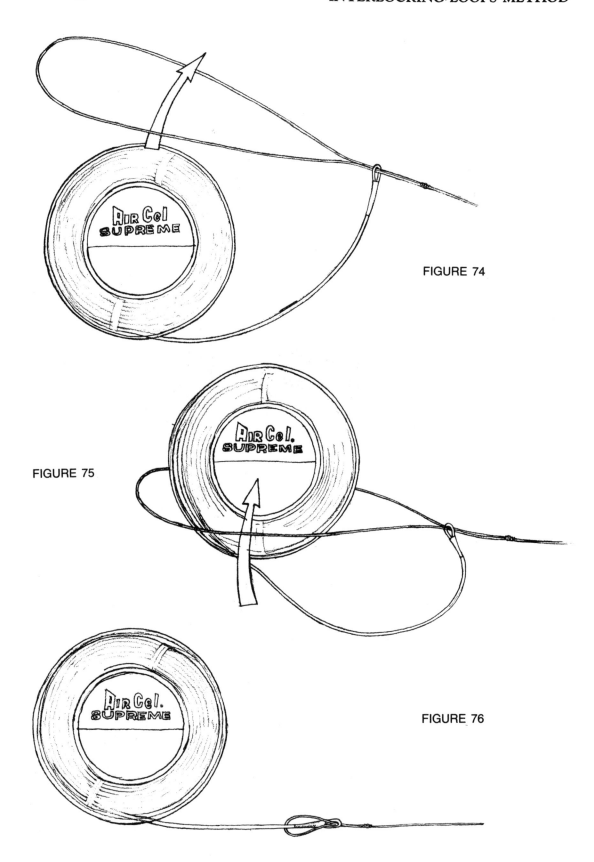

FIGURE 74

FIGURE 75

FIGURE 76

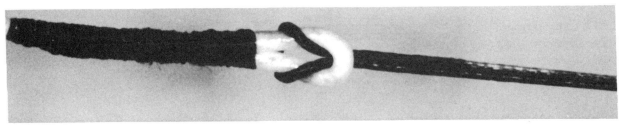

**FIGURE 77**

**FIGURE 78**

*Interlocking-loops method for connecting line to backing. Make a large loop in the end of the backing. The Surgeon's knot loop is appropriate for this, as the backing is limp. The loop thus created should be large enough to allow a fly line mounting spool to pass through comfortably. Run the backing loop through the line loop and form the interlock by passing the entire line through the backing loop (Figs. 74–76). When drawing the loops tight, be sure they interlock in the proper configuration. The correct and incorrect configurations are shown in Figs. 77 and 78 respectively.*

## THE NEEDLE KNOT

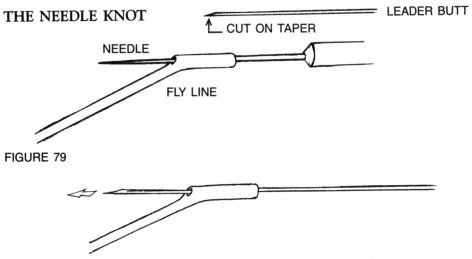

**FIGURE 79**

**FIGURE 80**

*The needle knot. This is an excellent knot for attaching leader butt to fly line. Run a stout needle into the end of a fly line for a distance of approximately 3/16", or 1/4", if you wish. Something with a handle works best, such as a fly-tyer's bodkin or a pin vise with needle inserted. Puncture the wall of the fly line as shown. Then withdraw needle and insert leader butt, giving yourself 3 to 4 inches of material with which to work (Figs. 79 & 80).*

FIGURE 81

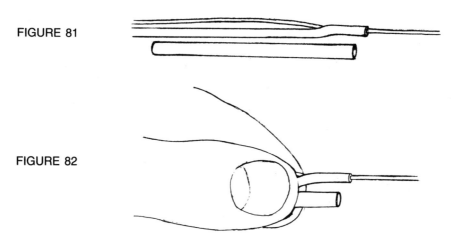

FIGURE 82

*Lay a small-diameter tube along the front end of the fly line—a fly tyer's thread bobbin is ideal. Seize with left thumb and forefinger, with tip of line slightly in front of the tube (Figs. 81 & 82).*

FIGURE 83

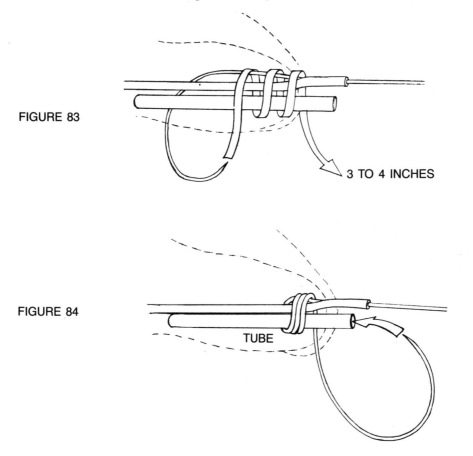

3 TO 4 INCHES

FIGURE 84

TUBE

*Wrap the end of the leader butt forward around the line and tube, catching it with the thumb and forefinger to hold material in place after each wrap. Three wraps is sufficient—however, that actually requires four passes, as one is lost in the tightening process (Figs. 83 & 84).*

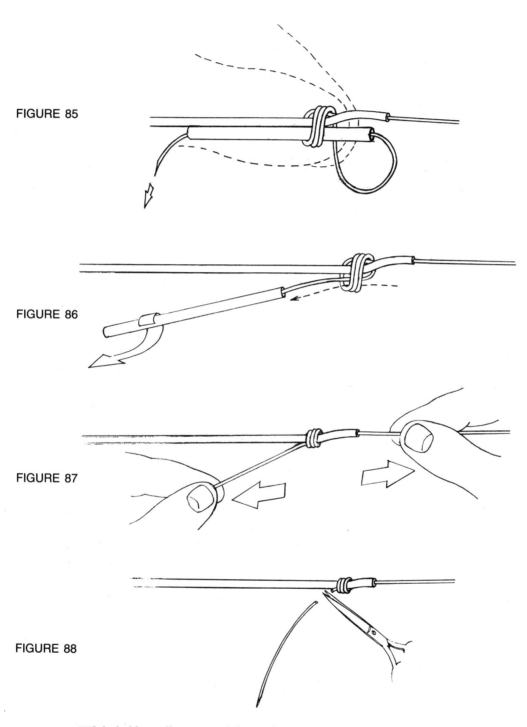

FIGURE 85

FIGURE 86

FIGURE 87

FIGURE 88

*While holding all wraps tightly in place, run the butt end back through the tube (Fig. 85). Then carefully withdraw the tube, taking care to keep wraps in original sequence (Fig. 86). Tighten and trim (Figs. 87 & 88).*

*KNOT NOTE: Some people use more than three turns in this knot. That's okay—however, it doesn't make the knot any more secure, and complicates the tying. When tightening, try to get the wraps over the needle hole.*

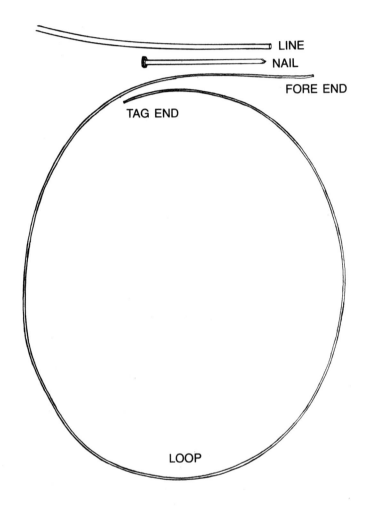

LINE
NAIL
FORE END
TAG END
LOOP

FIGURE 89

The nail knot, simplified method. This is also an excellent knot for attaching leader to line, if one isn't concerned with the leader actually being inserted into the line. The only tool required, other than clippers, is a thin nail or heavy needle for backbone.

Form loop with leader, as shown in Fig. 89. This loop can be practically any size, as dictated by the length of the leader material. In fact, an entire knotless leader can be attached in this manner.

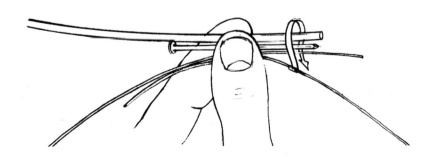

FIGURE 90

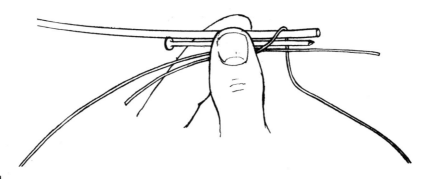

FIGURE 91

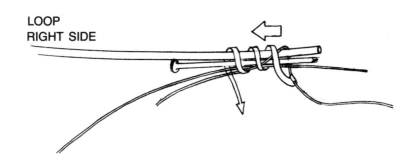

LOOP
RIGHT SIDE

FIGURE 92

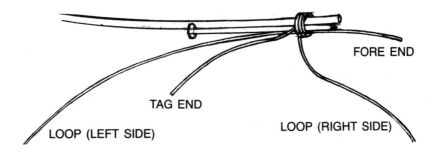

FORE END

TAG END

LOOP (LEFT SIDE)

LOOP (RIGHT SIDE)

FIGURE 93

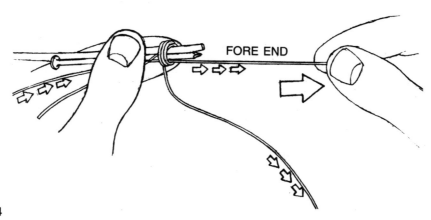

FORE END

FIGURE 94

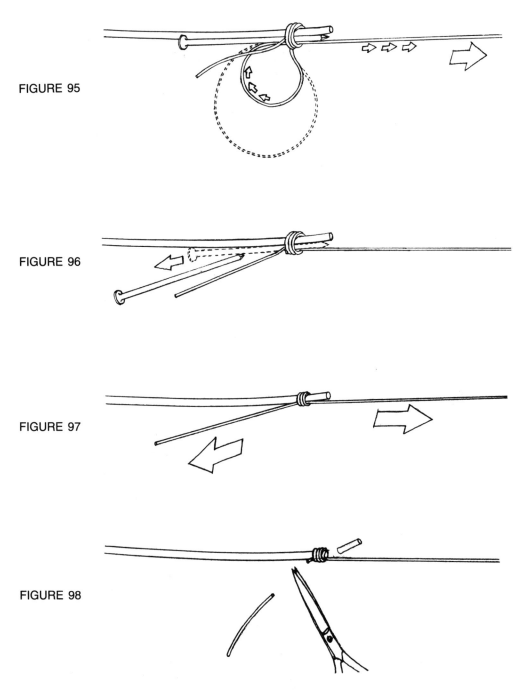

FIGURE 95

FIGURE 96

FIGURE 97

FIGURE 98

*Seize the right side of the loop and wrap it around the nail and line, working back toward the fingers so that the leader material also passes over itself (Figs. 90 to 93). Again, four wraps are required to get three after tightening. Tighten by pulling on fore end while holding the wraps in place, as shown in Figs. 94 and 95. Withdraw the nail, finish tightening and trim both the leader butt and the tip of the line (Figs. 96 to 98).*

*KNOT NOTE: It's essential when tightening that the wraps remain in proper configuration and don't overlap each other.*

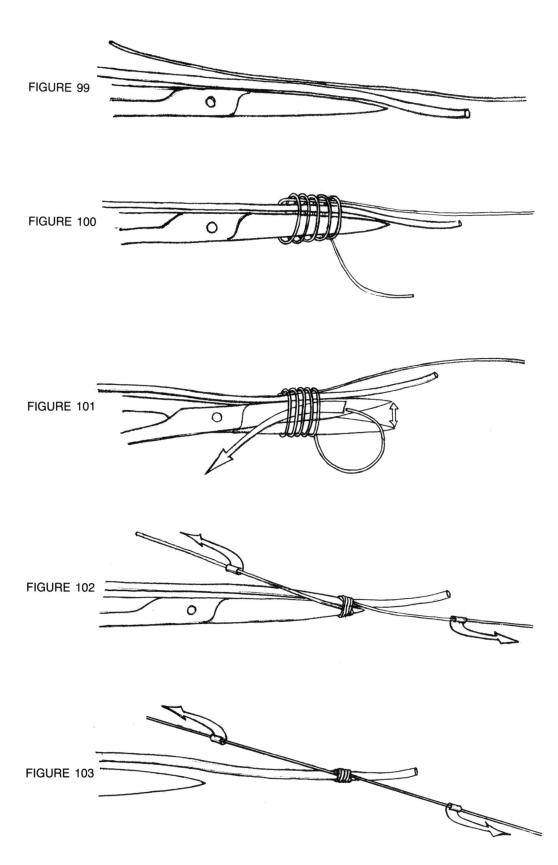

FIGURE 99

FIGURE 100

FIGURE 101

FIGURE 102

FIGURE 103

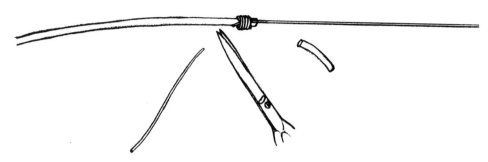

FIGURE 104

*An alternative method for tying the nail knot, with which the leader doesn't have to be knotless. The knot is tied in a manner similar to the needle knot, in that the tag end is passed back beneath the wraps. A fine tipped pair of scissors is required. Note that when it is time to run the tag end beneath the wraps, the scissors are opened slightly to create a channel through which the leader material is passed. The scissors are then closed and in the tightening process, the knot follows the taper of the scissor's point and slips off the tips.*

In closing, I'll give you a couple of illustrative leader formulas, in addition to the one described earlier:

| Longer leader | Length | Diameter |
| --- | --- | --- |
| Section 1 (butt) | 42 inches | .20 inch |
| Section 2 | 36 | .17 |
| Section 3 | 24 | .14 |
| Section 4 | 18 | .12 |
| Section 5 | 12 | .10 |
| Section 6 | 9 | .08 |

11'9" plus tippet

| Shorter leader | Length | Diameter |
| --- | --- | --- |
| Section 1 (butt) | 30 inches | .20 inch |
| Section 2 | 18 | .17 |
| Section 3 | 12 | .14 |
| Section 4 | 10 | .12 |
| Section 5 | 8 | .10 |
| Section 6 | 6 | .08 |

7'0" plus tippet

These leaders are designed around a weight-6 line and work fine on 5's and 7's also. For weight-3 and weight-4 lines, change sections 1 and 2 to .18 and .16 respectively. This works very well on a 5-weight also.

# CHAPTER VI _____

# *Wading Gear and Assorted Paraphernalia*

Proper wading gear is as essential to fishing comfort as proper tackle is to fishing success. Today, there is quite an assortment of waders, wading shoes and hip boots available. While quality has improved considerably over the last couple of decades, it has not been a linear progression. There have been many problems, both in new makes and in older brands which have gone through evolutionary changes. Unfortunately, anglers have suffered countless days of soggy socks and pants as a result.

All other considerations set aside for the moment, the one all-important attribute of any wader or boot is that it doesn't leak. With today's technology, there is no excuse for a product not being dependable and durable, yet we still encounter this. As recently as 1985, I had to return two pairs of waders that leaked the first time out. That's inexcusable. Sure, all better-brand waders are strongly warranteed, but what good does that do an angler who is standing sopping wet in a cold Alaskan river, hundreds of miles from the nearest dealer? It seems to me that a world which can equip people for space walks should be able to keep fishermen and fisherwomen dry.

With that, let's get on with our orientation. Waders come in two basic styles: boot-foot and stocking-foot. Each has its advantages and disadvantages. Boot-foot waders are more convenient, are faster to get into and may be somewhat less costly overall, since they are complete, in and of themselves. Stocking-foot waders require a wading shoe and usually a wading sock of some sort, and it is a bit more time-consuming to put these components on. However, they generally provide better support, are less cumbersome, are easier to walk in and offer less water resistance. They also are modular to a degree, in that different wading shoes with various types of soles can be used interchangeably.

Stocking-foot waders have become very popular these days. They are available in a number of different materials, the characteristics of which vary considerably. There are lightweight models made out of synthetic materials which I find quite comfortable, particularly in warmer weather. They don't have much stretch, so it's necessary to buy them slightly oversized. Being of thinner material, they are more vulnerable to leaks from abrasions and punctures, so it is wise to carry a repair kit. Confer with your dealer on this, as the repair adhesive must be compatible with the wader material. Incidentally, one can protect lightweight waders against damage from rough brush and other hazards by wearing a pair of inexpensive, oversized trousers over them.

Pure latex rubber waders are also available, and they have several desirable attributes. They have sufficient give to allow freedom of movement, are easy to put on, are fairly lightweight and can be patched with practically any adhesive. They hold up quite well, provided you avoid direct contact with sharp objects. As they are made of natural rubber, care must be taken to store them away from direct sunlight and also not to let them freeze in the winter. I feel these are perhaps the best waders for a beginner because of their reasonable price and ease of repair.

Neoprene has come on strong as a material for stocking-foot waders in recent years. Neoprene is a synthetic material similar to that used in making wet suits. The first models were unlined and were a horror to put on. This problem was relieved considerably by the addition of a lining. Neoprenes are flexible and quite comfortable if a good fit is obtained. They have excellent insulating properties, which is a plus for cold-weather fishing but a definite negative in warmer climates. In fact, they could cause overheating to dangerous levels if any significant amount of walking is required in hot weather. Under such conditions, roll the upper portion down to your waist—this helps a great deal.

As neoprene material is fairly thick, no supplementary wading sock is required. Many models have a gravel guard, which consists of a cuff which turns down over the tops of the wading shoes. This is an excellent feature. Patching adhesive is readily available, and it is effective though somewhat overpriced. Neoprenes are the most expensive of all stocking-foot waters, but the cost may be offset by longer life. At this writing, it's

*Neoprene stocking—foot waders.*

too early to accurately assess the life-span factor, as neoprene waders are still relatively new to the market and have undergone several model changes and improvements since their introduction.

The increased popularity of stocking-foot waders has generated a rapid evolution in wading shoes, one which will certainly continue. At this writing there are a number of excellent models available. Some have plain felt soles; others offer felt with metal cleats or studs. Felt offers comfort and is much less slippery than rubber soles. However, felt is not effective on certain types of rock, particularly where layers of silt or algae are present. Metal cleats are vital here; they can save you many impromptu baths and perhaps a broken bone or two.

Whether you opt for plain felt or studded felt, check to see that it is securely affixed to the undersole. Most of the better-quality shoes have sewn-on felts, or sewn plus adhesive. I am a strong advocate of the sewn-on process, as plain adhesive may come unglued. This is a real problem today, because the new synthetic materials are not compatible with the traditional shoemaker's cements used to bond felt to rubber or leather.

Wading shoes are currently manufactured out of synthetic leather, natural leather and canvas or synthetic mesh, in various combinations. Personally, I favor those made entirely of synthetic leather. The material is sufficiently flexible for comfortable walking, yet rugged enough to protect the feet against contusions from sharp rocks in the streambed. Also—and this is a large plus—the synthetic material doesn't stiffen up after drying out, as natural leather does. I expect natural leather to be phased out in the not-too-distant future.

*Felt-soled wading shoes and gravel guards.*

Except in the case of neoprenes, wading socks are required with stocking-foot waders. These are worn over the wader feet. Their function is to provide a buffer against gravel and small stones, which will chew up waders in short order. These socks should be heavy, stretchy and preferably of a synthetic material. They must also be large enough not to cramp the feet. Ideally, they should be of a dull color, such as brown or olive, but that may be difficult to find. Just be sure to avoid something light and bright, such as white or yellow.

Neoprene wading socks are available, made out of the same material as the waders, and featuring a gravel guard—a good idea, perhaps, but personally I don't like them at all. For one thing, they are awfully hard to get into. Also, they are overly bulky and tend to cramp the feet. Perhaps if the fit were a bit loose and one had oversized wading shoes, they would work—but who wants oversized wading shoes? Those things are clumsy enough as it is. I wear a normal-width size 11 street shoe, yet the extra-large-size neoprene socks are still too small. Try them if you must—just remember that feet swell from walking and wading, and there's nothing worse than cramped toes. These socks are very expensive, so if they don't work out, you're stuck with a rather costly mistake.

There are a few supplemental items which come in handy. Neoprene gravel guards are quite functional—these aren't socks, but merely cuffs which encircle the ankle and fold over the tops of the wading shoes. These come in sizes, so be careful to get a proper fit, not so tight as to cut off circulation. Two models are available, one with zippers and one without. Suit yourself.

Wading sandals offer flexibility regarding type of sole. They strap on over wading shoes or boot feet; thus, you can quickly change from felt or plain rubber to felt with metal cleats. This is an advantage when hiking into a remote spot—you simply carry the sandals in a vest pocket or shoulder bag and put them on when it's time to wade.

There is also a supplementary wading shoe which consists of an extra-heavy rubber similar to the kind worn on rainy days, with cleated-felt soles. They slip on over wading shoes or boot feet. They work fine, except that they have a tendency to come off if you get stuck in the mud or wedged between a couple of rocks. They are slightly ungainly but tolerable, provided you remove them during longer walks. One cautionary note—they do not fit well over insulated boot-foot waders.

As I mentioned, boot-foot waders don't offer the snug-fitting security around the ankles that wading shoes do; however, you may not mind that, especially if a good fit is obtained. They are somewhat less comfortable on long walks—but not everyone does that much walking. From a convenience standpoint, they have it all over stocking-foots, as they are a single unit and simply slip on and off.

Boot-foot waders are made of several materials, notably rubber, rubberized canvas and, most recently, neoprene. The pure rubber and rubberized canvas models patch well with various adhesives. They don't stretch much, so allowance must be made to accommodate walking and bending. Soles are offered in choices of felt, cleated felt and, in some models, plain rubber.

If one does opt for boot-foot waders, patchability becomes an important consideration. If a stocking-foot wader goes, you need only replace the wader, as the shoe is not affected. When a boot-foot wader goes, all is lost. You will want to satisfy yourself that an effective patching material is readily available.

As I mentioned, boot-foot waders are available with insulation. This is a great asset in cold-weather fishing but quite the opposite in milder temperatures. Unless you do a lot of fishing in frigid conditions, noninsulated waders with warm layers of socks and underwear should suffice.

No matter what type of waders you choose, fit is all-important. This affects comfort, mobility and longevity, for poorly fitting waders will chafe and wear prematurely. Additionally, waders which are too tight may spring a seam leak. If compromise is required—and it usually is, wader fit being less than perfect—it's advisable to go slightly large rather than slightly small.

It's better to purchase waders in person, although mail order is okay if you are sure you know exactly what you want. Plan on spending some time in the store. Dress as you would under typical fishing conditions. Be particularly sure to wear the socks you would wear onstream. Put on the entire assembly—waders, socks, shoes, sandals, gravel guards, and so on. Then walk around some, stretching and bending into the various positions required in actual fishing situations. Think about what additional clothing you might want to wear. Remember that your feet will swell a bit during long walks and wading sessions.

Some waders offer choices of inseam lengths, which is a definite plus. Too short an inseam limits mobility and is uncomfortable. Too long an inseam results in bagginess around the knees, with resultant wear and chafing. A few manufacturers offer custom-fit waders, at extra cost. If you happpen to be an off size, like me, it's worth the money. I am long-waisted and short-legged, 6 feet tall with a 30-inch inseam. No standard wader is going to fit that weird a body really well. But keep this in mind. If you decide to order custom-fit waders, be very sure you and the manufacturer understand each other regarding dimensions. Often, custom-fit waders are made too snug, which reduces mobility and makes it difficult to add clothing in colder weather.

Today, many waders come with built-in suspenders, lacking which you will need to buy a pair. Get the real article. While a dollar or two might be saved by purchasing brand-X suspenders in a discount store, they may not all be appropriate for holding up waders.

Some people like to wear an exterior belt to prevent the waders from filling up with water in case of a fall. That's fine, but remember, the idea is to avoid falling in. It's an old adage that a belt is dangerous because it traps air in the waders, and if you get swept down stream, the buoyancy makes it difficult to regain footing. Having fallen in lots of times with and without a belt, I can't say that I agree with that, so it's up to the individual.

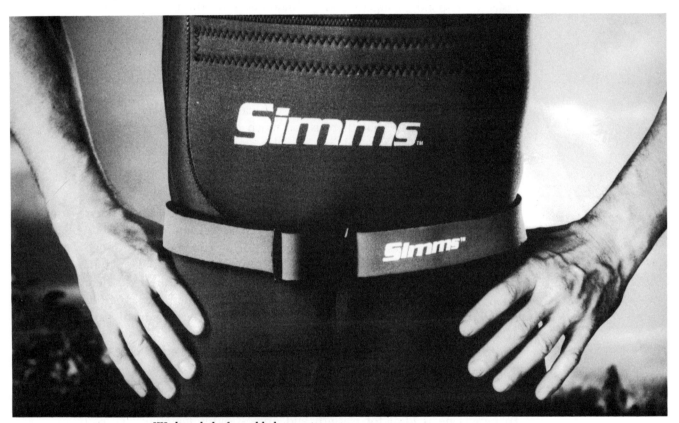

*Wading belt for added security.*

There's also the question of whether or not to carry a wading staff. Today, it's far more convenient to do so, what with collapsible staffs like Joan Stolliar's Folstaff and the new Trac staff. Still, it's one more thing to drag around, and I only use mine under the roughest of conditions. There is no question that they aid stability—three points of balance are better than two. In fact, there is a danger of becoming overly confident, as a wading staff may enable you to get to a place that's dangerous to be in. If you want to try a staff, simply cut yourself a nice, straight, heavy stick, preferably of green wood so it doesn't float well. Tie on a piece of heavy twine as a lanyard and knot it to your waders, perhaps to a belt loop or suspender strap. Thus you'll find out whether or not you're a staff person.

Before moving on, mention should be made of hip boots. These are also available in stocking-foot or boot-foot models—I definitely recommend the boot-foot on the basis of convenience, unless a lot of hiking is anticipated. Hippers are great for shallow wading—that is, up to midthigh. They are much more comfortable in hot weather, and make it far easier to respond to urgent bodily functions. One thing—after several months of frequent fishing in full-length waders, have your wits about you when switching to hippers. Last summer I put mine on and proceeded to wade right out into waist-deep water. Color me soaked.

I really hope waders are getting better from a quality standpoint. In years past, they have caused more anger and frustration than everything else combined. It is strictly a matter of quality control. The greatest problem, I believe, is that there is too much change going on, brought about by competition. As with any complex and critical product, it's very difficult to perfect something that's being constantly redesigned. A period of stability in the wader business would benefit everyone at this point.

A final note. If you plan an extended trip, be it to the Rockies, Alaska, Labrador or wherever, spend some time fishing in the waders you'll be taking. Most manufacturing defects, such as seam leaks, show up right away, sometimes on the first day of use. If you stay dry through several long days astream, those waders are probably going to be good for quite a while. It's advisable to take two pair, both field-tested. Here again, stocking-foots offer a distinct advantage, as they are easier to transport, and only one set of shoes is required no matter how many pairs of waders are taken. Bring lots of patching stuff also.

So much for waders—what should be worn underneath them? Let's address—or should I say undress—the neoprenes first, as they are somewhat unique, in that you do not wear regular trousers under them. Neoprenes are form-fitting, and go on over some sort of long underwear. Polypropylene is ideal for warmth and dryness—this material acts as a wick to remove moisture caused by perspiration. When maximum warmth is not desired, a pair of women's tights makes an excellent undergarment. Don't bother with anything expensive, like dancer's tights; the economical discount-store variety is perfectly serviceable. And don't be self-concious about wearing them. We running-boomers broke that barrier years ago when we found out how great tights were for winter workouts.

Not to hype a brand name but merely to pass along something of value, the best polypropylene-type underwear I've yet found is that of the Damart Company. They call it Thermolactyl, and while I'm not sure how that might differ from plain polypropylene, I can tell you it's great stuff.

Single-ply and double-ply are available, for whatever degree of warmth one requires.

Of course, you can still wear polypropylene longies and tights under non-neoprene waders, along with whatever trousers are preferred. The only critical point regarding trousers is that they aren't too tight for easy movement. It's nice if they taper a little, so that the cuffs can easily be tucked into your socks. Incidentally, I recommend that a fairly substantial pair of socks be worn inside the waders, even in hot weather, for foot comfort. The boot socks worn by hunters are an excellent choice. They come in various weights, so you can adjust to temperature.

Up top, a polypropylene undergarment is great for cold-weather fishing. Incidentally, these should be worn against the skin to maximize wicking action. We runners have found that turtlenecks are significantly warmer than plain crewnecks, but not everyone can tolerate a turtleneck, so have a care. Outer garments can be whatever the weather dictates— denim, wool, down, and so on. I prefer shirts and jackets to sweaters, as they have pockets and don't catch on every little snag.

Unless you're going to be strictly a fair-weather angler, a rain jacket will be an essential part of your wardrobe. Essentially, the choice boils down to the traditional rubberized or synthetic material and Gore-Tex. Both shed water. Gore-Tex is somewhat pricey, but very comfortable and quite stylish. It serves double-duty when a windbreaker is required. A hood is a must. Don't buy too long a jacket; it will drag in the stream during wading. Be sure it is sufficiently loose-fitting to accommodate the stream vest, which is worn underneath.

Sometimes you want to pack a rain jacket in the pouch of your wading vest, just in case. There are specially designed jackets available which are cut extra-short and are made of thinner material, so they may be folded into a small, neat package. This is a very handy article.

Even if you aren't a hat person, there will be times when this item is an absolute necessity. For wet, cold weather, I recommend a long-billed cap which integrates with the hood of the rain jacket so that the face and entire head are shielded. Broad-brimmed hats offer protection from both sun and rain. In high winds they tend to get blown off, so if you opt for a western hat or something similar, a chin strap is suggested. I happen to be one of those people who can't tolerate much sun, so a warm-weather hat is essential. This needs to be of lightweight material which ventilates well.

With hats and, in fact, all garments worn above the waist, we become concerned with color. Anything light, bright or shiny is more visible to the fish. Fluorescent colors are particularly bad—I cringe when I see people fishing in hot-orange jackets and caps. The problem is that most people tend to be style-conscious, myself included. Knowing this, the manufacturers design products to please us rather than the trout. Thus we still have pale tan and beige hats and stream vests, instead of subdued shades. Incidentally, the underside of a hat brim should be dark green or black, so as to absorb reflection from the water.

I'm not quite ready to give up my beige vest, even though I realize the color is not optimal, because it has a Silver Doctor embroidered on the back. When I do retire this article, I'll switch to olive or camouflage. I wear dull green or camouflage hats and shirts or, in warmer weather, blue demin, which is a sky color. I seem to be passing inspection. Subdued plaids are nice also.

Those who fish in really cold conditions will want something for the hands. I sort of hate gloves of any type and so have adopted a personal rule that I won't fish in weather so cold that I can't go bare-handed. Fortunately, I have a fair tolerance, so I don't miss out on all of the excellent cold-weather angling. For those who want gloves, I would suggest the Glacier Glove. It is constructed of closed-cell neoprene and nylon for maximum warmth and comfort. The ends of the thumbs and index fingers are exposed to facilitate knot tying and other operations which require dexterity. For those who wish to cover up these extremities, a set of finger covers are included at no additional cost. All in all, a fine product, one which may change my mind-set about gloves.

Having mentioned stream vests, let's further examine that important item. There has been a great deal of evolution in vests over the last decade or two; consequently, there are many fine models available now, and very few inferior ones. Since they all must serve the same purpose, stream vests are generally similar, but there are variations—numbers of pockets, size of pockets, weight of fabric, type of pocket fasteners and coloration are the main considerations. I have a preference for velcro-type fasteners as opposed to zippers, which can be a bit tedious to open and close when standing in midstream, rod in hand. Other than that, my only recommendation is that you consider how the vest is organized, in terms of the size and number of fly boxes and other items you intend to carry. And choose a dull color—don't be a clothes horse, like yours truly.

Now you have your stream vest with all those generous pockets. How wonderful never to have to worry about capacity! Don't be too sure. If you are like most of us, those pockets will fill up faster than you'd ever believe. It's not just the fly boxes, it's the multitude of essential and/or irresistible tools and accoutrements you encounter in the shops and catalogs.

Fly-fishers tend to be gadget addicts, and the entrepreneurs are outdoing themselves to see to it that we don't run out. You must use some discretion, lest a caddy or bearer be required to haul the gear. It then becomes a matter of what you are able and willing to carry.

I've just dumped the contents of my vest onto the floor. Here's what came out, exclusive of the fly boxes:

| **Item** | **Application** |
| --- | --- |
| Clippers | For cutting leader material, trimming knots, and so on |
| Hemostats, small | For extricating flies from fish |
| Knife | Various tasks; has scissors blade |
| Bottle/can opener | *Very* essential |
| Tiny pliers | For debarbing hooks and pinching sinkers |
| Hook hone | For sharpening hooks |
| Small split shot | For adding weight |
| Wader patch | In case of disaster |
| Stream thermometer | For taking water temperature |
| Small tape measure | For measuring fish |
| Lip balm | For the chops |
| Sunscreen | For the nose and face |
| Fly floatant | For treating dry flies |
| Dessicant | Ditto above |
| Small flashlight | For walking after dark, also knot tying at dusk |
| Ferrule cement | For fixing loose tip guides |
| Miniature notebook | I'm an author, right? |
| Ballpoint pen | Ditto above |
| License holder | Keeps me legal |
| Sunglasses | For bright days, polarized |
| Leader material | For tippets and front sections of leaders |
| Pocket camera | For recording beautiful sights and heroic deeds |
| Emergency pack | Includes toilet paper, bandages and mercurochrome |
| Narrow tape | For emergency guide reattachment |

There's also a net suspended from the back. More on that later. Then, of course, there are fly boxes. I may carry from one to four, depending on how much variety is anticipated.

That's not all. I have a tackle bag which serves as a warehouse for additional items which accompany me on my excursions. Having emptied it also, I list the contents:

| Item | Application |
| --- | --- |
| Leader kit | For tying and rebuilding leaders |
| Extra reels and spools | For line changes, also to accommodate variety of rods |
| Fly boxes | For additional variety |
| Heavy pliers | For various and sundry tasks |
| 35mm film | As required |
| Tiny screwdrivers | For fixing reels, eyeglasses, etc. |
| Line dressing | For dry-fly lines |
| Compass | Should I decide to strike out for unexplored regions |
| Hand lotion | A godsend |
| Handiwipes | Great for removing fishiness |
| More wader patch | For backup |
| Spare sunglasses | For loaners or in case of loss |
| Bug dope | For discouragement of hostile winged beings (transfer to vest during bug season) |
| Heavy knife | Just in case |
| Thermos | For coffee and whatever |
| Butane lighter | I don't smoke but do require flame occasionally |
| Corkscrew | In case I meet someone with a bottle of wine |
| Plastic bags | For those rare occasions when a fish is taken home |
| Duct tape | For quick fixes on waders and rain gear |
| Aquarium net | For collecting insect samples |
| Teflon grease | For lubricating reels |
| Nail-knot tool | For emergency replacement of leader butt |
| Needle-knot tool | Ditto above |

This is a lot of stuff; however, all of it has a purpose and does get used, at least occasionally. The idea is to set up a four-stage rotation system: house, car, tackle bag and vest. With a little forethought and planning, you can then have on hand what's needed, without toting a lot of extra items. In this system, the house equates to the base camp in a mountain-climbing expedition. The vest equates to the high camp—you go as light as possible, taking only what is needed.

In the car I always have at least one extra rod for backup and variety, also a second pair of waders. A cooler is usually present for keeping food fresh and drinks cold. Also, if a fish is killed, prompt refrigeration is very important. The car also carries rain gear and any extra clothing I might require. In colder weather, I generally carry a full change of clothes in case of a dunking.

There's so much out there today that it's really not feasible for one person to test everything. I do have some thoughts and observations on some of the listed items, however, which I will pass along.

Clippers                    Ordinary nail clippers will do nicely; however, Orvis puts out a really fine tool which

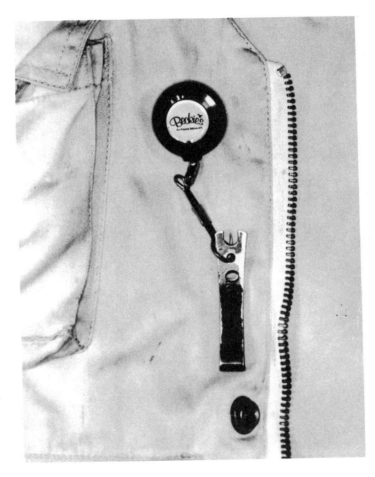

*Clipper with stiletto, mounted on retriever.*

also has a stiletto for picking head cement and little pieces of leader tippet out of the eyes of hooks. Should you opt for nail clippers, remove the fold-out lever—you won't need that much leverage for cutting leader material, and it constantly gets tangled in the line. Mount this tool on a small retriever and hang it on the vest.

Hemostats      There's nothing better for removing hooks. An ultra-light pair will do for average-size flies. For huge streamers, salmon flies, etc., a heavier tool is required, or perhaps long-nosed pliers. Hemostats can also be mounted on a retriever. I pin mine inside the vest, so as to avoid having multiple objects dangling in front with high tangle potential.

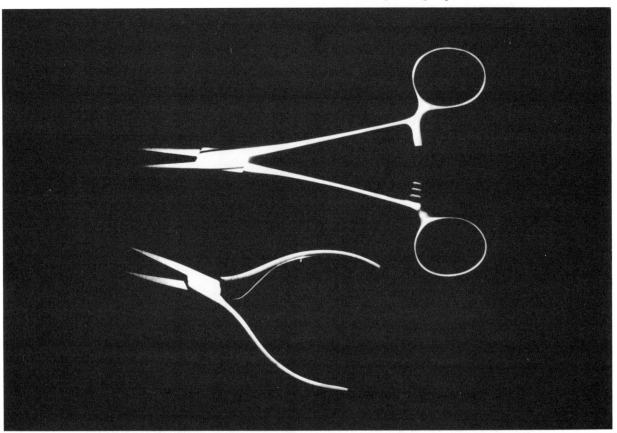

*Hemostats and de-barbing pliers.*

| | |
|---|---|
| Knife | A large one is not required for typical trout fishing. A blade of 3 to 4 inches is adequate. A scissors blade sometimes comes in handy. |
| Tiny pliers | The tiniest, for hook debarbing and split-shot pinching. Also mountable on a retreiver. |
| Hook hone | Ceramic, diamond and very fine-grit stone are all serviceable. |
| Stream thermometer | It's worthwhile to keep track of water temperature. Select a model with a sturdy case. Attach a 5- or 6-foot piece of cord with a safety pin on the end, so it can be pinned to the vest or elsewhere during periods of use. |
| Fly floatant | Both pastes and liquids are available. I prefer the liquid, but carry both, as the paste does double-duty as a line dressing. There are numerous brands—get some advice from experienced dry-fly addicts. |
| Dessicant | A powdered substance for drying and restoring flies. Great stuff. Carry it in a small vial or bottle. |
| Small flashlight | I carry a two-AA-cell version which I have outfitted with a neck strap for hands-free operation. It works much better than any angler's nightlight I've yet tried. |
| Sunglasses | A quality pair of polarized glasses will protect the eyes and help you see into the water. Plastic lenses are lighter and cheaper, but glass has less distortion and resists scratching. There's now a model with small clear magnifiers located just below the polarized lenses. Wonderful for those of us who require reading glasses. |
| Pocket camera | Really nice to have. The fully automatic 35 mm models are ideal for the casual photographer, offering self-focusing, autowind and rewind, automatic film speed setting and pop-up flash. For the more serious photographer, the Olympus XA is hard to beat. |
| Emergency pack | Don't forget that toilet paper unless your love of nature extends to a preference for |

|                    | leaves. And should that be the case, be sure you know what poison oak and poison ivy look like. |
|--------------------|--------------------------------------------------------------------------------------------------|
| Narrow tape        | Carry a small spool of some brand with good adhesive qualities for binding down guide feet when wrappings come off. This does happen occasionally. |
| Extra reels/spools | As required. Think about what types of fishing you will be doing. It is sometimes advisable to carry a spare spool in the vest, if a situation is anticipated where a different type of line—such as sink-tip instead of floating—is required. |
| Fly boxes          | I prefer medium to small sizes—they fit vest pockets better. But if you carry very large dry flies, get a good deep box for them— |

*Flies in closed-cell-foam fly box.*

they should not be compressed. Avoid fly books and wallets. Carry streamers in boxes designed to accommodate them. The new boxes that have closed-cell foam inside are terrific for wets, nymphs, streamers, and so on.

| | |
|---|---|
| 35mm film | Carry several speeds for varying light, 64 ASA to 400 ASA. On warm days, do not leave it in the car; it gets hot in there. Trunks are somewhat better, as they don't get the greenhouse effect. Best, store spare film in the ice chest. |
| Screwdrivers | Those little sets of a half-dozen sizes are a valuable addition to the tackle bag. I guarantee you'll use them and be grateful for their presence. |
| Teflon grease | The best substance for lubricating fishing reels I've yet used. Good for automobile antennas also. |
| Needle/nail-knot tools | Perhaps not essential in the traveling kit, but they take up so little space, why not include them? I seem to frequently end up working on people's leaders, so I keep these tools handy. |

I believe you will not have any trouble making intelligent selections of the other listed items, what with the information provided on the packaging plus advice from the dealer. I suggest you acquire things gradually as they are needed and as you become more aware of your requirements.

There are several other items which I personally find most serviceable and which I recommend. There is a device for carrying liquid fly floatant which consists of a small elastic harness mounted on a leather pad to which is attached an alligator clip. It will accommodate a 2-ounce bottle and clips conveniently to the vest. In order to avoid losing bottle caps, I drill a small hole in the cap, insert a screw eye and attach a piece of cord which is safety-pinned to the vest, on the inside of a pocket flap perhaps. Thus I can douse my flies without having to worry about hanging on to a slippery cap.

Incidentally, my two favorite liquid floatants at this writing are Flyta, produced by F. A. Johnson, Inc., of Lyndenhurst, N.J., and Fly-New, a product of B.T., Inc., Cortland, N.Y. Both do a terrific job of cleaning,

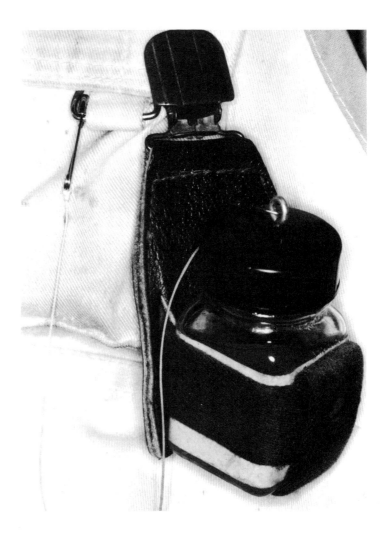

*Harness and bottle for carrying liquid fly flotant. Note arrangement for securing lid, so as to avoid accidental dropping in water.*

restoring and enhancing flotation. What tomorrow's technology may bring I can't say, but I do know that I can heartily recommend these two products.

About nets, there's been some controversy here. One camp maintains that a net makes it easier to handle and release fish without hurting them. The other says that the mesh of the net can disturb the protective mucous which covers a trout's body, resulting in the contraction of fungus-type diseases. My thought is that while net mesh does hold a potential for scraping off body mucous, that can be avoided with careful handling. This places me in the pro-net camp. We will discuss landing and releasing fish in a later chapter.

A trout net doesn't have to be very large, unless we're talking steelhead, giant Alaskan rainbows or something on that order. What is important is that the bag should be deep and of a fairly fine weave. Better-quality bags are of a graduated-type construction—that is, the mesh at the bottom starts out very fine, then gradually becomes larger. The bag should be of the softest material available; hard, rough material is tougher on the fish, and lends some credibility to the anti-net position.

The most widely used method for hanging a net from your back is via a spring-loaded retriever, similar to that used for carrying a bunch of keys. That's fine, but I have an arrangement I like better. It involves a little craftsmanship, some Velcro and one of those elastic shock cords. First, sew a small patch of male Velcro to the back of the wading vest up near the collar, adjacent to the cloth loop from which the net is sus-

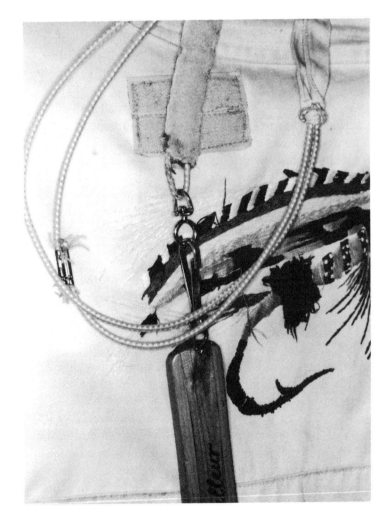

*Net mounting arrangement with Velcro and stretch cord.*

pended. Sew a piece of female Velcro to the shock cord at the end where the net will be attached. Connect the shock cord and the cloth loop, using the interlocking loop technique, then connect the net to the other end. When not in use, the net is held against your back by the Velcro, with the handle just behind the neck, where it can be grasped easily. The cord and net bag ride against your back, minimizing the bothersome snagging that occurs when walking through brush. As an option, a loop of female Velcro can be attached to the front of the net frame, which causes the net to ride upside-down, with the bag folded underneath. This is even more snag-proof, though not as convenient as the other method.

I'm one of those farsighted people who doesn't need bifocals but must have magnification and focusing assistance at reading distance—which, of course, is also knot-tying distance. My solution is to hang a pair of reading glasses around my neck on a Croakie. A Croakie is a neck strap made out of neoprene, expressly designed for holding reading glasses. It is manufactured by the Simms Co. of Jackson, WY., which produces quite a line of angling products, including excellent-quality neoprene waders. The Croakie is one of those marvelously simple problem solvers you wonder why you didn't think of yourself.

Another neat device for those who need magnification astream is the Flip-Focal. This is a double-lens magnifier which mounts beneath the brim of your hat. When not in use, it folds up out of the way via a small hinge. Magnification is approximately 2X at 14 inches focal range.

The original model affixes to the hat brim with two small pins, onto the ends of which slip a couple of stays—not the greatest arrangement. I believe a model featuring a simple alligator clip is just becoming available. I modified my pair by epoxying a couple of heavy-duty bobby pins to the mounting plate. Now I simply slide it onto any hat brim and adjust until the focus suits my eyes. A real improvement.

As a compulsive bearer of multiple spools of leader material, I've always longed for something that would help organize this. Now such a product is available. It consists of a four-compartment pouch, each one of which holds a spool. They are closed with Velcro, and the monofilament feeds right out through the Velcro, without damage. It works great. I have color-coded the compartments, in order to readily identify the four different diameters enclosed. I see that certain fly-fishing vests are now available with such a feature built in. Good idea.

I could go on and on. The other day I received a catalog from a new mail-order supply house, one I wasn't previously aware of. It contains page after page of paraphernalia, including most of the items mentioned in this chapter. Some of them make me smile. Anyone want a stomach pump for analyzing the contents of a trout's stomach before releasing the

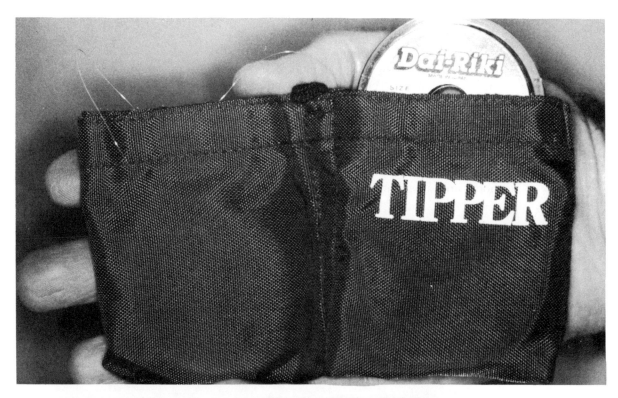

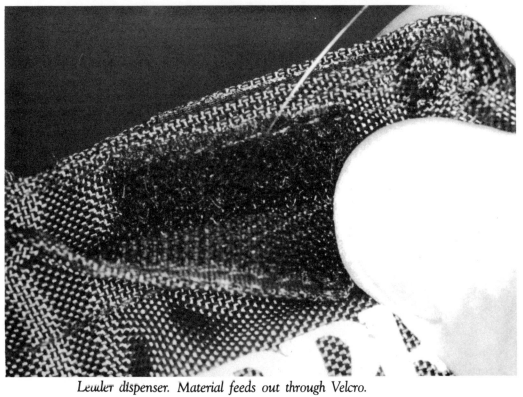

*Leader dispenser. Material feeds out through Velcro.*

poor creature? How about a blood-knot tool so you can complicate a simple operation? Perhaps I'd best stop right here—I shouldn't knock products which others may find useful.

I'll leave you with this admonition: don't become a gadget-freak. You will enjoy purchasing and using functional, good-quality tools, as we all do, but make sure the items you purchase meet those criteria—function and good quality. Otherwise you'll end up with an angling junk shop at home and a wading vest Superman couldn't stand up in.

# CHAPTER VII _____

# An Appreciation
# of Aquatic
# Entomology

Insects are the trout's main dietary staple and thus of great importance to the fly-fisher. A basic knowledge of stream insects, both water-based and land-based, is essential to effective fishing. While not a guarantee of total success, such knowledge will enable even the newcomer to catch some of the fish some of the time, a great improvement over catching hardly any fish at any time.

The field of entomology, even that small segment of it which affects the angler, is vast. It's rather intimidating—demoralizing, in fact—for an aspiring fly-fisherperson to look at a fishing book catalog and see one title after another on insects. Most of the books currently in print have merit and value, but remember, the way to eat an elephant is one bite at a time. In this chapter, I'll feed you some delectable and nutritious morsels. The banquet goes on for the rest of your angling life.

We shall concentrate on three major orders of aquatic insects—Mayflies, caddis flies and stoneflies. We will take a brief look at several others which can be of great importance at times, and at a few significant terrestrial, or land-based, insects. We will study the life cycles of stream insects in terms of the importance of these phenomena to the trout and the angler. Thus, we shall send you streamward with sufficient orientation to successfully identify, imitate and emulate the behavior of the more common types of insects trout feed on.

Let's start with some general information which is essentially common to all aquatic insects. They begin life on the stream bottom as a tiny fertilized egg. Soon the egg becomes a nymph or larva, at the same time becoming potential trout food. The larva grows in its watery world until maturity is reached, one year being a typical period. Then a remarkable event takes place—a winged insect, which has been slowly developing within the larval shell, emerges. Anglers refer to this as a hatch, a term which can create more excitement than almost any other in fly-fishing: "The Salmon flies are hatching on the Madison!" "The Green Drakes are hatching on the Beaverkill!" Otherwise sober and responsible men sneak out of work and miss dinner to be on the water at hatch-time.

The winged insect will feed no more—its only remaining task is to reproduce. The adult may or may not go through a final transformation before mating, depending on the particular type of insect. The males and females join, and the eggs are quickly fertilized. The female deposits her precious cargo back into the stream, and the cycle begins anew. The spent insect may fall to the surface, perhaps to be sucked in by a feeding trout, in total fulfillment of its destiny.

## MAYFLIES

The order of Mayflies—Ephemeroptera to the entomologist—is a very old and prolific one. Mayflies are present in some abundance in trout waters throughout the world, extremely cold areas excepted. This is the classic aquatic insect—many of our most historic and popular fly patterns are modeled after one Mayfly or another.

Despite the name, Mayflies occur in other months besides May. In the eastern, northeastern and central range of trout habitat, we begin to see them in April. May and June are peak months, with various major species making their annual appearance. The summer months are less productive, although certain small Mayflies can generate excellent fishing where conditions are favorable. September and October hatches, while less prolific than those of spring, can be very important at times.

In the Rockies, May is not Mayfly time, although a few species begin to emerge on spring creeks, where snowmelt is not a factor. Generally, major hatches begin in mid to late June and continue into October. There is a summer slump in August, with activity commencing again after Labor Day. Again, the spring creeks are an exception—the stable environment in these streams supports hatches right through the summer.

I'm going to pause here for just a moment and give you some extremely important information—in fact, I'm hard pressed to think of

*Mayfly dun (sub-imago).*

anything that has a greater bearing on angling success. It's simply this: trout waters differ greatly one from the other—individually, by locality and by region. The more I travel the trout beat, the more I marvel at the diversity. And it keeps changing, as conditions change and the insects, flexible creatures that they are, adapt accordingly. Therefore, it is impossible to make absolute, specific statements about aquatic insects which are accurate all of the time over large geographic areas. *It is vital to have specific information on the streams you intend to fish at the times when you will be fishing them!*

Back to Mayflies. The insects of this order have a three-stage life cycle, not counting the egg: nymph (larva), dun (subimago) and spinner or spent (imago). I give you the Latin terms as well as the common ones, because while they are meaningless to the trout, they are most helpful in discussions with other anglers and when reading angling literature.

Nymphs definitely *are* important to the trout, and therefore to us. Trout take a much greater percentage of their insect diet in the sub-aqueous form than the dun or spinner form. Sorry, dry-fly purists.

Mayfly nymphs fall into four basic categories: crawlers, clingers, swimmers and burrowers. In my experience, I've found the swimming nymph types to be the most productive from a fishing standpoint, the

burrowers the least so. This has to do with exposure and attractiveness to
the fish. All nymphs get exposed to the trout at some point, even if only
briefly during periods of emergence. At that time, they may not appear as
a true nymph, but as an emerging insect, which accounts for the success
of raggy-looking wet flies.

Nymphs extract oxygen from the water via a set of gills located on
either side of the abdomen. These gills vary considerably in appearance
and functional characteristics. Clinging-type nymphs have proportionately large gills, which serve the dual purpose of acting as suction cups
which grip the rock's surface and taking oxygen from the current. These

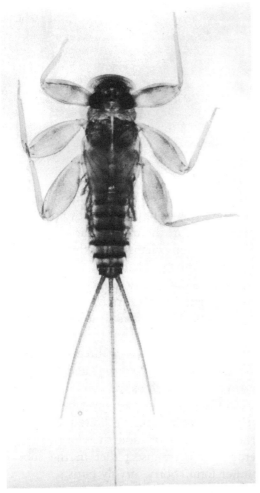

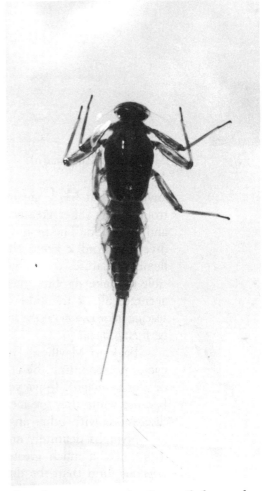

*Clinging-type nymph. Note powerful legs.*          *Crawling-type nymph. One tail damaged
in capture.*

flat-bodied nymphs must live in fast water, because they rely on water passing through the gills for breathing. In still water, a true clinging nymph would drown.

Crawlers' gills are less pronounced than clingers', and although they rely somewhat on the current for assistance in breathing, they can do quite well in quieter waters, at least for limited periods. This varies in degree among species. Thus, crawling nymphs are found in more diverse water types.

Swimming nymphs breathe very efficiently, even though they have the smallest gill structure of the four types. This, coupled with their ability to swim, allows them to survive in various water types.

*Burrowing-type nymph. Note prolific gill structure.*

*Swimming-type nymph. Note streamlined shape, webby tails, conservative gill structure and relatively weak legs.*

Burrowing nymphs, by necessity, are most efficient at extracting oxygen. Their gills are proportionately large and plumagelike, and constantly in movement. Thus, sufficient oxygen is obtained from the seepage which passes through the silt, sand and detritus in which they live. Several very large and important Mayflies which inhabit still waters, such as lakes and ponds, come from burrowing nymphs.

Mayfly nymphs, with a few exceptions, live in the stream for one year. During this time, they grow. Their skin or shell does *not* grow, so it is shed periodically. These are called instar periods. A typical Mayfly nymph goes through about twenty of these in its lifetime. Lobsters do the same thing, but only once a year—they are called shedders then. Sometimes you will encounter a nymph that is very pale in color and soft to the touch. That nymph has just shed its skin.

Instinctively aware that the denizens of their underwater world are out to get them, nymphs attempt to stay out of harm's way. The swimmers, crawlers and clingers hide under and around rocks and other stream-bottom structures. The burrowers, best equipped of all for survival, bury themselves in a soft, silty or sandy stream bottom. Burrowing nymphs are found only where the stream bed is hospitable to their lifestyle.

With all their stealth, nymphs still become exposed to trout. Clingers become dislodged; crawlers lose their grip on their home rock; swimmers dart into the current foraging for plankton. At certain times, once or twice a day, major nymph activity may occur, when a great many nymphs are carried downstream by the current. The biologists call this an invertebrate drift. Apparently, it is triggered by a compulsion to migrate. During these drift periods, trout have the opportunity to feed heavily on nymphs, and fishing with an artificial nymph can be very productive. In warmer weather, nocturnal drifts are common, often occurring just after dark. This can be an exciting time, with larger trout moving out to feed.

Another major period of nymph exposure is just before and during a hatch. Nymphs become active, moving about as they prepare for migration to the surface. Thus, they are more easily dislodged. As hatch time nears, nymphs begin to drift, wriggle and half-swim upward, sometimes making abortive attempts before embarking on the final journey. This activity and the large concentration of nymphs at one time encourage the trout to feed voraciously. Incidentally this is about the only time the fish get a chance at the burrowing nymphs.

The manner in which nymphs hatch varies considerably from type to type and from species to species, and has a profound influence on the feeding behavior of the trout. Some nymphs rise very quickly to the surface, where the winged insect emerges from the shuck in short order, but must ride the surface for a spell, while full circulation occurs in the wings and they become dry enough to permit flight. The trout take the nymph in its true nymphal form, and also the adult during its helpless preflight drift. Typically, the trout start feeding on nymphs, then become interested in the duns as the hatch progresses. Sometimes, they will feed on either form.

Early-season Mayflies often ride the surface as duns for long stretches. The water is still cold, and the air perhaps colder still, so it takes a while for the insects' circulatory system to fill the wings, and for the wings to dry. Spring rains greatly inhibit the emergent duns' ability to fly, and dry-fly fishing to a hatch on a rainy day can be absolutely wild.

Other species make it to the surface only to encounter difficulty completing the emergence. The adult has trouble emerging from and casting the skin. It struggles along, often dragging or riding the empty shuck for some distance. They are extremely vulnerable at such times, and visible rise forms appear in great numbers. This can be a confusing time for the angler, because what he sees may be quite different from what the trout sees. The dry-fly fisherman ties on what appears to be a credible imitation, and the fish refuse it, because they are looking at semi-emerged insects or shuck-draggers. A special-purpose fly is often required at such times.

Still other species seem to anticipate reaching the surface and actually cast the nymphal shuck on the way up. The trout then become selective to the emergent insect, and wet-fly or emerger patterns work wonderfully well. Again, appearances can be very deceptive, because the angler sees a great many adult Mayflies in the air. Rise forms are visible, as trout intercept the insects just beneath the surface, virtually shouting "dry-fly" at the trembling fisherman. But close observation reveals that the flies hardly spend any time on the water surface at all—they take right off for the bushes!

The phenomenon just described is of tremendous importance to the angler. There is no greater frustration than having visible—and sometimes audible—rise forms all over the place and not being able to prick a single lip. The key is to ascertain whether the duns are actually drifting on the surface or flying off into the air. This hatching behavior is employed by several important late-spring, early-summer Mayflies in the east and midwest. By the time they appear, water and air temperatures are warmer, circulation in the wings takes place very quickly and the dun makes a clean getaway.

The swimming nymphs can create a lot of excitement at hatch time. Several large species common to eastern and midwestern waters swim into the shallows and congregate around rocks and logs. When ready to emerge, they crawl onto the rock or log and hatch in the air. The trout follow the nymphal migration, and often large fish are to be seen turning and slashing at rocks as though trying to devour them. They are after the nymphs, of course, sufficiently stimulated by the hordes of darting prey to abandon their normally furtive habits.

Not all swimming nymphs crawl out of the water to hatch, so the trout do see duns at times, to the delight of the dry-fly enthusiast. On dark, rainy days, even the species that normally crawl onto the rocks may start popping out in the stream. It's essential to find out precisely what goes on in the rivers in your locality.

The Mayfly dun, or subadult, flies to cover, if fortunate enough to escape the hungry fish and birds that lie in wait. The life span of the dun ranges from under an hour to several days, depending on species and weather conditions. Then another of nature's incredible phenomena occurs—the dun casts a final shuck and steps forth as a shining adult or

*Mayfly spinner (imago) and empty shuck from which it has just emerged.*

spinner. This is the "metamorphosis of the sub-imago", a melodic term that stirs my soul. The wings are clear or hyaline; the eyes are bright and enlarged; the body coloration brilliant; the tails long and delicate.

The males and females meet and couple, sometimes in the trees or bushes, other times out over the stream, where their love making is viewed by a breathless group of expectant anglers. The eggs are quickly fertilized and the lifework of the males is done. The females have one final mission—to deposit the fertilized eggs in the stream. They hover over the water and either eject the eggs or touch them to the surface.

Nature, in its apolitical efficiency, wastes little. The spent adults drop to the stream surface, some flush, others with a wing raised in a final feeble but victorious quiver. Once more, the waiting trout are encouraged to feed and the well-prepared angler has an excellent dry-fly opportunity. Not all Mayfly spinners create fishing potential. The males of some species never leave the trees; the spents of certain species make it back to land. This is another aspect of fly-fishing where study and awareness of the aquatic insects indigenous to the rivers you fish is of great value.

## CADDIS FLIES

Caddis flies—order of Trichoptera—are at least equal in importance to the more glamorous and popular Mayflies but only in recent years have they been accorded the recognition they deserve. Initially this may have been a carry over of the British influence. Their sedge, as it is called, is very much subordinate to the Mayfly. Also, caddis flies are more difficult for the angler to relate to. They do not have the distinctive appearance of the major Mayflies; therefore, few of them have nicknames, like the Ephemeropterae do. And they can be very confusing in behavior. But make no mistake—they are of monumental importance.

The life cycle of the caddis differs somewhat from that of the Mayfly. The fertilized eggs hatch into a larval form called a caddis worm. These vary in color from waxy cream to various shades of green and olive to tans and browns.

Most caddis worms build protective cases out of a variety of minute matter from the river or lake bed. This includes sand and gravel, tiny twigs and strips of bark. The cases are held together by a secretion, and quite effectively so. The worm adds to the case to accommodate growth. The cases are very interesting to look at—some are even pretty. It's difficult to believe a dumb little worm could do that.

Those caddis worms which do not build cases rely on camouflage and secretiveness for survival. Fish will take them readily, given the opportu-

*Adult Caddis fly.*

nity. They will also take the cased ones, cases and all. I have a couple of cased caddis imitations which work very well at the right time and place.

As the time for emergence draws near, the caddis worm goes through an underwater transformation and becomes a pupa, after which it no longer eats or grows. Soon after pupation, the insect wriggles from its case, rises to the surface and flies off into the streamside foliage. During emergence, the caddis are extremely vulnerable, and trout gorge themselves on them as they struggle to reach the surface. Pupal imitations, including the simple soft-hackle wet fly, are deadly at such times.

With certain exceptions, the adult caddis spends little or no time floating on the water—they have the facility to be gone in a hurry. Often they will make several abortive takeoffs, hopping and dancing along the surface. This drives the trout wild, and rise forms are generally rather startling. The appearance of these adult caddis is not difficult to simulate, but emulating their behavior can be a bit tricky.

One of my favorite techniques is to drop the fly directly on top of the rise form, as fast as I can get it there. Quite frequently, the trout will miss a hopping caddis and will be hanging right in that spot, disappointed and angry. Given what is perceived as a second chance, the trout gulps your counterfeit caddis without hesitation. I also like to make down-stream or down-and-across casts, letting them fall slack, then twitching the fly in a subtle, provocative manner.

I've noticed in my Rocky Mountain fishing experiences that the caddis out west seem to ride the surface longer. I have no explanation for this—apparently it's just the way those species evolved. In any case, the anglers should be thankful, because the caddis fishing out west is marvelous, both dry-fly and subsurface.

The adult caddis is rather mothlike in appearance, with the wings proportionately oversized for the body. It does not go through a final molt, as the Mayfly does. The adults are relatively long-lived, many species surviving for as long as twenty days. This is deceptive, because the angler may see caddis in the air and assume there is hatching activity, when actually that particular species is done for the season.

Caddis don't immediately die and fall spent after mating—in many cases they survive to mate two or several times. The females deposit their eggs on or beneath the water, some species actually swimming to the stream bottom, ovipositing and reemerging. This creates some interesting and exciting fishing. Apparently, certain anglers found this out a long time ago. The Grannom, a wet-fly pattern which features a pea-green egg sac, has been around for ages.

There are about twelve hundred species of caddis classified at this time. Fortunately for the angler, only a modest number of them are important from a practical fishing standpoint. The range of sizes is almost as wide as the Mayfly. There are micro-caddis which are only a few millimeters in length, large lake-dwelling caddis which run to an inch or more and everything in between. There are also wide variations in color, which range through shades of tans, grays, brown and black. The wings may be mottled or solid-color. Sometimes the true coloration is deceptive, as the insect in flight may appear to be of a lighter shade than it actually is. Capturing a specimen is the solution, but this can be difficult, for the caddis is very elusive, much more so than the Mayfly. Anyone wishing a close look at caddis is well advised to carry an insect net.

## STONEFLIES (ORDER OF PLECOPTERA)

As with caddis, stoneflies have received far less documentation in angling literature than Mayflies. It is the smallest of the three major orders, approximately five hundred species having been classified in American trout waters. A select number of these are of first-magnitude importance to the fly-fisher, several achieving super-hatch status.

The stonefly has only a two-stage life cycle, nymph and adult. The nymphs of the smaller species live one year, while those of the larger species live two or three years. This is interesting, for it means that these nymphs are available to the trout in a wide range of sizes.

*Typical Stonefly nymph, top and bottom views.*
*Tail broken in capture.*

Stonefly nymphs are distinctive, easy to identify and often strikingly beautiful. Unlike Mayfly nymphs, they have no gills along the abdomen—rather, they are smooth-bodied. The gills, consisting of hair-like filaments, are located in the thoracic area. These nymphs invariably are two-tailed. Most Mayfly nymphs have three tails, although there are a few two-tailed species.

Another distinguishing characteristic is the presence of two distinct wing cases, which are needed because the adult has two pairs of large and fully functional wings. In front of the wing cases is a protothorax, which carries the foremost set of legs and some of the gill filaments. The head is large and flattened and the jaw structure rather powerful, especially on the larger species, which are carnivorous. The giant Pteronarcys stonefly nymphs not only feed on other insects, they are known to kill small fish and suck the fluids from their eyeballs.

Stonefly nymphs have high oxygen requirements and are invariably found in fast-water sections of streams. Populations are considerably greater in the Rocky Mountain and western rivers; however, there are quite a few stoneflies in the central and eastern regions also, and they are given less attention than they deserve. I believe this is primarily due to the fact that they seldom generate any dry-fly fishing. The nymph fisherman, however, can score well on certain eastern freestone streams where good stonefly populations exist.

When ready to hatch, stonefly nymphs march along the streambed until they find a rock or log to crawl up onto. Emergence occurs above the waterline, with the tell-tale shucks left behind. This stream-bottom migration exposes the nymphs to the trout, as some are dislodged by the current. Bottom-fishing with a weighted nymph can be absolutely marvelous at such times.

After mating, the female adults fly out over the stream to oviposit. Adult stoneflies are easily recognized in flight by the double set of wings. Some shake the fertilized eggs into the water; others ride the current and allow the eggs to be washed off. This, of course, is dry-fly time. However, much of this activity is nocturnal and of value only to the night-fisherman.

A notable exception is the huge Pteronarcys Californica stonefly, which is found in the rivers of the Rocky Mountains and Pacific Northwest. This species is known as the salmon fly, because the underside of the abdomen is reminiscent of a fresh salmon filet in color. These giants often reach 2 inches in body length, with the wings creating an even larger silhouette. It is an early-season fly throughout its range, coming off from around the end of May into early and even mid-July, depending on the particular watershed. Weather conditions have a pronounced impact on emergence, which makes it difficult to predict exactly when prime fishing will occur in a particular locality. This is a problem for the vacation fisherman, who tries to pick a time months in advance.

When the massive females are ovipositing, all hell generally breaks loose, and rises can be spectacular. One of the benefits of having such an enormous insect on the water is that the trout often come to the feast in high or off-color water conditions, when a smaller fly would not bring them up. And of course, they make it worthwhile for really large trout to surface-feed.

Such is the reputation of the salmon fly hatch—actually, the egg-laying flight—that it is thought of as the Mardi Gras of angling, an

*Stonefly adult.*

opportunity to realize one's fantasies. As an eastern-based fisherman who has made many western trips, I want to pass along my perceptions. As mentioned, it's tricky to predict precise timing, and even trickier to pin-point where a flight will occur on a given day. Generally, activity first begins in the lower portion of a river, where water temperatures get warmer sooner, then progresses upstream. Drift-boating is very effective, as it allows the angler to cover a lot of water in search of peak activity. Floating with a reputable guide who knows the area is most worthwhile.

Another peculiarity I've noticed in fishing the salmon fly is that the best fishing often occurs during a modest ovipositing flight, rather than a heavy one. I've found this to be true in the case of certain other insects also. I think it's because the trout have to be opportunistic. With many big flies on the water, the trout have no problem getting all they want. When there are only enough insects to get the trout's attention and stimulate the urge to feed, they are likely not to let many go by. Also, I believe that even very large trout can get stuffed early on when feeding on such large flies, especially in early season, when colder water temperatures cause the fish's metabolism to be lower, and digestion is retarded. For this reason, it is often advisable to use an artificial which is slightly smaller than the natural.

## MIDGES (ORDER OF DIPTERA)

This order is a very large one. It includes the various craneflies, a host of true midges and such ominous characters as the blackfly and the mosquito.

The pseudonym "midge" is a derivative of "midget" and thus implies diminution. True, many members of the order Diptera are tiny, but some are good-sized. There are giant craneflies so large that the leg span will almost reach across a tea saucer.

I like to think of midges in just that manner: gangly-legged. My old angling friend Dud Soper was intrigued by these insects and designed a pattern to imitate the craneflies he encountered on the Battenkill. He named it the Gangly-Legs. A bizarre-looking creation, it was generally scoffed at within conventional angling circles, but let me tell you, it worked, especially when handled by a master like Dud.

The true or nonbiting midges are of significance to the angler, and while not in a league with Mayflies or caddis, they can be very important at certain times. The midge goes through a two-cycle subaquatic existence, larva and pupa, similar to the caddis. They vary greatly in coloration and size. They are most abundant in silty, soft-bottomed streams which contain heavy plant growth. The larvae are wormlike in appearance. The pupae are slender-bodied and long-legged, with a slightly enlarged thorax and visible wing cases.

Trout will take both larva and pupa, the adult less frequently because it does not ride the water. Just before emergence, the pupae drift in the surface film, their bodies hanging downward. Their extreme vulnerability makes them fair game for trout and important to fishermen.

The spring creeks of the west have tremendous populations of Diptera. While we all love to fish the bountiful Mayfly hatches which occur on these streams, midge fishing can be just as exciting. Often, it fills out the day, providing morning action before the Mayfly hatch begins and evening fishing after it's over. It also offers winter fishing opportunities— one can midge fish the spring creeks almost any day the weather is tolerable. I once had a ball on Armstrong's spring creek in a virtual blizzard.

Occasionally, other Diptera flies than the nonbiting midge come into play. I've mentioned Dud Soper's Gangly-Legs, which is used to imitate the craneflies we sometimes find around the streams. These insects are easy to identify—they look like big mosquitos. In trout ponds, mosquito and blackfly larvae are fed upon by trout. The latter are also present in streams and can produce in the early season, before major hatches begin.

One final word on midge fishing. Often, as the emergence progresses, there are so many tiny pupae in the water that a single scoop with an aquarium net will capture a dozen or more. The great density entices the trout into feeding in gulps, much the same as a whale feeds on krill. Successful presentation then becomes very much a matter of timing—one tries to get in synch with the trout's feeding rhythm, and seeks to cast the pupal imitation amongst a group of naturals that are about to be devoured. Accuracy is also important, because the trout have no reason to move laterally to obtain food.

## OTHER AQUATIC INSECTS

Occasionally the angler encounters a situation where insects other than those previously described are being taken by trout. This tends to be quite localized, which accounts for the shortage of documentation. I'm sure that eventually the angling entomologists will get around to telling us more about the off-beat insect species, but meanwhile we must rely primarily on observation, experience and perhaps a hot tip from a local expert.

The little back-swimmers and water-boatmen of the order Hemiptera are found in many ponds, lakes and slow rivers. Typically, they are active in early season, just after ice-out. The tipoff that trout are taking them is the energetic rise form with no insects visible on the water. These insects are capable of quick movements, so the trout often have to chase them. An active, jerking retrieve with a wet fly is the recommended technique.

Several members of the order Sialis are worthy of note. One is the American alderfly, Sialis infumata. This insect is frequently mistaken for a caddis, which it closely resembles. It dwells in both streams and ponds. I've had very good fishing to the alderfly in a number of northeastern streams, notably the Housatonic in Connecticut and Grand Lake Stream in northern Maine, where it provides dry-fly fishing for land-locked salmon.

While dissimilar in appearance, the dobsonfly is also a member of the order Sialis. Its Latin name is Corydalis cornuta. The larva is the hellgramite, commonly used as bait by bass and trout fishermen. Hellgramites tend to inhabit very swift sections of streams, and, while omnivorous, they are essentially predators, eating other nymphs and larvae. If you pick one up, watch out—they bite!

I often used hellgramites in the Esopus Creek in my bait-fishing days, and they were very effective on the resident rainbows. I honestly do not know whether the dobsonfly is indigenous to the Esopus—I've done a fair amount of rock rolling there and have yet to find a hellgramite. However, the Esopus has a good population of large stoneflies, and I believe the hellgramites were taken for stonefly nymphs.

Two members of the order Odonata offer good potential for sport. These are the dragonflies (suborder Anisoptera) and the damselflies (suborder Zygoptera). Both are quiet-water dwellers, inhabiting lakes and streams. The nymphal form produces the fishing, as trout seldom get a chance at an adult.

I haven't had the opportunity to do much with dragonfly nymphs, although it's probable that I've caught trout which took my large, deep-fished nymph or Muddler for one of those. The damselfly has been very good to me in the Rockies, where the large, elongated nymphs produce great fishing in several lakes I frequent. My imitations worked best along the shorelines, where the nymphs congregate before hatching. A darting retrieve suggests the swimming style of the naturals.

Even though they are not insects, I want to briefly mention the shrimps and scuds. These freshwater crustaceans are found in a great many ponds, lakes and slow-moving streams, often in proliferate quantities. They favor waters with heavy aquatic vegetation. Sizes range from about a sixteenth to nearly three-quarters of an inch. Colors run to grays, yellows, olives and ambers.

I am always glad to find shrimp or scud in trout waters, because quality angling is virtually assured. Trout love crustaceans, and there is no healthier food for them. Trout which have a large complement of crustaceans in their diet are generally well-colored, deep-bodied and powerful. And for those very rare and special occasions when we dare take a trout for the table, there's none so delicious as the crustacean-eater.

## TERRESTRIALS

Land-based insects have gotten considerably more recognition than the lesser aquatic forms, with at least one major book and a host of chapters and articles devoted to them. I believe this is because of their visibility and ubiquitousness, along with the fact that nearly all fishing to terrestrials is dry-fly.

There are several problems with terrestrials regarding trout fishing. One is that much of the major insect activity comes during summer months, when streams are in poor condition. Another is that terrestrials are just that—they don't willingly go into the water. If they should happen to end up there it's by accident—they fall from the bank or are blown onto the water by a gust of wind. Usually, this means they don't get far out into the current. Terrestrial fishing is mostly bank fishing, using grasshopper, cricket, beetle and ant imitations.

Low-water conditions exacerbate the bank-fishing problem, quite obviously. Trout are reluctant to move into shallow water, even for a grasshopper feast, because they expose themselves to their enemies. Also, there are a lot of fisherpeople around today, which increases the bank traffic and spooks the trout. Still, there are good opportunities for fishing terrestrials, if you pick your shots carefully.

Grasshoppers are common all over the continent, and where streams are in proximity to pasture, meadow or farmlands, hoppers can be of great importance. In the Rockies, hopper fishing can be just dynamite, given a good year (these insects are rather cyclic) and favorable weather and water conditions. The great thing we have going for us out there is that western streams are usually in excellent condition in August and September, when hopper fishing is prime.

Like many insects, grasshoppers vary widely in size and color. It's of value to know what type of hoppers predominate in the area you're fishing. This is somewhat confusing, because in prime hopper country you're liable to see quite a variety. I generally favor a smaller fly, especially on a quiet stream. On big, wild rivers, a larger fly might be a better choice.

Crickets have potential. I confess to almost total ignorance about these insects, but I do carry black cricket imitations, and if I see crickets in a locality, I don't hesitate to fish the pattern. I've done remarkably well with it on occasion.

I also carry a few simple beetle patterns, and, like the cricket, they come in very handy in doldrum periods when nothing's hatching. I get the distinct impression that there's something about beetles that trout like, because I've been able to get them to rise to my artificials on summer dog days, when the river is dead as a doornail.

There was a time when the Japanese beetle created a lot of excitement in angling circles. This insect was introduced to the United States in the mid-1930s, live larvae being present in the soil used to package shrubbery imports from Japan. Allegedly, the first beetles hatched from the roots of a bunch of Banzai trees planted along the perimeter of a golf course near Riverton, New Jersey. In no time, they were defoliating the trees in the area, and in a few years were infesting the entire northeast. That may be what precipitated World War II, Pearl Harbor notwithstanding.

Disaster though it was for the foilage, it was a windfall for the angler. There were so many beetles that large numbers of them ended up in the water, and trout gobbled them like kids gobble M & M's. The beetle fishing on the Pennsylvania limestone streams was sensational, as documented in the writings of great anglers like Charley Fox, Vince Marinaro and Ed Shenk.

In time a biological control was developed, and beetle populations were decimated. I got in on the tail end of the bonanza, as I always seem to do—there were still some beetles in the Catskills in the mid-1950s. As a matter of fact, there still are a few.

Ants are very interesting. They are part of a vast insect order, Hymenoptera, which encompasses some fifteen thousand species, including sawflies, bees, wasps and ants. Actually, the latter three fall into a large suborder, Apocrita. The ants themselves are called Formicidae, and there are over seven hundred species recorded in North America.

Ants come in a wide range of sizes. Ant-conscious anglers may carry imitations from hook size 28 to size 10. Colors vary—black, fiery brown, cinnamon, yellow. Some species have multicolor bodies—for example, reddish head and thorax and black or dark brown gaster, or rear section.

The amazing thing about ants is that trout often take them when there is apparently no reason to do so. On a number of occasions I've been able to take trout on ant patterns during a Mayfly hatch when I couldn't get them to believe my hatch-matching pattern consistently. In larger sizes, ants make excellent "pound-them-up" flies for between-hatch fishing. Apparently, trout just love them.

The great ant-fishing extravaganza is at mating-flight time. This is not easy to anticipate—some species swarm and mate even in early spring and late autumn, given a balmy day. A select community within the ant colony, called sexuals, grows wings for this event. The queens are much larger than the sexual males. After mating, the queens seek to found new communities, while the males flutter helplessly and soon die. Many of them are carried onto the water by the wind, where they can bring on a rise which rivals any super-hatch.

The first time I fished Henry's Lake from my belly boat, I lucked into a mating swarm of flying ants. It took me a while to figure out what the fish were after, because there was a fair Mayfly hatch going on at the same time. Finally, I saw them. Some were spent males; others were couples, still in copulation, blown to the water. Fortunately, I had my ant box on board and enjoyed an afternoon of super dry-fly fishing.

On that note I conclude this dissertation on stream entomology. In a
sense, I feel like the well-meaning older gentleman in the movie *The
Graduate*, who took the young honor student aside to tell him about Life
and Success. His many years of experience and wisdom were compacted
into one word: "Plastics."

In a few pages we have examined orders of insects totaling many
thousands of species. Luckily for us fisherpeople, only a small percentage
of them have meaning in our game, and many of them are sufficiently
similar that they may be lumped together. My idea of the ultimate lumper
is the angler who decides (1) dry-fly is the *only* way, and (2) an Adams
covers everything. God bless those people! But that's about as much fun
as eating a fast-food burger three meals a day—and even less nutritious.
For the rest of us, a lifetime of reading and on-stream observation lies
ahead.

## THE SEASONAL CYCLE

Now let's take a trip down a well-worn but still exciting path. Walk with
me through the seasonal cycle of a typical eastern/midwestern trout
stream. I choose that region because it's my home beat, and I am therefore more familiar with the particular insects and the dates when we
might expect to see them. Those of you who live in other parts of the
country—the Rockies, the far west, the Pacific northwest—will encounter seasonal cycles on your rivers also. The insects and periods of emergence will be different, but what's important is that the cycle is repetitive,
and more or less predictable, depending on environmental conditions.

Oh yes—it is essential to take weather and other factors into account when trying to anticipate the insect emergence schedule of a
particular stream or region. This varies considerably with topography. In
mountainous country, where snowmelt and spring runoffs make a heavy
contribution to water conditions, the effects of weather may be dramatic.
In a more stable environment—the spring creeks or the rivers of relatively flat upper Michigan, for example—temperatures and precipitation
have much less of an effect.

In addition to natural phenomena, we also must take into account
the effects of human alteration and intervention on many of our rivers.
Historically, the Beaver Boys of the Army Corps of Engineers have kept
themselves busy between wars with dam-building projects, many of which
were unjustifiable on any rational basis. Big cities, notably New York,
have reached out and seized water resources far away which they then
proceeded to waste and abuse. But enough of that for now. From the

anglers' standpoint, it is important to realize that downstream fisheries below impoundments, particularly where flows can be altered at will, are apt to have atypical hatching cycles.

With that, let's be off. Assume that my model typifies the New York–New England streams and those of northern Pennsylvania. Hatches and dates differ, depending on how far north or south you travel, so be aware that certain emergences occur much sooner in North Carolina than in the Adirondacks.

It's early April, and signs of spring are everywhere. Winter was about average weather-wise, and the snow fields in the mountains have pretty much melted. The trout streams, while still somewhat high, are running clear and getting warm enough for one to think about venturing forth with a fly rod.

One of the earliest hatches you might encounter is the Early Brown Stonefly. Actually, there are two species, but they are very similar. The late Art Flick, in his classic *Streamside Guide to Naturals and Their Imitations*, indicates this is the first insect of the season in which the trout show real interest, and my notes over the years confirm that. Some years the Early Brown Stone is of no value, because stream conditions are still horrendous at the time of its emergence, but with any kind of a break, it is productive of some very worthwhile fishing.

As with most stoneflies, the nymphal form is the most productive. These handsome little nymphs run to shades of brown and fiery brown, and average 11 to 14 millimeters in length. They are daytime emergers, frequently becoming active as the morning sun warms the streambed. On occasion, these flies will produce a little surface activity, given favorable water conditions.

As the stoneflies wane, the hopeful angler begins to anticipate the appearance of early-season Mayflies. The weather, while unpredictable, is improving, moving things in the right direction. In mid to late April, we begin to see some small slate-winged Mayflies, perhaps the little Iron Blue Dun (Paraleptophlebia adoptiva) or an early Baetis with a dark olive body. These flies are productive in several stages of emergence: nymph, emerger and dun. The adults average 6 to 8 millimeters, making a size 16 or 18 dry fly appropriate.

These small Mayflies are harbingers of greater things to come. Very soon we can expect to see Quill Gordons, Hendricksons or both. Usually, the Gordons come first. I once encountered an excellent hatch on a small Catskill stream on April 9, but that was a most unusual spring, following one of those rare non-winters. Normally, mid to late April is the time for Quill Gordon, or Epeorus pleuralis.

The Quill Gordon is a gray-winged insect with distinct light-dark body markings. It is often slightly greenish in shading, there being some variation from stream to stream in that regard. The angler's name—actually the pattern name—for this fly dates back to Theodore Gordon, a legendary if somewhat reclusive man who lived and fished in the Catskills from the late 1800s until his death in 1915. Gordon was an astute observer of stream insect phenomena, and his letters and magazine articles constitute a rich legacy to succeeding generations of anglers, in lieu of the book everyone wishes he had written.

The key to hatching activity is water temperature. Once the streams have reached 50 degrees Fahrenheit consistently for a few days, the Gordons will start coming. Emergence is usually concentrated around midday, when the sun is at its zenith. A nymph may work in late morning, but an emerger or dry-fly pattern during the hatch is the ticket. The traditional Quill Gordon is still effective during an Epeorus pleuralis emergence. The adults run 9 to 12 millimeters, so sizes 14 and 12 are recommended.

It displeases me to have to report that the Quill Gordon is no longer as ubiquitous as it once was. The fast-water-dwelling, clinger-type nymphs will tolerate very little pollution, and many streams are simply no longer pure enough to support them. Their presence in quantity in a river is an indication of good water quality.

Usually we look for Hendricksons right after Gordons, where there are Gordons. Traditional emergence dates range from late April to early and mid-May. However, this can vary a great deal either way. In the spring of 1985, following a virtually snow-free winter and exceptionally mild March, we got Hendricksons in mid-April on some Catskill rivers. Someone tipped me off, and I had fabulous dry-fly fishing for two weeks. The hatch had just about petered out by the first of May, and we began to see late-May insects which were also accelerated by the unseasonable weather. Thus, late May and June were a bust. Short-term bonanza, long-term disaster.

The year before had been quite the opposite. Cold, rainy weather persisted throughout April and May—and so did the Hendricksons. We were still fishing these hatches in late May, which means that with their very early emergence the next spring, the insects had only been in the rivers for about eleven months. This dramatically indicates how profoundly thermal conditions can affect seasonal cycles.

That miserably cold May generated another phenomenon of great interest. Bill Dorato and I were shivering through a particularly mean afternoon. The water temperature never got above 45 degrees Fahrenheit, and there were no bugs. We were very disappointed, because the previous day had been quite pleasant, and we had gotten reports of a major Hendrickson hatch.

At last I spotted a trout dimpling in a slow backwater, and I managed to take it on a number 18 dry fly. The fish's belly was distended, as though stuffed. I decided the river could afford to give up one trout to science, so I dispatched the fellow and performed an autopsy. To our great amazement, it was chock full of subvaria duns that looked so fresh they could take wing—yet we hadn't seen ten flies all day! Lesson: it had gotten so cold the trout hadn't been able to digest yesterday's dinner. That's what frigid temperatures can do to a trout's metabolism.

The so-called Hendrickson hatch actually is composed of three closely related Mayflies: Ephemerella subvaria, E. invaria and E. rotunda. Any or all of these may be present in a given stream. Subvaria is considered the classic Hendrickson. It is the largest of the three, and the first to appear. The slightly smaller and paler rotundas and invarias follow, often contiguously, giving the appearance of a continuous hatch to what is actually two or three consecutive hatches.

An interesting characteristic of subvaria is that the male and female duns differ in body color, to the extent that different fly patterns are used to imitate them. The male has a darker body with distinctive reddish-brown segmentation. Art Flick designed the Red Quill to imitate the male subvaria. The female has a lighter-colored body, often tinged with an elusive rosy-pinkish hue when newly emerged. Roy Steenrod, a legendary angler of Livingston Manor, New York, developed the Hendrickson, naming the pattern after Al Hendrickson, a fishing companion. Bill Kelly, who also lived for a time in Livingston Manor, showed me a sample of the original Hendrickson fur blend which Steenrod had given him. The elusive pinkish case was present. Incidentally, Roy Steenrod was one of Theodore Gordon's few intimates.

Normally, we would expect to see subvarias start popping in early afternoon, but weather and water conditions affect this, sometimes drastically. Hot, bright weather will retard the hatch until late afternoon or evening, whereas a warm spring rain may get the bugs going early. Incidentally, there are few happenings in all of angling which compare to fishing a Hendrickson hatch in a drizzling rain.

Last spring I hit a dour day during the subvaria hatch, and therein lies a story worth telling. I arrived early at the river, wanting to get into position before the crowd arrived. It was about 11:30 in the morning. I waded across a thigh-deep run to an island, from whence I could gain access to the enormous pool below. There were several cars on the far shore, and I saw people climbing into waders and assembling tackle.

No sooner had I reached the island than thunder began to boom, and I could see a storm coming my way in a hurry. I do not care for electrical storms around water, especially when I'm carrying a graphite rod, so I hunched down on a rock and laid the rod on the bank. Soon the rain began pelting down in large heavy droplets. I marveled at how they splashed when they hit the stream—but wait! No raindrop ever made a splash like that—or that, or that. Good Lord, there are Hendricksons struggling all over the water and the trout have moved up into the riffle to get them!

That's when I pulled a real sneaky. A glance over my shoulder confirmed that the gang on the far shore was sitting it out in their cars, intimidated by the thunder and lightning. I eased myself over to the rod, picked it up and began making little side-arm casts, as surreptitiously as possible. Fifteen or twenty feet was far enough, and immediately I was into fish, which I snuck into the shallows and released. The rain lasted about three-quarters of an hour, during which time I landed eight trout and lost that many more. It was wild! I'm sure I was observed, but no one made a move.

The rain abated, and instantly car doors began to slam. I could see fish working in the main pool, so I moved down. Soon I was joined by five other guys, a couple of whom sort of glared at me. I proceeded to catch two big rainbows in quick succession, which served to darken their countenances several shades. Sated, I decided to leave the pool to them, especially as I could see the hatch beginning to dwindle. By the time I got my waders off, there was hardly a ring on the water.

Back to the bugs. Subvaria subadults measure 10 to 12 millimeters, which translates to size 12 and 14 dry flies. Invaria and rotunda duns run slightly smaller, so 14s and 16s are needed. Traditional patterns are still productive—the Hendrickson and Red Quill for subvaria, the Light Hendrickson for the other two. The hair-winged Comparadun-style dressing is also excellent, and very durable.

The invarias and rotundas are liable to come off later in the day as the emergence progresses throughout May and perhaps even into early June. This may run them into an overlap with other species to which they bear some resemblance. More on this in a bit.

Much as I crave the dry-fly action, I must mention that Hendrickson time holds great potential for nymph fishing. An hour or two before hatch time, the nymphs start to become restless, and their activity increases as the moment of emergence nears. Brownish nymph patterns in sizes 10 to 14 can be deadly at these times—in fact, I've seen the trout gorge themselves on nymphs to the point where they were very picky when the duns appeared. Sometimes an emerger pattern fished just under the surface solves that problem.

The Hendrickson holds yet another reward for the informed and persistent angler, that being the spinner fall, which begins a day or two after the hatch commences. The first subvaria spinner falls normally occur between 4:00 and 5:00 P.M., then come progressively later, into the evening and at dusk. Invaria and rotunda spinner falls are generally evening affairs.

Hendrickson spinner-fall fishing is one of the great delights in all of angling, and when conditions are right, I love it more than fishing to the dun. The pieces of the puzzle must be in place—there cannot be much wind or rain, or the delicate imagoes will not leave the trees.

Usually, the spinner fall is of short duration, lasting perhaps a half-hour. Therefore, it behooves you to be prepared. There is generally a period of inactivity between the end of the hatch and the beginning of the spinner fall, but should they be contiguous, it is easy to tell when the trout have switched to the spents—the rise form changes. The fish generally slash at the duns, whereas they gently sip the spent flies, apparently aware they aren't going to get away. Usually, it's easy fishing.

The spinners congregate over the riffles to oviposit, after which they fall to the surface and are carried downstream. The trout like to congregate near the heads of pools where the current slows and they can sip the helpless spents at their leisure. The sight of expanding rings on a quiet pool will quicken the pulse of the most blasé angler.

A spent fly pattern is required to properly match the silhouette of the naturals. It is very important to present the fly precisely to the trout's feeding position, because with so many naturals on the water, the fish have no reason to move left or right to take a fly. When a fish is hooked, try to lead it out of the prime feeding lanes, so the others aren't put down.

One more Hendrickson war story and we'll move on. In the spring of 1970, several of us drove out to Michigan to catch the opening-day Hendrickson fishing. We arrived to find near-summer conditions—the weather was so balmy we fished in short-sleeved shirts. That was nice for us, but the Hendricksons didn't care for it at all. Afternoon hatches were very spotty, and the fish skittish.

Several things saved the trip. The spinner falls started in mid-evening and went on well after dark. One moonlit night I fished until 1:00 A.M., and trout were still rising when I finally left. The question then became, where were all those spinners coming from?—we hadn't seen that many duns. Art Flick, who was there with another party, solved that one. A habitual early riser, Art got out on the stream at 8:00 A.M. to find a Hendrickson hatch going on. I've never seen that happen before or since.

So we fished early and late, and slept and tied flies during the day. By the end of the week we'd had our fill, and decided to leave a day early.

That was a mistake. The hot, dry spell broke, and a wet front moved in—Hendrickson weather! A couple of days later I called out there to see what was happening and was informed that the rain had brought on the greatest hatch in anyone's memory, with big fish slurping all over the place. Story of my life.

We always hate to see the Hendricksons go, but go they will, and we must look to other hatches. By now, we will have seen some caddis, notably the Brachycentrus, which anglers call the grannom, or in the western Catskills the shad fly, as its appearance generally coincides with the great Delaware River shad run. There are several types of Brachycentrus which hatch throughout the month of May. Emergences may be sporadic, or concentrated in early morning or afternoon. Pupa fishing is worthwhile, and so is dry-fly fishing with a hair-wing caddis tie or the improbable but murderous Dorato Hare's Ear, in sizes 14, 16 or 18. Several body colors are used to match the variations between species, including apple green and subdued ambers and olives.

Several species of Hydropsyche caddis may also be expected at this time. If there is an angling name for these caddis, I don't know what it is—I think they get lumped with the grannom. These insects are slightly smaller than the grannom and have grayish olive bodies. Hook sizes range from 16 to 20.

Incidentally, the hook sizes used for caddis imitations belie the overall size of the insect. The bodies are much shorter than the wings, which lie tented over the body. The so-called down-wing or tent-wing patterns which are designed to imitate caddis are tied in just that manner—smaller body, longer wing. Hence the smaller hook.

Caddis fishing can't compare to Hendrickson fishing—but then, there is little that can. Still, it can be very rewarding, and I've done well over the years. I love the dry fly, but would probably score more consistently if I fished more subsurface pupa imitations, such as the common soft-hackle wet fly. I'm working on that. And don't forget the Grannom wet fly with the green egg sac. Massive flights of caddis all headed upriver indicate that mating is taking place. However, that does not mean good wet-fly fishing right then. These caddis do not oviposit immediately, sometimes delaying the act until after dark.

The next major Mayfly we look for is the March Brown, or Stenonema vicarium to you Latin scholars. It is quite large as Mayflies go, the adults measuring 14 to 16 millimeters. This is the first Mayfly of the season which has other than plain gray or slate wings. The wings are tannish and splotched with brown, and lie back at approximately a 45-degree angle, which is characteristic of the Stenonema family. The body is also tan with dark brown markings along the top.

The emergence style of the March Brown is quite unlike the orderly regatta of the Hendrickson. They begin to hatch sporadically in mid to late morning and continue throughout the day and sometimes into the evening. Once having reached the surface, they have a terrible time becoming airborne. Their awkward fluttering on the surface creates disturbances which often bring savage rises from large trout, and between that and the toll taken by birds, I'm amazed that enough March Browns survive to procreate.

A good place to look for struggling duns is in side eddies and pockets, where they can attempt to get their act together in slower currents. One of my favorite March Brown spots is beneath an old railroad trestle. The huge concrete abutments create perfect backwaters for the duns to collect in. These happen to be deep, but don't ignore the shallows—often a sizable trout will come into calf-deep water to get in on the feast.

Preston Jenning's American March Brown is still an effective pattern during this emergence, as is the Caucci-Nastasi Hackled Comparadun. A variant-style dry fly works well in broken water. Emerger patterns are very good also, fished just beneath the surface to rises or in likely-looking spots. These are big flies, and a size 10 or even an 8 isn't too large.

The distinctive March Brown nymph is quite a tempting morsel for a hungry trout, and therefore of value to the angler. It is a clinging-type nymph, flattened, long-tailed and with strong legs, making it appear as though the insect pumps iron. Generally reddish-brown in color, these nymphs become somewhat orangey as hatch time approaches. They tend to crawl across the stream bottom a few days before emergence, positioning themselves as best they can. As those times, a nymph fished on the bottom will take trout.

The vicarium spinner fall is a great one which sometimes is obscured by coincident hatching activity of other species. It starts around dusk and goes on nearly until dark. The riffles are the place to be. You will see the big reddish males beginning to swarm, inviting the females to the party. When they oviposit and fall spent in any significant quantity, heavy trout will work up into the current to intercept them.

Close on the heels—or should I say tails—of the March Brown comes its lighter brother, the Gray Fox, or Stenonema fuscum. Generally, it follows by about a week, but it's quite common to see them overlap. Even for the fledgling stream entomologist, it's easy to tell the two apart. The Gray Fox is slightly smaller and considerably lighter in color in all three stages—nymph, dun and spinner. A ripe Gray Fox nymph is amberish, whereas the March brown is orangey. The dun's body has an amber cast, and the wings are sometimes flecked with amber. The spinner is rich ginger in color.

The three forms of the Gray Fox are fished in the same manner as those of the March Brown. The Gray Fox, Gray Fox Variant and Fuscum Comparadun are all effective imitations of the subadult. The spinner is matched by a ginger or amber-colored spent-style pattern. Figure one hook size smaller than the corresponding March Brown artificials.

Typically, the two big Stenonemas start in mid-May and carry into early June. In late May we can expect to see the beginnings of several other Mayfly hatches. Not all of these appear on the same streams at the same time, of course, but they are quite common throughout the region.

One of the loveliest Mayflies of all makes its appearance around Memorial Day, give or take a week, depending on weather and locality. This is Ephemerella dorothea, the Pale Evening Dun. It is also called the Sulphur Dun, but I reserve that name for another Mayfly.

E. dorothea is on the small side, the duns measuring 6½ to 7½ millimeters. The bodies are yellowish in color, the wings pale gray. Dry flies having that color scheme, sizes 16 and 18, will match the duns. But one should not overlook the potential of emerger patterns during this hatch, for the subimagoes often drift long distances in the surface film before popping loose from the nymphal shuck. With duns all over the surface and many visible rise forms, even the veteran can be duped into thinking dry fly when most of the feeding is actually subsurface.

Dorothea hatches occur in the evening, usually not before 7:00 P.M. What fooled anglers for decades, myself included, was the appearance of similar-looking flies in the afternoon or early evening. These are the smaller, lighter Ephemerellas generally associated with the Hendrickson hatch—invaria and rotunda. It is not uncommon for these insects to overlap with early Dorotheas. By that stage, their emergence is late enough in the day that they can easily be taken for the Pale Evening Dun, and while not as yellowish and a size larger, the resemblance is close enough to support the deception.

If you are onstream some time in late May and are suspicious about the true identity of the yellowish Mayflies you're seeing, here are a few guidelines. Invaria and rotunda generally hatch in faster water than Dorothea. They are larger, running from a full size 16 to a small 14. The wings are slightly darker as a rule, and the bodies not quite as yellow.

Dorothea spinners produce excellent fishing, often better than the duns. They come late—at dusk, and as the emergence progresses, after dark. Look for sipping rises in quiet pools below leisurely runs.

As we move into June, variety will truly spice your life. If it were up to the Americans instead of the British, the order Ephemeroptera might have been called June Bugs instead of Mayflies, such is the bounty. As we work through the month, a pattern which you have perhaps already perceived becomes increasingly evident—the major insect activity concentrates in morning and evening. Intuitively, these microbrained creatures are programmed to go for the nicest times of the day, avoiding midday heat. In the early season, when midday and early afternoon was the most pleasant, the hatches occurred then. Something to file away under "empirical knowledge."

Around the end of May or first of June a major caddis will make its appearance. This is Psilotreta. There are two species, but they are so similar we won't worry about individual Latin names. These are good-sized caddis, measuring 13 to 15 millimeters overall. The body coloration is dirty gray-green, the wings dark gray.

I call this one the Polaris caddis, because it seems to come shooting up out of the water, never staying on the surface. Emergence usually takes place in the evening, or on a dark day, in afternoon. Dry-fly fishing can be frustrating, because most of the splashy rises seen by the angler are follow-throughs, the trout having just made a pass at an escaping insect. I look for a caddis flying virtually out of a rise, and pop my artificial right on the fish's nose, the rationale being that the trout just missed that particular insect.

Pupa fishing before and during the hatch is, I believe, a more consistently-productive method. Soft-hackle wet flies and similar patterns can be fished dead-drift on the bottom with telling effect before the hatch actually starts. When the insects appear in the air and trout begin to leap with abandon, fish the pupal imitation to the rise form, using the rod tip to impart an escaping sort of movement as the fly swings down in front of the fish. This technique is killing for most species of caddis and for many Mayflies as well.

There are probably some stoneflies in our model river, and at least a couple of them should start hatching now. These are two closely related members of the Perlidae family, Paragnetina immarginata and Phasganophora capitata. Don't let the Latin throw you—we can lump these under Yellow Stonefly.

The nymphs are about as beautiful as anything you might encounter underwater, short of a mermaid. They are intricately marked in browns, yellows and ambers, looking like miniature mosaics. Shades will vary with the overall tones of the streambed, for protective coloration is very much in effect here.

I've yet to encounter dry-fly action to these flies, although I'm reliably informed that it can occur on certain rivers. However, I find the nymphs to be wonderfully effective. Artificials may be fished on the bottom, into pockets and to shoreline holding lies. A variety of sizes is recommended, as these flies are on a three-year life cycle, and the nymphs go through thirty-odd instars. Mature nymphs can reach 35 millimeters in length, but I generally like to fish my artificials a good deal smaller. That's an awesome mouthful for the average trout, and besides, the bigger a fly, the harder it is for the tyer to make it look realistic.

The two tipoffs that Yellow Stonefly time has arrived are (1) empty shucks on the rocks and (2) adults flying in the air. You can hardly miss seeing them—they are large and rather clumsy flyers. This is prime time for nymph fishing. However, don't be afraid to try a Yellow Stonefly nymph at other times, when there's nothing going on and the river seems dead. These nymphs are always down there, and the trout are waiting.

Several lesser-known but often valuable Mayflies may appear around this time and contribute to the fishing. One is Epeorus vitreous, which I call the Sulphur Dun. The male has a delicate olivish yellow body and pale gray wings. The female has a similar basic coloration, but also has a distinctive undershading of rosy-orangey-pink in the abdominal area, caused by the mass of eggs inside. These little ladies are absolutely gorgeous!

These flies are about the same size as a Quill Gordon, to which they are related. I like to fish a dry-fly imitation of the female, because of its unusual coloration. There is an obscure Catskill pattern named the Catterman which calls for a pink fur body. It is fished around the Beaverkill-Willowemoc area of the western Catskills, and it works. I'm convinced it was originated to imitate the vitreous female.

We can expect to see Ephemerella cornuta any time now—in fact, it often starts hatching in mid-May in the more southerly part of its range. This Mayfly is a real sleeper, for some reason not having been accorded the recognition it deserves. It can be a major hatch, almost a super-hatch on many rivers.

The nymph is of the clambering type and resembles the Hendrickson, in a lighter shade. It is found in various water types, from leisurely to fast. Average length is about 10 millimeters. Behavior is similar to Hendrickson—a lot of prehatch activity and trial swims. This activity starts rather early in the morning, for cornuta is essentially a morning hatch.

The duns come off some time between 8:00 A.M. and noon, whenever the insects feel the water temperature is optimal. They seem to like it cool, between 50 and 60 degrees Fahrenheit. The subadult is a size 14, and it is a blue-winged olive—that is, olive body and medium-gray wings. There are many blue-winged olives in the order Ephemeroptera, with a wide range of sizes and shades. Many are of tremendous significance to the fly-fisher.

It's time now for a large Mayfly to pay its annual visit—one of the real biggies, in fact. This is the eastern Green Drake, Ephemera guttulata, arguably the most famous Mayfly in the world. Many anglers consider this hatch the high point of the season. In the Maryland-Pennsylvania region, the Green Drake usually gets going in mid to late May. In the Catskills, it's late May into early June, and in the Adirondacks and northern New England mid to late June.

Green Drake hatch fishing is a lot like lovemaking; when it's hot it's hot, and when it's not it's not. Many times I have stood in a stream on a pleasant June evening with succulent Green Drake duns struggling all around me, and nary a rise. Other times I've encountered a moderate hatch and the trout went at them with a "take no prisoners" attitude—none shall escape! I've noticed this behavior typifies the trout's response to a blanket hatch of other extremely large insects, particularly after the hatch has been on for a few days. As a rule, all hatches fish better when they first appear.

The casual angler might have a little problem identifying E. guttulata, there being some similar insects which may overlap the emergence. One confusing characteristic is the unusual range of size—Green Drake duns run from around 18 to 30 millimeters, the males being much smaller. Coloration also varies—in fact, some Green Drakes aren't very green at all. Water characteristics and food supply have much to do with this. The bodies run cream to yellow or greenish-yellow, with brown markings along the top. The wings are heavily veined and blotched with brown. Basic wing coloration is similar to the abdomen. Often, the leading edges have a bright greenish cast.

One of the toughest things about fishing the Green Drake, or, for that matter, any really large insect, is coming up with a credible imitation. The larger the bug, the harder it is to replicate, a problem which is greatly exacerbated by slow currents, where the trout get a chance to inspect potential meals closely. The Gray Fox Variant works reasonably well, especially in faster water. If the drakes really are green in your locality, it helps to have a few turns of yellowish-green hackle wrapped in. The winged Gray Fox pattern is even better. I suggest the wings be tied out of teal or mallard flank feathers dyed greenish-yellow, rather than plain, or tinted to that shade with a felt marker. The Caucci-Nastasi Green Drake Comparadun is a great fly also. I favor sizes 6, 8 and 10.

Trout are excited by any struggling movement of these majestic duns, so if you aren't getting the strikes you think you should, try twitching the fly a bit—that's *twitching*, not *dragging*. Popularized by several contemporary authors, this is actually an old technique. I first picked it up from Bill Dorato around 1965, and he had been using it for decades.

The spinner flight of the Green Drake is a truly awesome spectacle, and productive of incredible dry-fly action if everything goes right. The imago is known as the coffin fly, because of its funereal waxy-white, somber-gray coloration. Except for size, it bears little resemblance to the dun, and was at one time generally thought to be a different insect. Many otherwise astute anglers of past generations went to their graves carrying this conviction.

Here again, we are concerned with obtaining a counterfeit which will pass inspection. I've been doing some experimenting, and so have a lot of other fly tyers. The best pattern I've yet found is quite simple: a single-feather extended body of pale cream, and barred rock hackle, tied spent. Another effective tie employs a white polypropylene yarn extended body and the barred rock hackle. These flies are very light, and I think the manner in which they land and float on the water has a lot to do with their effectiveness. The trout are quite critical of the behavior of these insects, as well as their appearance. They seem to show a heavy preference for the large females, which are almost twice the size of the males, so I use really big artificials.

My approach to Green Drake fishing—and this is true of most "enormous fly" fishing—is to concentrate on catching one or two really large trout. This is in contrast to, let's say, a dorothea hatch, where I'm looking for action and numbers. Even the largest trout find the energy exchange favorable for surface-feeding on these flies, but it doesn't take long for them to get filled up. After all, it's evening, and they've been chowing down on various things all day, including perhaps some guttulata emergers in the early stages of the emergence. And after a few days of experiencing the hatch and subsequent spinner falls, they seem to realize that there is lots of food, plenty of time and no need to take chances. Thus, larger fish are apt to lie back, waiting for failing light, when they feel less vulnerable—and, incidentally, when water temperatures are most comfortable. Very often, the last fifteen minutes of the spinner fall, as darkness descends, is when the lunker makes his move. It is a time to emulate the trophy hunter and look for a prime head.

Around Green Drake time, or shortly thereafter, we begin to see another big Mayfly which is a particular favorite of mine. There are a number of colloquial names for it—the Mahogany Dun, the Slate Drake, the Leadwing Coachman, the Dun Variant. Entomologically speaking, we are talking about Genus Isonychia. Two species comprise the late-spring, early-summer hatches, I. bicolor and I. sadleri. In late summer, Isonychia harperi appears. While neither as prolific nor ubiquitous as the two earlier Isonychias, harperi can be very significant on certain eastern and mid-western streams at a time when little else is happening.

The Isonychia naiads epitomize the swimming nymphal type. They are quite large, ranging in length from 13 to 16 millimeters. The shape is distinctive—they are sleek and streamlined, with short, webby tails, an ideal physique for such talented athletes. Coloration is mahogany brown with a slight purplish tinge. The nymphs of Isonychia bicolor feature a distinct dorsal stripe which runs their entire length. Sadleri has a similar marking, but it is much less pronounced.

As hatch time nears, the nymphs gather in the pockets and side eddies around rocks, boulders and deadfalls. At first glance, you might mistake them for tiny minnows, because of their quick, darting, swimming movements. They are very skittish and will streak for cover if threatened. As you might expect, trout find these active creatures irresistible, and follow them into the hatching areas. The angler must proceed carefully, lest he spook sizable trout which are feeding in the shallows. If the contour of the stream allows, I prefer to wade the center and fish to the banks.

The Isonychia nymphs crawl out onto rocks and dead limbs to hatch, just like stoneflies. Once committed to emergence, they are tenacious. I recall a day when I was sitting on a rock taking a rest, and an Isonychia nymph crawled up beside my leg. I seized it and threw it back into the stream. It no sooner hit the water than it did a U-turn and sped back to the rock. It is unbelievable how fast these nymphs move in the water. Thus, we generally fish the artificials with short, rapid twitches.

The Isonychia nymph is well imitated by two patterns which feature bodies made of peacock herl—the Leadwing Coachman nymph and the Zug Bug. I prefer those with a purplish, rather than greenish, coloration—some herl has that shading. Fur-bodied nymphs work well also.

Emergence usually takes place in late afternoon or evening, but on dark days you are liable to see these flies at any time. Despite the stonefly-like hatching method, enough of the large slate-winged duns may fall or get blown into the water to get the trout excited. On stormy days, particularly during periods of high water, the nymphs may be forced to hatch out in the stream proper, which they can do if they have to. Sadleri is much more apt to hatch in this manner than bicolor. This produces some great dry-fly action for the angler lucky enough to hit it right. Art Flick's Dun Variant or the Comparadun are first-class imitations.

Spinner flights take place in the evening and are quite spectacular. I recall that during my early years astream the old-timers used to refer to the Isonychia bicolor spinner as the White-Gloved Howdy, because of the handshake attitude of the forelegs and the little white feet. The body color of the imago is reddish-brown, the wings clear or hyaline. Sadleri is very similar, except for the feet. I mention that because it is intriguing and also because it is helpful in distinguishing bicolor from sadleri. You don't have to worry about imitating the feet.

The spinner flights often take place concurrently with the hatching activity, and if there are duns on the water, you must determine which form the trout are taking. The rise form is not a sure tipoff, as it is with some other hatches, for the trout will move into the riffles and slash at the falling imagoes. A compromise pattern is often a good choice. You must be ready, for these mating flights are rather brief.

Mid-June brings us an important morning hatch, one worth getting out of bed for. This is Ephemerella attenuata, another cousin of the Hendrickson. It is a blue-winged olive and is often confused with cornuta, which it closely resembles, except that attenuata is a size 16, while cornuta is a 14.

Emergence generally begins around 9:00 A.M., but I have seen it come much earlier. I vividly recall my introduction to this species, back in the mid-1960s. Dudley Soper and I were sharing a cabin on the Vermont Battenkill. It was early July, but the river was in very fishable shape, as compared to the streams of the Catskills and Adirondacks, which were suffering from a prolonged drought. Dud was never one to beat the sun in the morning, particularly when the fishing talk and liquid refreshment had lasted well into the night, so I was surprised to find him gone when I was stumbling around with toothbrush in hand. After keeping me in suspense for a couple of days, Dud got me out onto the stream and introduced me to the Blue-winged Olive. I'm reasonably sure it was attenuata, because a number 16 matched it perfectly.

Because of its unique style of emergence, attenuata fishes best wet. The nymphal shell is split on the streambed, and the subadult drifts to the surface, wings swept back, looking somewhat like a caddis pupa with shorter legs. This period of extreme vulnerability attracts the trout, which often take them on the rise, creating a visible rise form. But don't despair, purists—they will usually take the floating duns with fair regularity also. For best results, carry an emerger pattern in size 14 and a bright-bodied Blue-Winged Olive dun in size 16. I like to go a bit larger with my wet flies.

Throughout June and into July, several other Mayflies make their appearance in varying numbers. Two Stenonemas, ithaca and canadense, usually produce some good, if sporadic, fishing. They look very much like the Gray Fox, but are paler and smaller. Generally, they are evening hatchers, but on cooler, darker days they may come off in two's and three's all day. The famous Light Cahill in sizes 12 and 14 serves as a credible imitation of the duns. Should a concentrated spinner fall be encountered, a pale spent pattern is required.

A very pretty Mayfly that is of local importance on many rivers is Potomanthus distinctus, the Yellow or Golden Drake. Some colder streams also have Potomanthus rufous, but the two are so much alike that one imitation covers all. The nymphs are of the crawling type, although their generous gill structure, which enables them to live in quieter water, is reminiscent of the burrowers. A tannish nymph or wet fly in a large size works well, fished deep and twitched a little. Use sizes 8 and 10 2X-long hooks.

Look for the Potomanthus duns in slower pools at dusk, or on hot evenings right around dark. This can be tough fishing. A large artificial is required because of the size of the natural—these bugs are the size of a March Brown—so the trout get a very good look at them. Water is low and clear by this time of year, and the trout have been fished hard for several months. Presentation is critical. I usually have to use a longer, lighter leader than I would normally choose for a large fly, and casting becomes more difficult. A large, yellowish dry fly is a good match. Carry a few pale spents also, should a spinner fall be encountered over the riffles as darkness falls.

Incidentally, there is another large, light-colored Mayfly prevalent at this time that often gets mistaken for Potomanthus. It is Ephemera varia, and it looks like a pale Green Drake. Anglers call it the Cream Variant. It is less yellowish than Potomanthus, and has Green Drake-like markings on the back, wings and forelegs.

All of this time, there have been other things going on. Various caddis come and go, some of which are quite productive. Less significant Mayfly species create opportunities now and then, as do certain stoneflies. And we shall have seen some terrestrials—ants, beetles, perhaps some green leaf-rollers, with grasshoppers yet to come. Be aware, and be prepared. These less publicized insects can save the day—or the evening.

With summer, many anglers hang up their waders and head for the beach, golf course or tennis court. The hard core hangs in, however, and with good reason—there is more going on than you might think. The most significant happening on most streams is the annual appearance of a tiny but extremely important Mayfly. I debated whether or not I should go into detail on this somewhat demanding and esoteric type of fishing in a book intended essentially for the orientation of beginners. I decided that I most definitely should do so, the hatch is that important. Besides, once you learn to work with fine leaders and tiny flies, this is easy fishing—or a least easier than trying to convince a skeptical trout that a size 8 Light Cahill is a Potomanthus dun.

The Mayfly in question is Tricorythodes. While there are a number of species throughout North America, the two which concern the eastern/midwestern angler are Tricorythodes stygiatus and T. attratus. Again, we shall lump them together. In angling circles, they are commonly referred to as "trikes." Some people call them Caenis, which is not really accurate, even though they are part of a larger family named Caenidae. The main difference is that true Caenis are evening hatchers, while the trike emerges in the morning.

Trike is prolific, occurring in both limestone and freestone types of streams. The little brown nymphs run 3 to 4 millimeters in length and have an oversized wing case which almost resembles a carapace. Small though they are, these nymphs can be devastating just before or during the beginning of a hatch, before the trout have switched to the duns. It's tricky fishing, though, even for the experienced hand.

The trike hatch covers a long time period. It begins in late June and carries on into early autumn, barring a heavy frost. This varies from stream to stream, of course. The emergence is rather temperature-controlled, which accounts for the early-morning activity—these bugs like it cool. In more stable environments—limestone and spring creeks, for example—you usually encounter trikes around 8:00 A.M., give or take a half-hour. On freestone rivers, especially warmer ones, the hatch may come earlier, sometimes not long after daylight. Streams that get really warm in the summer may not have any trikes. As far as I know, there are none on the Schoharie, although there may be a few in the headwaters.

I have noticed that on freestone streams the trike hatch tends to come off later in the day as the season progresses into late August and early September. This, I believe, is because of the chillier night air and later sunrise, which affects water temperatures. In the Adirondacks and northern New England, I've seen late-morning trike hatches and early-afternoon spinner falls, a convenience for the socially inclined angler.

The trike duns also run 3 to 4 millimeters, and are tied on hook sizes 22, 24 and 26. Size 24 is a good compromise, but I've seen the trout get a bit size-concious during this emergence. The duns have very dark, prominent thoraxes, slightly lighter abdomens and pale watery wings which are somewhat oversized, compared to the legs and bodies.

Tricorythodes populations occur in a surprising variety of water types. My first encounter with the species, back in the early 1960s, was in the slow-moving upper sections of the New York Ausable. In time, I was to find them all over the river, even in faster runs. Optimal conditions are moderate currents and silty or sandy bottoms. The upper reaches usually hold the heaviest populations, undoubtedly because of cooler mean temperatures.

The trike dun changes into the spinner very quickly. Metamorphosis can occur within minutes, and usually takes place within the hour, so that often the insects that came off at the beginning of an emergence are returning as spinners while the hatch is still in full swing. This may bring on a measure of selectivity, although I find the trout will usually take either dun or spent if both are plentiful. I use a compromise fly quite frequently which was conceived by my friend Del Bedinotti, a premier trike-o-phile. Its distinguishing characteristic is the combination wing/ hackle, which consists of regular dry-fly-style hackle with the bottom half trimmed off. Thus, Del has obtained a spent and upright wing silhouette simultaneously. Incidentally, trikes cast their shucks over the water, although they will take refuge in streamside bushes to escape the wind.

Male Tricorythodes spinners are dark gray, almost black. The females, after having extruded the egg mass, have transluscent abdomens, but the prominent thorax is still very dark. I don't see that two distinct dressings are required, because these flies are so small the fish do not get that kind of a look at them. Size is the main criterion, along with pale, hyaline wings.

Positioning and presentation are all-important. Station yourself in a pool below a riffle, where the trout will be waiting. These are minute insects, and the fish aren't inclined to fight the faster water to get at them, as they would with March Brown or Green Drake. Try to fish as short a line as you can get away with, because even a minimal amount of drag will defeat your efforts. The water will be covered with tiny spinners; consequently, the trout have a tendency to gulp them in bunches. In the presence of steadily rising fish, try to estimate the timing of a particular trout's feeding rhythm, and attempt to synchronize your presentations with it.

Besides offering great sport, the Tricorythodes hatch emphatically underscores a most important point; it is much easier to fool a trout with a small fly than with a large one. I don't say that fishing is necessarily better—I'm talking about deception. But I will say this—trout are liable to feed more consistently on small flies than on large ones, given conditions which are conducive, especially when they are more or less stuffed. It's like those after-dinner mints we can't leave alone.

While trike provides us with summer fishing at one end of the day, a strange, little-known white Mayfly offers us an opportunity at the other. Genus Ephoron encompasses two species—leukon and the slightly smaller album. Again, we can lump them together for fishing purposes, even though E. album is slightly smaller than E. leukon and has a bit more of a yellowish tinge to the body.

Ephoron is not known to many anglers, even though the hatches are often prolific. I believe there are several reasons for this. The hatch doesn't start until mid or late August, a time when few fly rodders are about, and it comes off so late in the evening, often in pitch dark, that those anglers who aren't specifically waiting for the hatch have probably left.

If you are of a mind to extend your angling day and season, look for

Ephoron in the large, slow, silty pools as dusk falls. The fly is white, for practical purposes. The hatch may not start until it is getting pretty dark, so you will need a light. Use a heavier-than-normal leader tippet, something like 4X or even 3X. A number 12 usually matches size quite well. Something like a White Wulff or white Comparadun would be an appropriate pattern.

One of the chief complaints about the Ephoron hatch is that often there are too many flies on the water. This is because the emergence and spinner fall are compressed into a short time frame. Like Tricorythodes, the subadults go through the final molt very quickly after hatching, and massive spinner falls soon blanket the water. This can be too much of a good thing. In such a situation, it sometimes helps to use a fly one size larger than the natural, just to provide a point of focus for the trout, and for yourself.

The dedicated angler who wants late-season daytime action may connect with some grasshopper fishing, if conditions are favorable. Two ingredients are required: the hoppers, of course, and a stream that has reasonably abundant and cool flows in August and September. Meadow streams with deep-cut banks are ideal, there being good holding lies near shore, where hoppers are most likely to come in contact with the water.

Grasshoppers don't go swimming by choice, and their presence in the water is strictly by mishap. The wind blows them off-course, or something scares them, and they jump the wrong way. Hoppers can't fly very far, so if they happen to get out over a stream, they may run out of gas before they can make dry land. If you wish to observe a hopper's reaction to water, catch one and, being careful not to damage the wings, toss it out over the water. It will either streak for the far bank or boomerang toward the shore from which it was launched.

This brings to mind a ploy which can be tremendously effective at hopper time—a bit of a dirty trick, perhaps, but legitimate. I refer to chumming with real grasshoppers. They are easy to catch in the morning, when the dew is on the grass. The idea is to collect a batch and keep them in a well-ventilated container of some sort. Position yourself above a likely run or pool and start pitching the hoppers onto the water, one at a time. If the wings have dried, you will want to wet them a bit, or many will fly off without landing on the water. If a trout is present, it shouldn't be long before it begins to take the hoppers. When the trout is feeding confidently, cast your artificial into the drift line and prepare for action.

It helps to match the natural hoppers found around the stream in both size and color. This can be confusing, as several different species may be present at one time. I would opt for the smaller sizes in such a situation, following the principles mentioned earlier.

As the season winds down, insect activity becomes less and less dependable. In some rivers, Isonychia harperi, the late-summer Leadwing, may provide some excitement. Minor hatches of other species can generate a little fishing here and there. Autumn is such a beautiful time to be on a river that it's worth the trip, even though prospects are slim. Remember that nymphs are always present. Often, patient bottom-fishing with a nymph pattern is very productive in late season.

While we have enjoyed the rich bounty of our model eastern river, much has been happening elsewhere. In the midwest, many of the same species have appeared, and also some others not generally found in the northeast, in significant quantities. Two huge Mayflies, the Brown Drake (Ephemera simulans) and the infamous Michigan Night Caddis (Hexagenia limbata) create a lot of excitement. Simulans generally appears around the end of May and continues for several weeks. Limbata, which is not a caddis at all but a giant nocturnal Mayfly, begins emerging in early June and continues into early July on some streams.

Other hatches also contribute. Michigan and Wisconsin have some little Blue-Winged Olives we don't see in the east, and they are of considerable importance in that region. These insects and many others are well documented in angling literature.

In the Rockies, the bugs may, for the most part, be different, but the phenomenon is the same—the appearance of Mayflies, caddis flies, stoneflies, other aquatics and terrestrials follows an annual cycle. There is much more diversity in this region. Wild, tumbling freestone rivers, majestic streams of the high plains, spring creeks large and small, tail-race fisheries below dams, cold-water lakes—all have their own unique ecosystems. I think of the Madison and the Henry's Fork of the Snake. Less than an hour's drive apart, they share some insect species, and also have some profound differences. The Henry's Fork has major hatches never seen on the Madison, which likewise has hatches unique unto itself. One need only look at these two rivers to understand, they are that diverse.

Eastern anglers often harbor serious misconceptions about fishing in the Rockies, the most common being that it's all big-river, big-fly fishing. The Madison and the Yellowstone get a great deal of publicity, what with their Salmon fly hatches and guided float-boat tours. But there is so much more to the Rockies—more than any one volume could describe. We think of the region as being a frigid subarctic wasteland seven or eight months of the year, yet there is winter fishing out there that defies belief, and it is enjoyed almost exclusively by the locals. While snow runoff may render the Yellowstone, Gallatin and Big Hole unfishable, the spring creeks and high-plains rivers are at their best, virtually unaffected by the melt.

When I first ventured west in the mid-1960s, there was not a great deal of specific reference material about the region in the angling library. With certain exceptions, the local tackle stores weren't exactly fountains of information either. Mostly, one was told to "fish these-here Girdle Bugs and Muddlers with a lotta sinkers." Now we have a wealth of documentation on insect activity throughout the area, and more on the way, I'm sure. Also, many of the fly-fishing shops in places like West Yellowstone, Livingston and Bozeman, Montana, and Jackson Hole, Wyoming, are manned by people with a great deal of expertise. Tremendous strides have been made in fly tying and fly design—in fact, the western tyers have stolen a march on the more traditionally oriented easterners. The guides are much more knowledgeable—some are even scholarly. Therefore, it's no longer difficult to prepare for a Rockies excursion in terms of knowing about insect phenomena, fly patterns and such.

There. I've had the audacity to compress into one chapter an orientation on one of the most prolific fields of study in all of natural science. The rest is up to the individual. One can pursue the subject of angling-related entomology to whatever extent he or she finds worthwhile—the literature is available today. Meanwhile, the newcomer can head streamward with an appreciation of what's happening there.

# CHAPTER VIII _____

# *Artificials*

The objective of this chapter is primarily to acquaint the reader with the principles of fly design and, secondarily, to familiarize him or her with a few proven fly patterns which typify various designs. Over the years, I've become a believer in the importance of having the right fly for a specific situation, and I've come to believe this is more a function of design than of pattern.

When I speak of fly design, I am essentially referring to two characteristics: shape or silhouette and amount and type of materials. When I speak of pattern, I'm talking mainly about color and texture. There is definitely an interrelationship between design and pattern, but also a degree of separation. Pattern has more to do with visual imitation of the natural foods which make up the trout's diet, and with making the fly visually attractive to the fish. Design has to do with the fly's behavior and attitude on or in the water. It is very much a function of the type of water in which the fly will be fished.

I want to emphasize that last point, because it is an extremely important one—the matter of matching one's fly to the characteristics of the stream, lake or whatever. For example, it wouldn't make sense to fish a no-hackle dry fly on a frothing, boulder-strewn river, because (1) it wouldn't float, and (2) the visual characteristics would be negative. Neither would it be good practice to use a fluffy, overdressed variant-style dry fly on a placid spring creek, because the image seen by the trout would be so unlike that of the natural insect on the water that the fish might actually streak for cover in alarm.

During my angling career I've met a number of one-fly fishermen. Many of them were also one-river fishermen. I think of an old fellow who used to haunt the Esopus—I can't recall his name—and fished one odd-looking pattern he had designed himself. It was a dry fly—he said that was the only way he enjoyed fishing. I remember the fly as being heavily dressed and having a lot of red in it. I'm sure he did fairly well—the Esopus is a fast, rough river, so the heavy dressing was appropriate, and for some reason the Esopus rainbows have always liked flies with a reddish cast.

Some one-fly fishermen are much more scientific than that. I know several people who fish an Adams constantly, but they use a full range of sizes to match the naturals. One could do worse. The Adams is perhaps the finest compromise dry fly ever—it is suggestive of quite a number of insects.

I have no problem with this approach, provided the angler realizes its limitations. To me, one of the great fascinations of fly-fishing is figuring out what will work. Thus, I carry a wide variety of flies of various types, for while I have preferences, I have no prejudices. If a nymph or wet fly or attractor-type streamer is what's required, that's what I'll fish—I simply can't see the point in floating dry flies over trout that couldn't care less when I can catch them on something else.

Incidentally, you may encounter people who are critical of the methods used by other anglers. Don't be intimidated by them. There is no moral or aesthetic superiority associated with, for example, dry-fly fishing as opposed to wet-fly fishing. Purism is a matter of attitude, not method. If a person treats the fish and other fisherpersons respectfully, I don't care what kind of fly he or she uses—in fact, I don't even care if they fish with worms.

Now let's discuss how flies are classified and become familiar with some of the terminology used to describe them. There are two major dichotomies: surface/subsurface and imitator/attractor. Surface/subsurface equates, quite obviously, to dry fly or wet fly. Imitator/attractor has to do with whether or not the fly is designed to imitate a specific food.

These descriptive terms are used in combination. For example, a Royal Coachman dry fly, which bears little resemblance to any specific insect, would be classified as a surface attractor. A Yellow Stonefly nymph, dressed to look like the real thing, is a subsurface imitator. Of course, the fish make the ultimate choice. If a trout thinks a garish streamer looks like a minnow and gulps it, who are we to argue? The classification system facilitates meaningful communication among anglers. The fish only know what they like.

As mentioned, fly design is more a discipline of angling habitat than of food imitation. For example, I have a box of Hendrickson dry flies which vary widely in style. Some have lots of hackle and plenty of tail fibers; others are very sparsely hackled thorax-style dressings; still others are hair-wing parachute ties. The reason for this is that I fish the Hendrickson hatch in both faster and slower currents. I want heavier-dressed patterns which float well on rougher water and also sparse flies with a clean, uncluttered silhouette which will pass close inspection on the slow pools.

Let's take a little fishing trip together, and I believe all will become clear. We're going to fish a typical freestone river which has various types of currents, ranging from slow pools to rapids. We shall begin in a stretch of faster pocket water. Nothing's hatching. You decide to fish dry; I'm going subsurface. You will want a high-floating fly of sufficient size to be seen by trout that aren't necessarily focused on the surface. A Wulff pattern might work, or a Variant, or perhaps a Humpy. I'm going to try a good-sized stonefly nymph. If that doesn't produce, I'll switch to a Wooly Bugger or maybe a streamer of some sort.

Moving along, we come onto a section where the currents are considerably slower. There are long glides downstream of large boulders and leisurely side eddies near the bank. You might switch to something like an Adams—a 12 or 14, perhaps. I might consider the time of year and try to select a pattern that looks like whatever nymphs should be active right then. For instance, if it's late May, I'll try a March Brown nymph.

Further downstream we find ourselves faced with a large, quiet pool—very slow currents here, and no deflections. If there's still no visible sign of feeding activity, this might not be a good place to fish at that time. However, should we decide to do so, you will want a very lean-and-mean dry fly. A parachute pattern might work, or a thorax type. I'm going to try a sparsely dressed soft-hackle wet fly, one which will undulate enticingly with very little inducement.

What we just did was to match our flies to the changing environment through which we moved. We took into consideration such factors as turbulence and speed of current, which drastically affect trout's vision and decision-making time frame. As we moved into the slower currents, we traded off visibility for credibility. That's the way it works.

Now let's consider how and what the trout sees. Fortunately for us, the medium in which a trout lives interferes considerably with its ability to see objects as they truly are. Were it not for that, I'm sure we would rarely fool one. Objects on the surface are seen as distorted images, with little dimples or impressions in the surface film creating light patterns. Objects beneath the surface are seen more or less in their true form. However, tiny air or gas bubbles surrounding an object can cause distortion. This is often the case with emerging insects, where gases are emitted as the nymphal shuck is cast, and also with artificial flies, where air bubbles are trapped in the rough furs and feathers commonly used as body materials and hackle.

Another problem created by water is that of light or, specifically, lack of light. As we know, light does not pass through water as readily as it does through air. Therefore, a significant amount is lost—the deeper the water, the less the amount of light that reaches the streambed. In deeper pools, especially when light is fading, it becomes more difficult for trout to see small objects near the bottom. Protective coloration contributes to this. I believe this is one reason why weighted flies fished deep seldom produce well later in the evening.

As the angler must look into the water to see a fish, so must the fish look out to see objects in the outside world. This brings into play another source of visual distortion known as refraction. This phenomenon, coupled with another called reflection, greatly affects the visual perceptions of both fish and fisherman.

Those of you who grew up in a rural area, as I did, may recall spearing suckers in the early spring when they were plentiful and the meat was tasty. What happened when you poked the spear into the water preparatory to skewering a fish? The shaft appeared to be bent or broken at the water line. This was caused by refraction, or light rays bending as they entered the water. Therefore, the head of the spear was not really where it appeared to be—and neither was the sucker. This also works in reverse—a fish looking out into the air from underwater does not see objects as they actually are either.

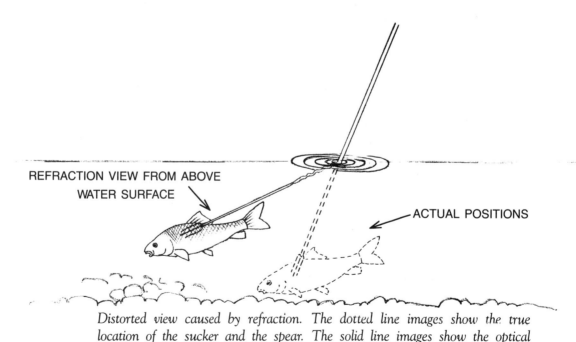

*Distorted view caused by refraction. The dotted line images show the true location of the sucker and the spear. The solid line images show the optical illusion.*

The light rays which enter the water come from all directions, but the ones which affect trout and angler are those along which their line of vision travels. The flatter the line of sight, the greater the amount of refraction, and also the lesser the amount of light which enters the water, because of deflection. Thus, the lower the vantage point, the harder it is to see a trout in the stream. The best view is from directly above. In other words, if you were to crawl out onto a tree limb and look directly down at a fish, you would see it in true perspective and at its actual location.

When we watch a trout from the bank of a stream, we are treated to a distorted view. The fish looks thinner than it actually is, because the light rays along which our line of vision travels are bent downward, so that we get more of a top view than a side view. For the same reason, the fish also appears to be farther away and shallower than it really is—after all, a bent line between two points is longer than a straight one. This should be kept in mind when you are presenting a fly to a nonrising fish which can be seen holding in a pool. The tendency is to cast beyond such a fish.

While the trout sees a distorted view of the outside world, it is nonetheless an acute one. Trout are very sensitive to any movement in the air, for this is where much of their trouble comes from, in the form of ospreys, kingfishers and such. They can see much farther than most anglers realize. In a calm pool under good lighting conditions, I've seen a trout spooked by a rod being raised 50 feet away. We shall revisit this topic in the chapter on tactics and streamology. For now, let's consider how a trout sees flies on the surface.

Another thing you may have noticed as a youngster is the strange view you get from underwater. I recall diving into a lake and peering upward. It seemed as though I was looking out at the world through a hole—and in essence I was. This is the window—the circle on the surface which comprises the open end of the cone of vision through which any submerged creature can see out into the air.

The window is surrounded by a mirror, which is the undersurface of the water. Objects in the air outside the window are not visible to the trout. Objects beneath the water may be seen in the mirror as reflections. Objects floating on the surface are seen in a somewhat distorted manner, as mentioned.

Let's consider a dry fly drifting along the surface of a pool. As long as the fly is outside the window, the trout sees it as dimples or indentations in the surface film. As the fly nears the window, the refracted light rays followed by the trout's line of vision intersect with the highest point of the fly—the wings usually. Because of refraction, the wings appear to be

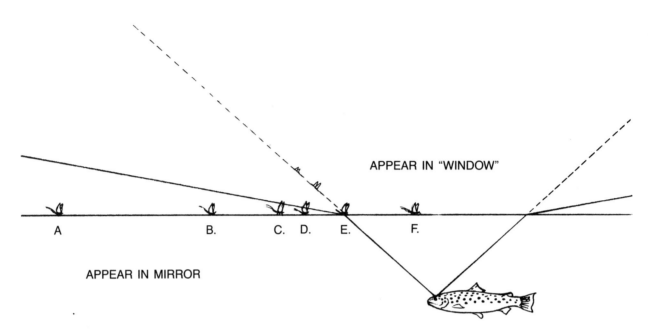

*Here we see the trout's "window" and "mirror". A fly drifting looks to the fish as though it is coming down an incline—another illusion caused by refraction. The upper parts of the wings become visible in the window first because of how the light rays involved in the trout's line of vision bend as they enter the water.*

suspended above the dimples where the fly touches the water—thus, the two appear to be dissociated.

As the fly moves into the window, more and more of its upper structure becomes visible, and the visual gap between it and the surface image becomes less and less. When the fly is in the window, the trout can see it in true perspective. However, other factors still create distortion and interfere with the trout's getting a perfect view, thank God.

During the drift, any portion of the fly which breaks the surface film can be seen by the trout, and it is seen double: the actual object and the reflection of it in the mirror. This must really appear bizarre to a trout. The most dramatically visible component is the hook. I once took some underwater photographs for a fly-tying book, and in all cases where the hook hung beneath the surface, it appeared as though the fly were tied on one of those double salmon hooks. Alarming, to say the least.

With this in mind, you might assume that one of the primary disciplines of fly design would be to eliminate, or at least minimize, the visibility of the hook. True, this is a consideration, one which I believe accounts for the success of certain fly designs. Yet we use other designs where the hook is blatantly exposed for all the underwater world to see,

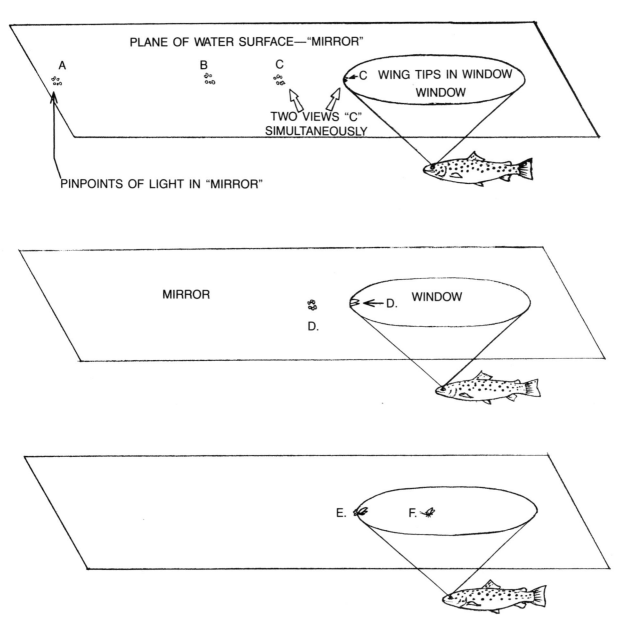

An underwater sequence of an insect drifting toward a trout. The parts of the fly which touch the water appear as small indentations or "points of light" in the surface film. As the fly comes into the window, the wing tips enter first, as stated previously. The distortion caused by refraction makes it appear to the trout as though the wings are disassociated with the indentations in the surface film. This illusion resolves as the fly drifts further into the window. When it is fully in, the trout sees it in proper perspective, still somewhat distorted by light from above.

and they work wonderfully well. I think particularly of the sparsely dressed parachute and no-hackle patterns which we employ on quiet pools, the most demanding arena of all.

How can this be? After all, real bugs don't have hooks sticking out of them. I can only conclude that if the trout likes the overall image it sees, it simply overlooks the hook, leader and whatever. This punctures another of trout fishing's sacred myths, that being how intelligent these creatures are. Actually, they are quite dumb—wonderful, resourceful, beautiful, but dumb. Praise God once again, for if they were at all smart, we couldn't fool them. There, I've said it.

Both of the images seen by the trout—the surface indentations and the wing silhouette—are important considerations in fly design. The key to an effective fly is how the components are structured to obtain the desired visual effect while satisfying functional requirements, such as floatability. As we shall see, there are a number of approaches.

Let's examine the anatomy of a fly—a classic, proven dry fly widely used throughout the east and midwest. This is the Red Quill, which represents the male dun of the true Hendrickson. We will look at this fly in partial stages of undress, so as to better appreciate the various components and see how they combine to make the finished product so effective.

We'll take the components in the order in which they are tied on. First, the wings. This pattern utilizes the popular wood duck flank feather wing type, which is also found on such other famous patterns as the Quill Gordon and Light Cahill. These feathers are dull gold barred with dark gray, not the exact color of the wing of the natural, but still suggestive of it. On a well-tied fly, the wings are substantial enough to provide a clearly visible silhouette, but not so heavy as to overbalance the fly. They should be separated into a distinct V, so as to abet the aerodynamics of the fly, helping it land upright in a nicely cocked position. The wood duck wing, if properly tied, is much more durable than it would seem, and retains its shape quite well over time.

Next, the tail. On many commercially tied flies, the tails are overdressed, which I consider a serious defect. The function of the tail is simply to provide balance and aid flotation, and it should be as unobtrusive as possible. In this case, we aren't much concerned with imitating the tails of the natural, because they seldom touch the water. A conservative wisp of very stiff hackle fibers is sufficient, about the length of the hook shank. They should be well spread, so they don't look like an extended body, and also to improve flotation. Tails with the fibers clumped in a bunch tend to soak up water like a blotter.

The body is made of quill, or stem, from a reddish-brown rooster

*The justly popular Wood Duck wing.*

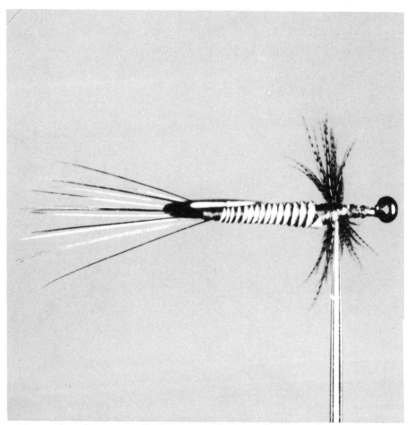

*An underside view with the wings, body and tail in place. Note the segmentation of the quill body and the spread of the tail fibers.*

neck or saddle feather, the barbs having been stripped off. This simulates the distinctive, rusty light-dark segmentation of the natural. A slight forward taper is desirable. The quill body should be well coated with cement or lacquer, as it tends to be somewhat brittle.

The final component is the hackle, which is formed by winding one or two stiff-fibered feathers from a rooster's neck or cape around the front portion of the fly. We take some turns in back of and in front of the wing, for proper balance and symmetry. On an average fly of this type, a moderate amount of hackle is appropriate—perhaps eight to ten turns. The pattern calls for medium gray hackle (dun, in fly-tying parlance), which blends with the wood duck wings to simulate the shade of the wings of the natural insect.

Curious, that last statement. Many anglers equate hackle with legs, so why be concerned about wing color? The answer is that while the hackle does contribute greatly to flotation, and while it does create indentations similar to the feet of the natural, it is also a major factor in wing impression.

Most anglers eventually become tyers, but until that time comes, you will want to be able to select good-quality flies wherever you purchase

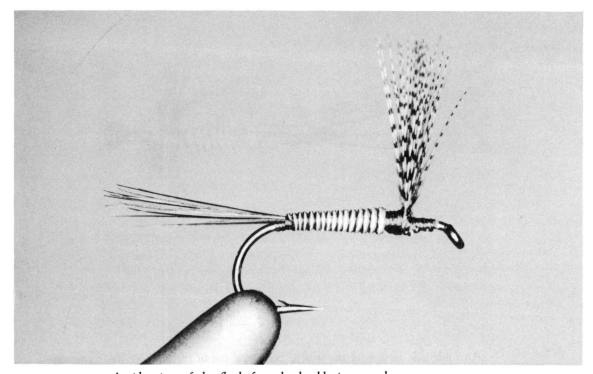

*A side view of the fly before the hackle is wound on.*

# Notes On The Color Plates

The flies depicted in the color pages are all great producers but that is not the primary reason I selected them for inclusion. The most important thing about them, in my opinion, is that they are representative—in fact, archetypical—of some of the most effective types of flies commonly used today.

The flies are dressed as I would normally fish them, except that I have taken a few liberties for photographic reasons. For example, the hackle on the Red Quill and Quill Gordon wouldn't be that dark and the hair wing on the Comparadun would probably be grey, although that can vary. I should also mention that the body color on the Grizzly Wulff was originally a bit more on the yellow side. A color-correction filter was used in taking these photographs to compensate for the tungsten lights and it didn't quite reconstitute that particular shade.

Some of these fly patterns are quite specific—the Light Cahill is a good example—and there is little variation from tyer to tyer. Others are more-or-less generic, and are dressed in a wide range of colors and shades—the Humpy and the Wulff series are prime examples of that. Also, flies are sometimes varied in style or construction, in order to adapt them to different situations. This involves such things as body thickness, body texture and amount of hackle. There really is no *absolutely* right way to tie a fly, It's very much a matter of the effect one is trying to obtain.

There are also many options. Notice that the two spinner patterns are dressed with wings of different materials, one synthetic yarn, the other hackle. Each has its advantages. Tinsel ribbing is also optional in some cases. I put it on the Hares' Ear Nymph and two of the Soft-Hackles, but often as not I fish these patterns plain. Again, it's a matter of what works best in a given situation. I wouldn't omit the tinsel rib on the Zug Bug—that's a specific pattern.

You will notice a unique eye-like feather on the Grey Ghost Streamer. That is a Jungle Cock feather. It is no longer legal to import Jungle Cock into the United States—hasn't been for some time, as a matter of fact. Substitutes are now being used which produce a comparable effect—notice the eye on the Edson Tiger. The optional painted eye on the Black-Nosed Dace is another alternative. That may well be the last Grey Ghost I will ever tie with real Jungle Cock, as my meagre stash is getting low and I want to save what's left for classic Atlantic Salmon patterns.

There's an incredible array of flies out there today and things can be awfully confusing. Just remember—presentation is more important than pattern, and silhouette is usually more important than color. As suggested in Chapter Eight, try to match your fly to the type of water you're fishing.

**Dry Flies:**

| | | |
|---|---|---|
| March Brown | Light Cahill | Blue-Winged Olive |
| Rusty Spinner | Dun Variant | Golden Spinner |

| | | |
|---|---|---|
| Sulphur Dun | Red Quill | Quill Gordon |
| Adams-Parachute | Adams-Standard | Dorato Hares' Ear-Dark |

**Dry Flies:**

Green Drake, Eastern-
Extended Body Style

Green Drake, Western-
Extended Body Style

Grizzly Wulff

Black Ant

Pheasant Hopper

White Wulff

Hair-Wing Caddis-Grey

Henryville Special

Comparadun-No-Hackle
Style

H & L Variant

Royal Trude

Humpy

**Wet Flies/Nymphs:**

| | | |
|---|---|---|
| Dark Cahill | Green Scud | Leadwing Coachman |
| March Brown-Emerger | Montana | Zug Bug |

| | | |
|---|---|---|
| Hares' Ear Nymph—Gold-Ribbed | March Brown Nymph | Pheasant Tail Nymph |
| Green Soft-Hackle | Dark Dun Soft-Hackle | Amber/Olive Soft-Hackle |

**Streamers:**

Wooly Bugger

Light Edson Tiger-Maribou

Hornberg

Black-Nosed Dace-Painted Eyes

Light Spruce Fly

Rabbit Matuka Sculpin

Grey Ghost

Muddler Minnow

*The completed Red Quill.*

them. The points touched upon in the anatomy of the Red Quill will
help you do just that. Also, look for feather quality in the hackle and tail
fibers. They should be resilient and lively. Touch the hackle to your
lips—it should feel stiff and bristly. Drop the fly on a countertop—it
should be quite bouncy. When the fly is resting on the tail and hackle,
the hook should clear the countertop.

Another "point," if I might be permitted a play on words—be sure
to inspect the hooks on any flies you purchase. Most commercial flies are
tied on mass-produced hooks, and we see a lot of blunted or broken
points, poorly formed barbs and the like. We also encounter malforma-
tions in the eyes of these hooks. If they aren't too serious, the tyer can
compensate when forming the head of the fly. However, eyes which are
not fully closed or which have rough edges of hook wire exposed are a
potential source of serious trouble. You will want to avoid flies which
manifest such problems.

I frequent several rivers where the Hendricksons drift into large,
quiet pools, where cynical trout of great size reside. While my standard
Red Quill or Hendrickson may work okay, I generally do better with a
leaner design. One I particularly like is the parachute style, with the

*Two views of the cut or shaped wing. Note clean silhouette.*

hackle deployed horizontally rather than vertically. An advantage of parachute hackle is that a little goes a long way. Having the fibers spread horizontally over the surface film provides adequate flotation and balance with a conservative amount of material. It works on the principle of the snowshoe, whereby a man's weight is spread over a large area, and he can walk on the surface of a snowfield which has virtually no compressive strength.

In the illustration, we see my so-called cut-wing parachute, in which I substitute shaped-feather wings for wood duck in order to obtain a very realistic, clear silhouette. I also alter the tail, using either a few widely spread barbules or three moose body hairs. Since the body of a parachute fly lies prone on the water, I want it to float well. Therefore, I use fur or synthetic dubbing, as it is called. The single hackle feather is wound flat around the base of the wings, thus completing the fly.

Deer hair, and that of other animals of the deer family, has become very popular as a material for making dry fly wings. It has several positive attributes—it is plentiful, durable and fairly easy to work with. It comes in a wide variety of interesting shades, and can easily be dyed any color. Its floatability factor is quite high, depending on what type of hair is used.

*The completed Cut-Wing Parachute. Note the dramatic difference in hackle deployment between this fly and the Red Quill.*

*An underside view of another Cut-Wing Parachute showing flat hackle and realistic tail. The tail is made of moose body hairs.*

Some hair-wing flies are tied in the no-hackle, or Comparadun style. Thus, they consist only of tail, body and wings. This economical dressing has merit, but proper technique is critical. The wings must be spread around the hook so that they form a wide wedge when viewed from the front, otherwise the fly will float on its side. A thorax made of the same material as the body should be added to enhance flotation, in the absence of hackle. Also, the wings should not contain too much material. Even the finest deer hair is bulky, and overdressing causes poor balance.

A version of this fly that has gained considerable notoriety recently is the Sparkle Dun. This style originated with Craig Matthews and his skilled staff at Blue Ribbon Flies in West Yellowstone, Montana. Instead of feather or hair fibers for the tail, Craig and company have substituted a small piece of polypropylene sparkle yarn. This creates the impression of an insect riding its nymphal shuck before taking flight, as many of them do. Great idea.

The Wulff series of hair-winged flies has been with us for some time, for which we owe a debt of thanks to Lee Wulff, the creative angling legend who developed the style. There are many pattern variations of the

*Two views of a No-Hackle Comparadun showing thorax and wing shape.*

*Wulff-type hair wings.*

basic Wulff. Typically, they feature hair wings and tails, fur or yarn bodies and lots of hackle. These flies were designed to float well in heavy currents, and they certainly do, if properly tied. They are durable and life-suggestive on the water. In the right situation—meaning faster, diffused currents—these flies are great producers.

The hair wing is also employed in constructing parachute-style flies. A single, upright clump of hair is used as a wing, with the hackle wound around the base. Here, we are again concerned that the wing not be overdressed, for reasons of balance and appearance.

One of the finest all-around patterns I've yet encountered is the Adams parachute. It features an upright wing of white calf hair, a tail of either barred rock hackle fibers or moose body hairs, a gray fur body and mixed barred rock and brown hackle. While not a specific imitation of any particular insect, it is suggestive of a great many of them. Thanks to the upright white wing, it is also a highly visible fly, a real blessing when light is failing.

I've alluded to barred rock several times, and would like to state my case for this particular material. Barred rock, commonly called grizzly, comes from the Plymouth Rock type of chicken. The feathers have alternate barring of white and dark gray or black. They are used for wings, tails and most notably for hackles, where a grizzly feather is often wound in with a hackle of some other color. The result is a mottled or variegated effect.

I am addicted to flies which contain a grizzly mix. I feel the mottled effect is more life-suggestive than a flat color, and trout eat living things, as Lee Wulff tells us. The traditional Adams, perhaps the most versatile dry fly ever conceived, features grizzly wings and tail and a brown-and-grizzly hackle mix. The enormous popularity of this pattern over many decades stands as a tribute to grizzly, and to the fly's originator, Len Halladay.

Several other grizzly-mix patterns are worthy of mention here, as they typify fly designs which are extremely valuable in certain situations. A favorite large dry fly is the Gray Fox Variant. The variant style of dressing features oversized hackle, a longer tail and a conservative-sized body. Wings are omitted, as the hackle serves to effect a wing silhouette. These flies are designed to float well and ride high. They land gently on the surface, and give a marvelous impression of aliveness.

The variant style is highly impressionistic, and works best in rougher water. Art Flick mentioned three variant patterns in the *Streamside Guide*: Cream, Dun and Gray Fox, the latter being his favorite. It employs a mix of light ginger, dark ginger and grizzly for the hackle, which is about three hook sizes larger than normal. This is balanced out by a longer tail of mixed grizzly and ginger. One of the hardest things in fly tying is finding feathers with barbules long and stiff enough for variant tails. The body is a stripped ginger quill, à la the Red Quill pattern.

Another grizzly-mix super-fly is the Dorato Hare's Ear, which was designed by my great friend and fishing buddy, Bill Dorato. Bill developed the pattern in an effort to solve the Battenkill caddis problem. We were having a terrible time getting the Battenkill browns to take a fly when caddis were jumping all over the place. It worked well—and, as we have learned subsequently, it is amazingly effective at other times.

To the critical eye, a Dorato Hare's Ear may not look much like a caddis. It doesn't have the tent-style wings of the natural, and it features an abbreviated tail, whereas the natural has none at all. The keys to this pattern's effectiveness are the tweedy dubbing used for the body, the grizzly-ginger hackle mix and the unique shape. The tails are quite short, in order that some aid to flotation be provided while effecting an essentially tailless silhouette. The body is mottled, and more rough than that of a typical dry fly. The hackle is trimmed slightly on the bottom, so that the fly sits squarely on the water and can be twitched effectively when it is desirable to do so. The trimming is optional—Bill tells me he generally doesn't bother with it these days. Personally, I favor it, but I wouldn't argue with Willie. Following him on a stream is an exercise in humility.

I'm sorry to report that the Dorato is not widely available—I believe the commercial tyers are put off by the requirement for wood duck and grizzly, both of which are premium materials. It's an easy fly to tie, so you shouldn't have a problem getting some made to order. The basic dressing is as follows: wood duck wings, short grizzly tail, rough hare's ear body, and mixed grizzly and ginger hackle. A paler version also works marvelously. We simply use a lighter dubbing mix for the body and a pale ginger or straw-cream hackle wound in with the grizzly.

Besides being effective as a caddis matcher, the DHE is a great probing fly, when nothing is hatching. For the latter application, larger sizes work best—12, 14, maybe 16 in clear and quiet water. When coping with leaping caddis, we simply match the size of the natural.

Speaking of caddis, there are other imitations which work well in various situations. The hair-wing styles are excellent, dressed in whatever size and shade are required to simulate the hatch. I particularly favor these patterns on western rivers, such as the Madison, the Gallatin and the Snake.

Currently, there is a style of interior decorating in vogue called minimalism, in which an absolute minimum of stark shapes is employed to create a sort of moonscape effect. Not to be outdone, the fly-fishing community has the no-hackle dry fly. We touched briefly on hackle-less flies in our discussion of the Comparadun, but the deer hair used on that style is very much a different ball game from the spare slips of feather used for the wings of a true no-hackle.

Typically, the dressing goes like this: fur body with pronounced thorax, two hackle-fiber tails spread wide, wings made from duck or goose wing quill sections. It takes some circumspect fly tying to produce a no-hackle fly that will set up properly on the surface and float reasonably well. Bonnie and Rene Harrop, the wife-and-husband fly-tying duo from St. Anthony's, Idaho, dress the most perfect no-hackles I've yet seen—and lots of other lovely flies, for that matter. Credit for the origination of the no-hackle style goes to Doug Swisher and Carl Richards, these flies having first appeared in Doug and Carl's landmark book, *Selective Trout*, around 1971.

While I believe an awareness is of value, I hesitate to recommend no-hackle flies to beginners. It takes some rather sophisticated handling to effectively present them. They can make quite a difference when fishing to extremely selective trout in slow, quiet currents, and when a modicum of skill has been achieved, you might try them on the most exasperating trout in the pool.

In the entomology chapter we learned about spinner falls and the value of spent flies. Now let's look at the artificials. At first glance, what you see is a very simple dressing—wings, body and tail. But there's more to the proper dressing of a spent pattern than that, and some of the critical points are rather subtle.

Spent flies that fall to the water have gone through the metamorphosis, becoming shimmering imagoes. They have mated, and as their final act, the females are engaged in or have completed oviposit. What's left is essentially a hollow tube with hyaline wings and long tails. The trout, looking upward through the water, get an impressionistic view, as whatever light remains in the sky passes through the diaphanous insects. Translucency becomes the byword.

In order to effect translucency in the body, the fly tyer uses materials with high sheen or gloss, such as imitation seal fur or Antron. The master tyer will scarify the sides of the body with a scroll-saw blade or similar tool, so as to obtain a fuzzy effect. When held up to the light, an aura is seen around the body. Under actual fishing conditions, this simulates light from the sky passing through the bodies of the naturals.

Many materials and techniques have been utilized in fashioning spent-fly wings, which are even more translucent than the bodies. The two most popular at this writing are synthetic yarns and trimmed hackle. Both produce the desired light pattern. I personally favor hackle trimmed top and bottom, wrapped over a thorax. The feathers should be of premium quality, very stiff and shiny. After all, there isn't much material to abet flotation, so hackle quality becomes critical.

Polypropylene yarn, or some other highly translucent synthetic material, makes presentable spinner wings, provided it is used sparingly and is flared as much as possible. I've looked at these wings from underwater, and the light pattern is brilliant and beautiful. The main problem with yarn wings is getting them to hold their shape under the stress of casting and fishing.

One word about tailing material on spent patterns. I see that some tyers are using stiff materials, such as animal whiskers and synthetic paintbrush bristles. They look great, but are quite dissimilar in texture to the softer tails of the naturals. I believe this could detract from the fly's effectiveness, causing missed strikes and rejections. Personally, I feel hackle fibers are a better choice.

There is so much more that could be said about dry flies, but this dissertation has to end somewhere. Now let's become familiar with the major characteristics of flies which are fished under the surface. Again, we have imitators, attractors and everything in between. We have flies designed for bottom-fishing and flies designed to be fished just beneath the surface. We have flies to imitate various stages of insect life—nymph, larva, pupa, emerger. And we have flies which imitate trout foods other than insects, such as crustaceans and small fishes.

Let's begin with an extremely simple style, the soft-hackle wet fly.

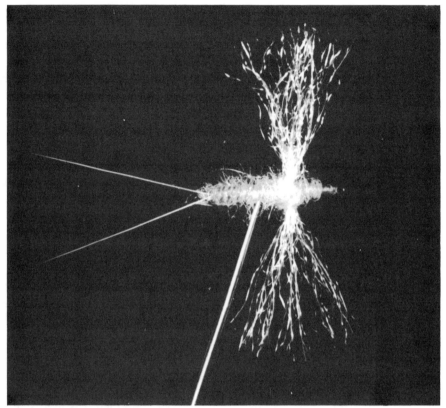

*A spent pattern with poly-type wings.*

Essentially, these flies consist of two components: body and hackle. On some patterns, a few wraps of a bright material called tinsel is added to create a sparkly effect.

Soft-hackle flies might best be described as being buggy-looking. They do not seek to closely imitate a specific insect, as realistic nymph patterns do; however, they are very suggestive of caddis pupae and the emerging forms of many insects.

The soft-hackle fly depends primarily on liveliness for its effectiveness. While the body materials contribute to this illusion, it is the hackle which really makes the fly. As the name implies, very soft, pliable materials are used, this in contrast to the stiff-hackled dry fly. The idea is that the soft fibers will absorb water readily and will wriggle enticingly, with a little inducement from the current and the angler.

Many types of feathers are used for hackling these flies; grouse, partridge and common hen are particularly popular. The main thing is to avoid overdressing, which detracts from the appearance of the fly. This is particularly true when such dense, fibrous feathers as grouse and partridge are used. Length of hackle varies with pattern. I prefer to make my

*A soft-hackle wet fly. Note sparseness of hackle.*

hackles a little longer than I would for a dry fly of corresponding size, and very sparse.

There is practically no end to the variations and combinations found in soft-hackle fly patterns. Many different body materials are utilized, both rough and smooth, some with tinsel ribbing, some without. Many different colors and shades are employed. Hackle materials vary considerably, as mentioned. A range of hook sizes is commonly used, 10, 12 and 14 being the most popular.

Personally, I like soft-hackles with somewhat fuzzy bodies tied out of translucent fur, either natural or synthetic. Olives, ambers and browns are very effective. I also recommend soft-hackles with bodies made of hare's-ear-type fur, which is rough and tweedy. Both the plain and gold-ribbed versions are effective. For hackle material, I favor game birds and soft hen chicken feathers.

In recent years, the traditional winged wet fly has waned in popularity a bit, mainly because of the upsurgence of the nymph and the special-purpose wet fly, such as the emerger. Still, they are worthy of mention. I carry several patterns that are murder at times.

The wings on a wet fly are tied down-wing style, over the top of the

*A traditional down-winged wet fly.*

body. Frequently used materials include sections of duck or goose feathers, wood duck, mallard and teal flank feathers and speckled turkey. Bodies and hackles are similar to those of the soft-hackle patterns. Most wet flies feature a tail of some description, and a few have a yellow or green egg sac.

The down-winged wet fly is an old style, having originated in England. Exactly what they had in mind is hard to say. Perhaps they sought to represent spent flies that had fallen into the water. In actuality, they were imitating emergers, and possibly egg-layers. In any case, the flies worked. In fact, they worked so well that wet-fly fishermen were held in scorn by the dry-fly clique, and heated arguments raged. Many British chalk streams allowed upstream, dead-drift presentation only, in an effort to thwart the subaqueous set.

As with the wingless soft-hackles, translucency and aliveness are two most desirable attributes. The pattern list is enormous, perhaps greater than that of any other category of fly. Many of the patterns are esoteric, localized, redundant, antiquated or all of those. Except in a few isolated areas, we can ignore the dozens of colorful attractor patterns designed to excite the gullible native brook trout of yore. Rarely would a civilized trout be inclined to take anything so unrealistic. These beautiful flies are of great historical and aesthetic interest, however, and certain master fly tyers dress them for framing.

My early mentors, such as they were, instructed me to use three wet-fly patterns—the Leadwinged Coachman, the Hare's Ear and the Light Cahill—and forget the rest. I did so, confining myself to sizes 10 and 12, and I didn't fare too badly. I was taught to fish two or three flies at a time, using droppers. A favorite ploy was to use one of each pattern and see if the fish were selective, in which case I would switch to three flies of the preferred pattern.

I still carry the original three, although I use the Light Cahill less than the others. In addition to 10's and 12's, I also use 14's and even 16's now, often with telling effect. To the list, I've added the Gold-Ribbed Hare's Ear, the March Brown and the Dark Cahill. The March Brown can be deadly during that hatch, in sizes 6 and 8. I also carry the Grannom, an egg-sac pattern which comes in handy during certain Caddis activity. These are in addition to the array of nymphs, emergers and weird experimental patterns I cart around.

For those who wish to learn more about the wet fly, I recommend a short but brilliant little book, *The Art of Fishing the Wet Fly*, by James Leisenring. The book is somewhat dated, and the illustrations aren't very good, but the patterns and tactical information are timeless and superb. The modern edition features an additional section by Vernon Hidy, "Fishing the Flymph." Winged and soft-hackle flies are both covered.

I've mentioned emergers several times, so let's briefly examine that style of tie. As the name implies, emergers are expressly designed to imitate insects in the act of hatching. As we learned in the entomology chapter, trout often are selective to insects in this transitory state, finding them an easy mark.

The unique characteristic of this style of fly is the construction of the wing. The idea is to convey the impression of an emerging wing, not yet fully blossomed. Therefore, the wing is tied shorter. Softer materials, such as down and marabou, are commonly used, because their tendency to move in the water simulates the natural insect's struggle to emerge.

It's very difficult to prescribe specific emerger patterns on a broad scale because they are so hatch-related. Some associations were made in the entomology chapter. As your fishing skills develop, your onstream experiences will assist you in determining when an emerger pattern is the optimum choice.

With the renaissance of fly-fishing, "nymph" has become almost a household word. A number of important angling books have treated the subject in depth. One in particular, *Nymphs*, by Ernest G. Schwiebert, is devoted entirely to the study of the nymphal, larval and pupal forms of aquatic insects and crustaceans.

Scholarly stuff, this, and properly so. The dedicated nymph fisherperson will surely read and study such material, and will also do a lot of rock rolling out in the stream. Probably, original fly patterns will evolve, as the nymphophile strives for more realism. But this is not the province of the beginning angler—a simplified introduction is what's needed.

Nymphs are very distinctive, but they also have several important similarities. The shape is generally the same. Coloration is dull, running to tans, browns, grays and black. And all nymphs live on or in the stream bottom until it's time for the winged insect to emerge.

There are many general nymph patterns that work well in the right place and time. Specific patterns become more important as emergence time for a particular species draws near, and the nymphs become active. Size is also a factor, as we attempt to simulate the natural. But for starters, I suggest you try a few generic nymph patterns in average sizes. With a little diligence and luck, you may be very pleasantly surprised. Patterns I would particularly recommend for beginners include the Hare's Ear, the Montana, the Zug Bug, the Muskrat, the Pheasant Tail and the Wooly Worm. If you fish in Hendrickson country, don't be without the Pheasant Tail during the early season—it's an excellent replica of that particular nymph.

Let us now examine a style of fly that isn't really a fly—the streamer. As stated in the beginning, streamers are suggestive of forage fish, not insects, so actually they should be classified as fly-rod lures. But who

*A nymph pattern. This one is dressed to imitate a common northeastern insect, Isonychia bicolor, thus the stripe down the back.*

*A quasi-realistic stonefly nymph dressing, with anatomical parts well defined.*

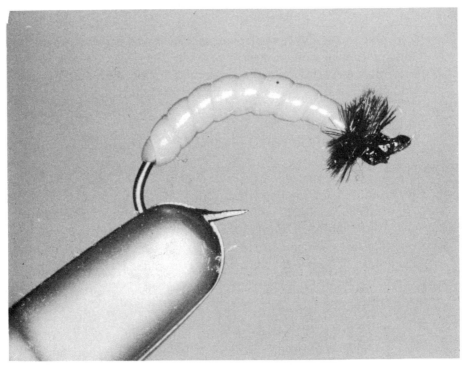

*A specialized type of "nymph"—the caddis worm.*

193

really cares? That's tantamount to hair-splitting, and one of the main objectives of this book is to simplify, rather than complicate.

As with other types of flies, many streamer patterns were designed to imitate specific bait fish. One of the most often copied is the freshwater smelt, which is abundant throughout the northeast. In the heyday of the native brook trout and land-locked salmon, ice-out in the lakes and ponds was also smelt time, which was synonymous with great fishing. Patterns were developed to imitate the coloration of local smelt, which varies somewhat from lake to lake. Many of these flies are still effective today, notably Carrie Stevens' classic Gray Ghost.

Many streamer patterns were *not* designed to imitate a specific forage fish. Two which readily come to mind are the Mickey Finn and the Black Ghost Marabou, both of which are allotted space in my flybox. What the designers of these patterns had in mind I can't say, but if it was imitation, they must have been thinking of a coral reef rather than the Beaverkill. Yet I've caught jaded, civilized old brown trout with these wild flies. It's a matter of knowing when and how to use them.

The key to streamer design, I believe, is to convey an impression of aliveness. The silhouette is that of a small fish, which is inevitably going to be swimming, perhaps in terror of what's swimming after it. Therefore, the materials, textures and configuration should support the overall illusion.

One of the most popular streamer materials is marabou, which actually comes from white turkeys. These soft, fluffy feathers look like nothing until they are wet, but in the water they slim out into a minnowlike form and pulsate with a lifelike action, under the tutelage of the angler. While not the choice for one who seeks realism, marabou is unbeatable when action is what's wanted.

Recently a new synthetic material called Flashabou was introduced, and it has caused quite a stir. While metallic in appearance, it is actually a polyester. Like marabou, it is extremely active in the water, with very little inducement required. A vast array of colors and color combinations are available, including all of the metallic shades and pearlescent.

While all-Flashabou flies are effective in certain situations, its greatest value is as a highlight. In the fall of 1985, Jack Gartside introduced me to his soft-hackle streamer, which is a unique blend of marabou with a couple of fine strips of Flashabou tied in. The effect is fantastic—I wanted to eat the thing myself! The pulsating marabou and the fluttering Flashabou drove the large browns and rainbows nuts in Yellowstone Park.

Therein lies a message: with certain exceptions, too much flash is not desirable in a streamer pattern. A lot of glitter is more apt to spook a trout than attract it. In Alaska, we found that the salmon running up the rivers craved straight Flashabou. My saltwater fly-fishing friends report great success with it in that element. And I would think a predominantly Flashabou streamer would be lethal on pike and pickerel—after all, anything that will eat a Daredevil is going to love Flashabou. For general trout fishing, however, conservativism is the byword when using Flashabou, tinsel or any highly reflective material.

Another popular streamer material is animal hair. While various hairs are used, deer tail remains on top of the list. It is inexpensive and readily available, being a by-product of deer hunting. Streamers tied with hair are commonly called "bucktails," even when something other than deer hair is substituted.

Animal hairs are used in their natural shades and also in a vast array of dyed colors. The inherent properties and characteristics vary considerably. Some are relatively soft, and therefore more lively underwater. Others are remarkably translucent—polar bear is a prime example. Some are much finer-textured than others, making them more appropriate for the smaller streamer patterns I personally prefer in most situations.

Since I mentioned that polar bear is called for in certain patterns, this is perhaps an appropriate spot to explain a couple of things. Traditionally, various materials have been used for fly tying which were once very common. Nearly all of them were by-products of other trades—for instance, the exotic plumage used for fully dressed Atlantic salmon patterns was a by-product of the clothing and hat-making industry. Other materials were by-products of sport hunting, polar bear being one of those.

As we all know, times have changed, and so have attitudes. Today, most people agree that the hunting of scarce and endangered species merely for purposes of decorating our garments or tying flies is simply not a humane thing to do. Consequently, we now use substitute materials in their place. Technology being what it is, there's virtually nothing which can't be copied. We now have artificial polar bear, seal and other exotics which are at least as good as the originals. Thus we may pursue our sport with a clear conscience.

Hairs are frequently combined in a pattern to create a likeness of some species of forage fish. An excellent example is Art Flick's Black-Nosed Dace streamer, which is designed to imitate a minnow of that same name. The three-part "wing" is composed of a layer of white, over which is tied a layer of black, which is topped by a layer of brown. This closely simulates the markings of the natural bait fish: white belly and flanks, black stripe down the lateral line, brownish back. This simple but effective pattern is still a valuable addition to your fly box, even though pollution has somewhat reduced the population of the environmentally sensitive minnow it represents.

There is yet another material widely used in streamer construction,

*A famous bucktail-type streamer, the Blacknosed Dace. Painted eye is optional.*

this being hackle feathers from the neck or saddle of a rooster. Again, both natural and dyed shades are employed. Some of the natural feathers have markings which create attractive effects. There are feathers with a dark stripe down the center, suggestive of the previously mentioned dace and other minnows. Others are mottled in soft browns, tans and grays, similar to the sculpin, a favorite forage fish. Thus, the fly tyer who is familiar with the appearance of these fishes is able to select feathers which produce a remarkable likeness.

Nature was considerate enough to cause the chicken to evolve in such a manner that certain of its feathers bear a marked similarity in shape to the small fishes found in the stream. Therefore, it wasn't difficult for the early innovators in streamer design to envision the effect obtained by tying these feathers down-wing style along the top of a hook. It is interesting to note that this component is called a wing, whether it is composed of feathers, hairs, marabou or some other material. This is an even bigger misnomer than calling a streamer a fly, but also one I wouldn't challenge, it having become accepted by usage.

The three types of materials just covered are all streamer wing materials. Generally, this is the most significant and visible component of the fly, but they also have bodies, tails, throats and ancillary parts which contribute to the overall effect. These are far too diverse and numerous to be described in a brief orientation.

In summary, I can say with a degree of confidence that the key ingredient in a successful streamer fly is how it behaves while moving in the water. Let's face it, even the most meticulously dressed streamer wouldn't fool a trout if the fish got a good look at it standing still. The fleeting impression transmitted to the trout is a combined function of shape, action, texture and coloration—an aquatic déjà vu, so to speak.

Given that premise, it follows that the streamer fly must be fished with plenty of movement. The main thing is for the trout to see the fly in such a manner that it believes (1) it's a small fish, and (2) it can catch it without too much effort. When a streamer fly is fished too slowly, the trout gets to scrutinize it, the probable result being rejection. If a streamer is fished too fast, the trout may simply give up. I try to fish my streamers with very brief pauses between the darting and swimming movements, so that the trout feels it has an easy chance to seize the tempting meal.

Picking your shot is also important in successful streamer fishing. I wouldn't use a streamer at a time when fish were feeding heavily on insect life, either on the surface or below. Trout are seldom deterred from insect feeding when the opportunity exists, and besides, I would prefer to be fishing an imitation of the insect myself. Instead, I would look for those slack periods when no bugs are apparent and insect imitations aren't producing. Early morning affords excellent streamer-fishing opportunities, before insect activity has begun. Night fishing can also be marvelous, as trout can see the larger fly and the disturbance created by its movements against the night sky. I fish my streamers just beneath the surface at that time.

Another high-potential opportunity is during periods of off-color water. I vividly recall a June afternoon on the Beaverkill back in the 1970s. I was fishing with Ralph Graves, an excellent fly tyer from southern New York State. We were more or less wasting time on a hot, bright afternoon in anticipation of evening hatching activity when a thunderstorm burst in, replete with a heavy deluge, which drove us to cover.

After the rains had abated, we returned to the river to find it up a little and slightly milky. I wasn't sure what to do, so I put on a nymph and started bottom-bouncing. Ralph tied on a yellow marabou streamer that I thought would scare every trout into the next county. Within a few casts, he hooked an enormous brown, easily a 2-pound fish, maybe 3. It broke him off. With appropriate comments, Ralph tied on another fly of the same pattern, and very quickly hooked another trout of similar proportions, which also broke him off. At that point, I asked Ralph what he was using for a leader, to which he sheepishly replied that he hadn't bothered to replace the 5X tippet he was using before the storm, because he really hadn't thought the streamer trick would work on the cerebral browns of the Beaverkill. A lesson long to be remembered by both Ralph and myself.

The high, cold, dirty water of early spring does not afford good streamer-fly opportunities, because you are fighting temperature. When trout are cold, their metabolism is low, and they are not inclined to chase after a meal. Neither do they want to eat in large gulps, as their rate of digestion is retarded. At such times, a nymph fished slow and deep is a far better choice.

I should mention that streamers often render excellent service as probing flies. Trout are territorial, and likely to chase or slash at un-wanted guests in their respective domains. While an actual take may not occur, you are now aware of the presence and location of a trout, possibly a good-sized one. Wait a bit, switch to a different type of fly, and you have a good chance at hooking that fish.

Because they are tied on larger hooks made of heavier wire, problems of engagement and penetration are often encountered with streamer flies. The same is true of very large nymphs. If you were to look at the point of a streamer hook under a microscope or even an 8X loupe, you would be appalled at how dull it is. All hooks could do with some touching up as they come from the factory, larger ones in particular. This is easily done with a small, fine stone or, better yet, a diamond hone. Try to work mainly from the inside and the sides of the point, rather than the outside, so that the point doesn't become overly curved inward, thus compromis-ing its hooking capabilities. Also avoid reshaping the point—it shouldn't become too short or stubbed. That's fine on a light-wire dry-fly hook, but with heavier iron, a more tapered point is required for effective penetra-tion.

I am a debarbing advocate, for a number of reasons. Obviously, it saves wear and tear on the fish. Not so obviously, it saves wear and tear on the fly. Least obviously, it enhances hook engagement, particularly in the case of streamer hooks with large barbs. That's a lot of metal to have to drive into a trout's jaw. You are much better off with a pinched-down barb.

I'll bet you thought that at the end of this chapter I was going to name a half-dozen sure-fire flies that you could take to any river, stream, lake or pond in the world and catch fish with all the time. Don't I wish I possessed such information! Rather than write, I'd hire myself out as a super-guide, success guaranteed, and get rich while having a grand time.

No, there are no panaceas. Even if you were to restrict your fishing to a single major river, the seasonal diversity and variations in water types would probably mandate a fairly diversified fly box. You would need to match the various stream insects in their several stages, and perhaps a few terrestrials as well. Other trout foods, such as crustaceans and forage fish,

*The Muddler Minnow, perhaps the most effective all-around fly pattern ever developed.*

would require imitation. And a few general patterns would be needed for those times when no identifiable food preference can be determined. This, just to fully exploit the potential of one fishery!

For the beginner, this is complicated, discouraging and counterproductive. After all, the thing is to learn the various techniques of presenting a fly, meanwhile enjoying yourself in the process. I believe it is best to start off with a few general, time-proven patterns suitable for the water types you'll be fishing. Concentrate on getting the fly to behave as you want it to. Develop confidence in your presentation, and don't become a compulsive fly changer. Pattern is important, of course, but presentation overrides everything else.

I would suggest that over a period of time you develop skills in the various types of presentation—streamer, nymph, emerger, dry-fly, whatever. Trout are usually willing to take *some* kind of fly, if you can simply make a proper choice and a convincing presentation. If at some point you decide you don't care for a particular type of fishing, that's okay, but why reach that conclusion without giving it a try? I enjoy virtually all types of fly-fishing, but I have no argument with the dry-fly purist who has given other methods a fair shot and decides to restrict himself or herself to the floater. As long as they don't pick on me for rolling a nymph along the bottom between hatches, I won't rub it in when I catch a fish that wouldn't rise to the prettiest dry fly ever tied.

# CHAPTER IX _____

# *Tactics and Streamology*

After eight chapters of orientation, it is time to move toward the stream. While en route, let's briefly discuss the trout we hope to encounter there, and the approach we must follow if we are to successfully infiltrate their domain.

There are a number of species of trout, and we shall examine the most common of them shortly. First, however, let's understand that there are also two classifications of trout: wild and stocked. Basically, a wild trout is one born to the stream, whereas a stocked trout is hatchery-reared and planted in the river by mankind. However, a stocked trout can become wild in character, adopting most if not all of the wily ways that enable the stream-born fish to stay a few fin-lengths ahead of its natural enemies.

Almost unanimously, serious fly-fishers consider stocked trout a necessary evil—in fact, there are some who would disagree with the term "necessary." True, they are a drab image of their wild counterparts. They have poor coloration, both inside and out. They are weak and soft-fleshed. They have virtually no flavor, and lots of spices are required to render them palatable. And they are very gullible, willing to take practically any fly or lure in their first days in the river after being stocked.

Do I paint a negative picture? Perhaps. Even so, artificial stocking represents a major program in the more populated eastern and northeastern states. Without it, there would be very limited or even no trout fishing in many streams and lakes. Even the hallowed Beaverkill would have only a modest trout population if it weren't for stocking, because the amount of fish produced by natural propagation wouldn't begin to satisfy the requirements of the thousands of anglers who fish there.

Artificial stocking works in several ways. It provides some level of sport in marginal waters, where trout will not survive for an extended period. This is put-and-take fishing in its purest form. The idea is to catch and keep as high a percentage of the stocked fish as possible, because they are going to die anyway. The value of such a program, in addition to providing recreation, is that it keeps large numbers of casual fishermen who want to kill a lot of fish away from the quality streams, thus extending the resource.

Artificial stocking also helps supplement trout populations where survivability is high but reproduction is limited. The Beaverkill program is a prime example. This beautiful river has good water quality and sufficient food to support a large number of trout. The idea, therefore, is to artificially populate the stream, protecting the trout via stringent regulations, so that they will carry over, grow to interesting size and take on the characteristics of wild trout. This type of program works well when properly managed.

In recent years, sophisticated artificial-propagation programs have been used to introduce different species and strains of fish into habitats where they would not occur naturally. The Great Lakes salmon and steelhead program is a prime example—you can now catch Pacific salmon and huge migratory rainbow trout in places like New York State and Michigan. There are lake trout once again in Lake George, where the native strain had been wiped out by DDT. A comprehensive program to re-establish brook trout populations in ponds and lakes throughout the northeast was also undertaken, and would have been successful if acid rain hadn't ruined the water quality. That's a problem which some day has to get solved—it's a national disgrace.

To the typical angler, the significant difference between wild and stocked trout is their behavior. Wild trout are totally tuned to their environment—food supply, water temperature, refuge from predators. Stocked trout, until they become acclimated, really don't know what's happening. They are used to having people around, and in fact depend on people for food. They are accustomed to crowded conditions. They have had no experience with otters, mergansers, king-fishers and the like. They don't even know how to survive when summer causes lower, warmer waters. All of this must be learned, and a large percentage of the trout will die in the process. Those which survive become pretty decent-quality fish.

Each season, many thousands of new and inexperienced anglers receive inaccurate indoctrination in what trout are really like, because they are encountering stocked fish almost exclusively. This is certainly better than having no fishing at all, but it is not the best preparation for dealing with wild trout which are fully trained in survival techniques. It can develop bad habits and careless tactics, as the following story serves to illustrate.

A number of years ago, I was spending a most enjoyable morning on one of New York State's premium trout streams. The pool I was fishing typified the character of the river—slow current, gin-clear water, a smooth, glassy surface. Sizable trout were rising to a generous hatch of olive-bodied Mayflies. With due caution, a long leader and a convincing imitation, they could be taken. It was demanding fishing, and most rewarding.

Immersed in concentration as I was, I failed to notice the approach of another fisherman. Suddenly, I heard a shout, "Hey, do you mind if I help you catch those fish? There's nothing happening over here." With that, the fellow waded noisily into my territory. Ripples lapped against the far bank, and instantly all rising ceased, as though someone had thrown a switch.

I was very angry, and I let it show just enough to indicate to the man that he had done something wrong. My ire subsided quickly when I realized he was genuinely sorry, and quite embarrassed. I suggested we back off and allow things to settle down. We sat on the bank, talking, watching. I explained about still pools and wild, wary trout. It came as a revelation—he was in his first season, and had been fishing almost exclusively over stocked fish.

With an irresistible procession of succulent insects drifting over their backs, it didn't take the trout long to forget about us. There was a rise, then two more, then a number of slowly widening rings on the surface of the pool. I had built out the fellow's leader to 6X and tied on a size 16 Blue-Winged Olive from my box. Together, we eased into the stream, inching across the pool to within casting range. The man cast surprisingly well, and was able to hook several nice trout before the hatch ended. Rarely have I seen anyone so pleased. He insisted on taking me to lunch, an offer I couldn't refuse.

Therein lies a message. Treat all trout as though they are wild, erudite, sophisticated, suspicious and virtually paranoid. You will do much better on the easy ones, and will become better prepared to deal with the really tough ones that know the game and, in effect, make the rules. This has become my greatest joy—to catch trout most other anglers can't catch, and may not even be aware of.

## TROUT SPECIES

Now, let's talk species. Most of us will be fishing primarily for brown and rainbow trout. Which species predominates depends on geography, essentially. In the east and midwest the brown is by far more common, while in the Rockies and Pacific northwest the rainbow generally dominates. This is not to say there isn't excellent brown trout fishing in the west—quite the contrary. The point is that the rainbow is a western species which naturally occurs in that region.

The brown trout, Salmo trutta, was transplanted to this continent in the late 1800s, in an effort to replace a badly depleted brook trout population. Fertilized eggs were transported from Europe—Germany, mainly, and the British Isles—which resulted in the introduction of two rather distinctive strains. The so-called German brown tends to be more colorful and has bright orange or red spots along the flanks. The more subdued Loch Leven strain lacks the red spots and is somewhat more silvery in appearance. In the one hundred years since brown trout were introduced to North America, these strains have become inextricably mixed. However, there are watersheds where the brown trout populations

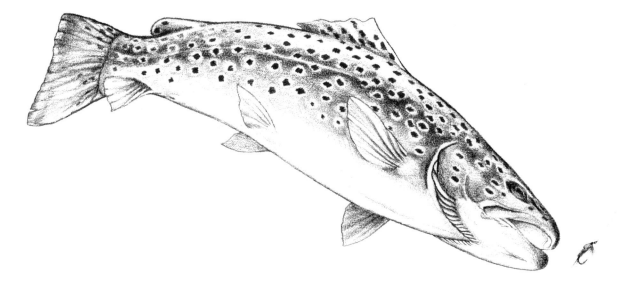

*Brown trout.*

manifest unmistakable characteristics of one strain or the other, indeed a beautiful thing to behold.

The enormous success of the brown trout on this side of the Atlantic is attributable to the resilient and resourceful nature of this marvelous fish. It can withstand higher water temperatures, more pollution and greater angling pressure than our native brook trout, and grows to larger size. As the cold-water resources of this country were dramatically altered by lumbering, tannery operations, impoundments and other poorly planned and ill-managed ventures, the brookie was driven toward extinction, its habitat reduced to the cold, pure headwaters and tributaries of our rivers, and to pristine ponds and lakes, far from the beaten path. Without the brown trout, stream fishing would be virtually nonexistent east of the Rockies.

Initially, Salmo trutta received a rather rude welcome from the rank and file of the angling clan. Brook-trout worshipers called them Sauerkraut Trout and Spotted Suckers, and denigrated them as both a sport fish and a table fish. Actually, the biggest problem was that few anglers of that era had the requisite skills to catch them. Today, the brown is almost universally accepted and acclaimed, although one can still hear a few faint derogatory echoes from northern New England and Michigan's upper peninsula.

Actually, the brown is a superior sport fish to the brook trout. It is much more inclined toward surface feeding, to the great delight of the

*Rainbow trout.*

dry-fly set. As mentioned, it grows to a larger size and has a longer life span. And it is quite delicious as table fare, provided the trout comes from pure, cold water and is either wild or has become fully acclimated.

The rainbow trout, Salmo gairdneri, is native to the great watersheds of the Rockies and Pacific northwest, its natural range extending well up the Alaskan coastal area. Its requirement for higher oxygenation causes the rainbow to prefer faster rivers with diffused currents; however, the rainbow is also quite comfortable in more sedate waters, including lakes, ponds and reservoirs, given sufficient oxygen content and alkalinity. Thus, the rainbow has been successfully transplanted to various watersheds of the North American continent, and has done incredibly well in foreign waters, including New Zealand, the South American high country and Yugoslavia.

Rainbows tend to be more migratory than other species of trout, which accounts at least partially for their abandonment of many waters where they were transported. However, there are many streams where the resident strain of rainbow seems perfectly content to stay at home. This, I believe, can be attributed to the eminent suitability of that particular resource, which has caused the fish to evolve as a nonmigratory strain. At one time, biologists classified rainbow trout separately, seeking to differentiate between migrators and nonmigrators. The nonmigrators were designated Salmo irrideus. However, since no distinctive biological difference could be defined, they are now lumped together as Salmo gairdneri.

This entire question of classification is curious and often confusing. Each species of salmonid has subspecies or strains which have distinctive markings, coloration and other characteristics. These are a product of countless generations of evolution in a particular habitat. Basically, it's still the same fish; however, some markedly different habits and behaviorisms may develop. For example, the steelhead is a migratory anadromous rainbow trout of the Pacific northwest. It is present in many rivers which also have a nonmigratory strain of rainbows. The two strains will not willingly interbreed in a natural environment. However, the eggs and milt may be mixed artificially and will produce fertile offspring.

Rainbow trout are reputedly less sagacious than the browns and more easily fooled. While I generally agree, I can also report many experiences with extremely selective and skeptical rainbows. No one who has spent time on the Henry's Fork or Silver Creek in Idaho would dispute the rainbow's capacity for discretion. In the right situation, they can be as tough as any brown.

I happen to love rainbow trout above all others. Their great strength and speed make them awesome battlers, and their inclination to jump produces matchless thrills. Rainbow rivers are generally noisier than

brown trout rivers, thanks to the exultant shouts and uninhibited expletives which emanate from excited anglers. My most pleasant dreams are a
kaleidoscope of mighty leaps, flips and tailwalks—which is why I'm
known to smile in my sleep.

At the time of the Pilgrims' landing, there were two species of trout
east of the Rockies: brook trout and lake trout. Their names are aptly
descriptive of their respective habitats. The brook trout, Salvelinus fonti-
nalis, abounded in the unspoiled streams and ponds of the New World,

Brook trout.

supported by a cold and abundant underground aquifer and shaded by a primeval conifer forest. Few creatures on earth can match their natural beauty, and their depletion is a great sadness, as well as a disturbing reflection of a societal attitude toward the natural resource which supports human as well as animal life on this planet.

The brookie, or speckled trout as it was sometimes called, was an easy mark, and the primitive methods employed by early fly-fishers were incredibly successful. Heavy bags of fish were the order of the day, most of which were wasted. This, coupled with the destructive industrial practices mentioned earlier, decimated the brook trout in an alarmingly short period of time. The period from the beginning of heavy lumbering, et cetera, to the virtual elimination of the brook trout from all but the most remote portions of its range encompassed only a few human generations.

Efforts to repopulate the brook trout have met with rather spotty success. They do poorly in competition with the tough, aggressive brown trout, and so are scarce even in rivers where the habitat is sufficiently pure to support them. Acid rain has raised havoc with the lake and pond restoration program, which otherwise would have been a spectacular success. Some streams and ponds have sufficient natural alkalinity to partially counterbalance the effects of acid rain, and fishable populations of brook trout exist there. For quality brook-trout fishing, however, you must go to the more remote waters of Quebec, Labrador, Newfoundland, Nova Scotia and other unspoiled areas.

The intellect of the brookie has long been slandered, and I feel unfairly so. The original residents were certainly an unsophisticated lot, but today I can show you brook trout that are more picky than you could imagine. Visit the Vermont Battenkill some time, and get refused by 7 to 12-inch brook trout all evening long—it makes you properly respectful. The lesson here is that any salmonid will learn to be selective and self-protective, given a conducive environment.

Technically, the brook trout is a char and not a true trout, like the brown, rainbow and western cutthroat. Biologists can explain the minute distinctions having to do with the formation of the vomerine, or tooth-bearing, bone and other subtleties. From an angler's standpoint, however, the brookie is every inch a trout, and a fine one at that—trout enough for this old Piscator, to be sure.

With due respect, we shall leave the lake trout, golden trout, Dolly Varden and Arctic char to others to describe. However, I want to devote a few words to the western cutthroat trout, as it is of major importance in many watersheds. It has been described as the brook trout of the west, a slight inaccuracy, since the brookie is actually a char, but apt enough, as both are indigenous to their respective territories.

The cutthroat, Salmo clarki, is a most interesting fish. It shares a common ancestry with the rainbow, although the separation is a very ancient one. Their original range included such diverse areas as Mexico and British Columbia, and the species is still widely distributed throughout the Rocky Mountains and the Pacific northwest.

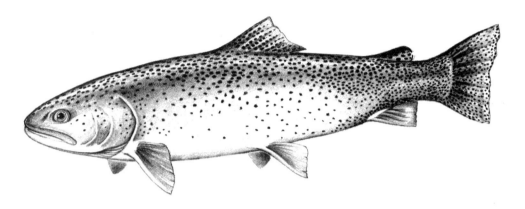

*Cutthroat trout.*

The geological forces which shaped the topography of the continent caused the isolation of the cutthroat into numerous watersheds. This influenced the trout to evolve into many clearly identifiable subspecies. Some of these are now extinct; others exist only in minute relict populations. However, two distinctive strains of cutthroat exist today in close proximity to one another. They are the Yellowstone cutthroat, which abound in the upper reaches of that famous river, and the Jackson Hole cutthroat, which thrive in the Snake River watershed, just over the Great Divide.

These trout are both cutthroats, true enough, yet they differ so strikingly in appearance that even a nonfisherman could easily tell them apart. The Yellowstone strain is perhaps the archetypical cutthroat, featuring larger black spots distributed mainly over the tail, lower back and dorsal and adipose fins. Colors run the gamut from golds, yellows and olives to reds, lavenders and even purples. The Jackson Hole strain features a multitude of small spots covering virtually the entire fish. The coloration is less exotic, and the overall appearance of the fish is more suggestive of its cousin, the rainbow. Both strains carry the distinctive vermilion slash beneath the jaw which is the prime identifying mark of their species.

The two strains differ in behavior as well as appearance. The Yellowstone trout tend to be gullible, although they can become exasperatingly selective to small flies later in the season. They are unspectacular but strong, game fighters. The Jackson Hole trout are much faster, make longer runs and will jump on occasion. They also tend to be somewhat more selective and harder to fool.

It is unfortunate that early biologists failed to grasp the significance of the many subspecies of cutthroat. In an effort to repopulate depleted watersheds, strains were mixed in the hatcheries and subsequent stockings, and much of the uniqueness was lost. The giant strain of cutthroat which once inhabited Pyramid Lake in Nevada and produced a record 41-pound specimen is extinct, thanks to indiscriminate irrigation and water storage practices. The cutthroat story is a sorry one, in some respects paralleling that of the American Indian. Still, healthy populations exist in a number of watersheds, and their beguiling beauty makes them a great joy to the angler.

Those are the fish that are out there, among all of the bugs and other denizens of trout country. The various species have their characteristics and idiosyncrasies, tolerances and preferences for temperature, affinity for water type, feeding habits, spawning habits, and so on. They also have common traits, particularly the instincts that protect them from predators, man included. This intuitive wariness is one of the major factors anglers must take into account if success is to be achieved.

## TROUT'S PROCLIVITIES

In heavily fished waters, trout become adjusted to human presence, to a large degree. That doesn't mean they are easy to catch—quite the contrary. What it does mean is that when approached with reasonable care, they will let you try.

There is a pool in the Beaverkill which has become a national symbol of contemporary trout fishing. It is known as Cairn's Pool. Old Route 17 borders its entire length, providing easy access and parking. The far bank rises abruptly into a steep mountainside, into which is cut the old abandoned railroad bed. The pool is very large—several football fields in length overall. The streambed is unobstructed and easily wadable, although high waters will confine the angler to the shallow side near the road. It is a quiet, slow-moving pool, with very simple structure and few impediments to casting and presentation.

Prime time on Cairn's Pool is like double-stamp day at the supermarket. I have seen dozens of anglers fishing it at one time, with still more on the bank, awaiting a slot. Fly lines form a virtual grid on the surface.

Multiple conversations are carried on, some via walkie-talkie. Yet amid this congestion and tumult, fish are feeding. Providing the anglers limit their movements and cast with care and delicacy, the trout behave almost as though no one were there. I've seen fish take up feeding positions above and below stationary anglers, using them as current breaks. All of which demonstrates that we can integrate ourselves with the trout's habitat—if we proceed properly.

Trout greatly fear things which are above them, and for good reason, for birds of prey are their mortal enemy. Thus, the angler must avoid alarming the fish when approaching the stream. We are much more visible and threatening to trout when standing on a high bank or rock than when hip deep in the current. Therefore, we must give careful consideration to how we approach a particular piece of water. Obviously, it's best to approach and enter the stream at a point where the water is very shallow and there is no significant structure, to minimize the possibility of spooking any fish. It is not good to scare even a small trout, for its panic-stricken dash for safety may cause others to take alarm.

Extremely slow, still pools are particularly demanding. After selecting the optimum point of entry, we are often faced with the task of wading out to where we can get access to the fish without frightening them. Waves and ripples on a quiet pool will alarm surface-feeding fish, putting them down, so you must move slowly, with very gradual movements. Quick, sudden movements scare trout—these are interpreted as predator-type movements.

The approach is not strictly a matter of visual camouflage—there is also the matter of detectable vibration. The lateral lines which run along the sides of the trout from just behind the gills to the base of the tail are equipped with a hypersensitive set of nerve ends. These serve as a highly-developed sonar system, enabling the trout to detect things it cannot see. Thus, fish can swim around obstructions in pitch dark, avoid other fish and evade the swift attacks of subsurface predators.

When we walk on the bank, vibrations are created. They may have no effect in a large, fast, noisy river, but in quiet sections they are a dead giveaway. I'll never forget the first time I fished the famous Letort spring creek in Pennsylvania. My heavy-footed approach put down a half-dozen rising trout, a fact made painfully clear to me by the two local experts who were casting to them. So have a care, and tread with stealth as you near the water.

Once an angler has entered the stream and has waded to a significant depth, certain factors begin to swing in his or her favor. We become shorter, in effect, so that our silhouette is obscured by the bank and bushes. Our overhead presence is diminished. Trout seem to be more

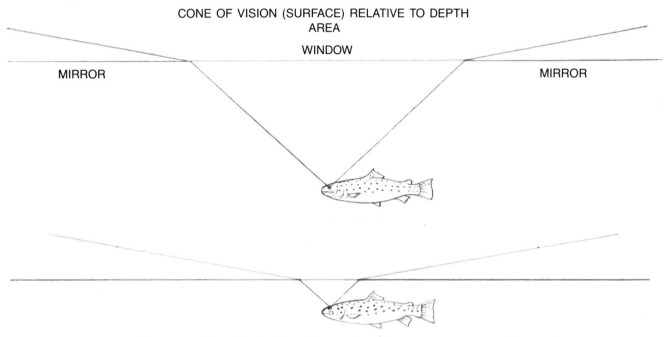

*The trout's "cone" of vision. The angle at the vertex is constant. Thus, when the trout is nearer the surface, the window is smaller, as illustrated.*

tolerant of things in the water, as opposed to objects outside and above, so the careful wader may ease his or her way around the stream with minimal disruption. And we have certain natural phenomena having to do with light and vision working for us—if we let them.

In the preceding chapter we examined the effects of reflection and refraction essentially in terms of how trout see flies on the surface. Let us now get further into how they see us. We have learned that refraction causes light rays to bend as they enter water. The more acute the angle, the more the bend. Also, the more the bend, the less the intensity of those particular light rays, to the extent that light rays which encounter the water at an angle flatter than 10 degrees are not a factor.

Because of refraction, much distortion occurs within the trout's field of vision. Again, the greater the angle, the more distorted the image. Light rays entering at flatter angles transmit a compressed image—in other words, the object appears more or less short and squat. The upper body of a wading angler looks like the view in those carnival funny mirrors. This, plus the darkening effect caused by the diminishing amount of light, can be used to advantage by the knowledgeable angler. The lesson is clear and simple—the lower your image, the less likely it is that the trout will take notice.

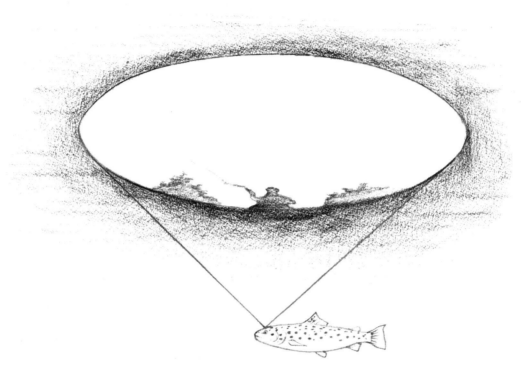

*The trout's view of an angler and streamside foliage.*

Please keep this message firmly fixed in your consciousness. So often we approach a piece of water from a high vantage point, making us readily visible to the trout. A little crouching, a lower profile, can get us into the water unnoticed. And move slowly—the key to approaching fish is "low and slow."

When preparing to fish any piece of water, you need to devise a plan. Usually, portions of the plan will be dictated by the situation—the presence of other anglers, the structure of the habitat, sun position, rising trout or lack of them, wading considerations, methods to be used, and so forth. Sometimes, the proper procedure is obvious, and planning is easy. Often, however, you are faced with a complex situation, full of subtleties. It is then advisable to take a few moments to figure things out, in order to optimize your opportunities.

One of the most common mistakes made by today's anglers is jumping into the stream and starting to fish without having made any assessments. This practice is on the increase, thanks to the tempo of our modern world and the numbers of anglers competing for pool space. True, there are times when you must establish a position, but it shouldn't be necessary to charge out there and start flailing away. Rather, you should sit on the bank or stand quietly in the shallows, making your intentions obvious without disturbing anything. It serves no useful purpose to win a beachhead if every trout in the area is spooked in the process.

Usually, the thing we look for first is visibly feeding fish. While there are times when feeding is obvious, there are also times when it is virtually undetectable. Even rising trout sometimes feed so delicately that the surface is barely disturbed. The diffusion of the currents can hide rises with surprising effectiveness, but even in quieter stretches there are circumstances where surface activity is all but imperceptible.

I vividly recall a day many years ago on the Esopus Creek in New York's Catskills. It was mid-August, not prime time for stream fishing in that region, but I had the urge. I chose the Esopus because water was being released into the upper portion of the stream via an aqueduct from a distant reservoir, which created an adequate flow of cool water. It was the only game in town.

By 7:30 A.M., I had reached my pool, but I wasn't the first, by any means. Several anglers were already in action, and a party of early-morning float-tubers drifted down the pool, to everyone's dismay. I sat down on a rock, poured a cup of coffee and took up watch. After a spell, I began to notice slight disturbances of the surface near the far bank. They were hardly visible—a déjà vu, so to speak—but unmistakable. It was apparent that the other fishermen had not noticed this activity—they were working the faster water in the head and tail of the pool.

I eased into the stream and waded into position. Looking upstream, I saw a silvery cloud of tiny insects hovering over the riffles, highlighted by the morning sun. Tricorythodes! I reasoned that the fish were taking spent flies in the slow water—and I was right. For nearly an hour, I had great sport.

To my amazement, the other anglers left me entirely alone, apparently unwilling to forsake the riffles and runs for the calm flats of the pool proper.

The lesson: don't assume that rising trout virtually scream "Feeding Time!" at the angler. Be observant, take notice of even the most subtle disturbances of the surface and be patient. Wait and watch a bit. Give the fish a chance to send a message—and be tuned in to receive it.

Rises can be even more difficult to detect in more diverse and turbulent currents. If trout are anything, they are effective feeders. Instinct and experience have programmed them to take their food with the least possible effort. This is the energy-exchange equation: energy obtained must exceed energy expended. Differently stated, it would not benefit a distance runner to run ten miles for a 500-calorie sandwich, because the 1000 calories burned in the process equates to a 500-calorie net loss. Thus, fish which live in rough water, which taxes their energy quickly, learn to use the little deflections and nuances of the current to make it easy on themselves when feeding.

The two main keys to identifying rises in broken water are (1) knowing what to look for and (2) knowing where to look. A mistaken perception is that fish which live in rough water rise to a fly with a vigorous slashing or boiling movement. Sometimes they do, during a heavy hatch when excitement is at a peak, but often they simply hold just off the heavy current and sip. I still marvel at the efficiency with which trout do this. Last summer I spent many days fishing the no-kill section of the Madison and was constantly amazed at how effortlessly and unobtrusively those trout could feed in that brawling river. You had to read the water, identifying the pockets, eddies and seams where fish could hold comfortably and pick at the movable feast brought to them by the currents. The rises were so gentle—a nose, a dorsal fin, a tail—that you had to watch closely. I saw many anglers walk right by a line of feeding trout, totally unaware of the activity.

Sometimes it is possible to detect trout feeding subsurface, even on or near the bottom. This is difficult in fast, broken currents, but reasonably easy in slower stretches, where visibility is not so obscured. Here again, it is important to know what to look for. Often, the only evidence of a feeding trout is the elusive wink or flash of a turning flank as an insect is taken.

G. E. M. Skues, the legendary champion of subaqueous angling on the chalk streams of Great Britain, called it "The sudden brown wink under water." In addition to being lyrical, Skue's description of subsurface trout behavior is as fresh and relevant today as when it was written many decades ago. I recommend *Minor Tactics of a Chalk Stream* and *The Way of a Trout with a Fly* to all anglers interested in what goes on underwater. May these classics stay in print forever.

As we learned in the entomology chapter, there is generally a lot of nymph activity before an emergence. Certain nymphs even take little practice swims in preparation for the main event. Many of those nymphs never live to fly from the stream as a dun, because the opportunistic trout gobble them first. This presents the angler with an opportunity. While it isn't essential to see feeding trout in order to fish the bottom currents effectively, it can help bolster confidence and assist in the development of a planned approach.

Incidentally, some of these winks and flashes are not trout. Suckers feed in this manner, and so do whitefish, which abound in western rivers. With experience, you will learn to identify feeding suckers with fair accuracy—their movements are generally slower than trout. Whitefish are much more troutlike in their behavior, and I'm still fooled quite frequently. Which isn't all bad—I've had some great battles with whitefish.

Having mentioned suckers, which are plentiful in many of our eastern trout streams, I should also mention that they play a role in stream tactics. Just because they are a so-called rough fish, don't treat them carelessly. Suckers are less nervous than trout, and are sometimes virtually under-foot. Try not to frighten them. A panic-stricken dash by a school of suckers sends a message of danger to the trout that share the pool.

## READING THE WATER

When no visible feeding activity is perceived, we do the next best thing and "read" the water. Actually, we are reading much more than just the water—we are reading the streambed, the rocks, the logs, the banks, the bridge abutments—everything which contributes to the character and configuration of a piece of water. What we are looking for is structure—that is, places which offer protection and, ideally, feeding opportunity as well. In addition to water quality and food supply, it is this structure which determines how good a habitat exists in a particular section of river.

Trout are apprehensive creatures, and do not willingly leave cover without a good reason. Usually, the motivation is feeding opportunity; however, trout tend to stay as close to home as possible, while still getting in on the chow line. Therefore, the ideal structure is one where protection and prime feeding lanes are in fairly close proximity.

Given a choice, trout generally opt for overhead cover—an outcropping of rock, a sunken log, an undercut bank. They tend to feel much more secure when their backs are covered, which is certainly understandable when you consider all the potential danger from above. The more aggressive fish will take the better covers, and will therefore end up living longer and growing to larger size. The rest of the trout in the area take second best, settling for lies which offer protection on one or both sides, or at least relief from the relentless current. In many situations, trout depend primarily on the water itself for shelter. Apparently, their instincts tell them they are less visible in frothing, broken currents or in the murky depths of pools.

While protection from predators goes hand in glove with relief from current, they are not necessarily the same. It does not take a terribly large object to provide a holding spot for even a sizable trout. I've seen 14-inchers finning away contentedly behind a rock the size of a grapefruit.

Such small obstructions don't afford much protection from predators, but can provide ideal feeding lies, offering relief from the current in prime feeding lanes.

One of the problems in reading water is that of identifying that kind of holding lie. The effect of refraction tends to make a stream bottom look flatter than it actually is, and quite often anglers assume that a pool has little or no structure when actually it has plenty. This comes with experience and knowing the streams you fish.

Water conditions have a profound effect on the deployment of trout, and on how they take their food. Spots which might provide good cover in higher water offer little protection when summer conditions prevail. Also, the prime feeding lanes may change because of the difference in current flow.

I've experienced this countless times; however, one particular instance remains vivid in my memory. I had taken some vacation in anticipation of the Hendrickson hatch, and was staying at a charming inn very close to one of my favorite streams. The insects arrived, right on schedule—but so did the spring torrents. It rained buckets, and the river rose and became off-color. Disconsolate, I figured the fishing was shot and my vacation wasted, but having nothing better to do, I got my gear together and walked down to the river. It was really roaring—the runs where I would normally have looked for rising trout resembled the Mississippi at flood stage. However, I began to see Mayflies in the air. Where were they coming from?

I sat down to watch. After a few moments, I noticed what appeared to be a rise directly upstream from me, close to the shore. Then there was a definite rise in that spot, and another. Normally, this water would have been only ankle-deep, and deserted. On this day, it was almost knee-deep. The insects were drifting out of the main current and into the quiet eddies, as they struggled to take off. Encouraged by the abundance of water, the trout followed them. It was my reprieve, and I enjoyed some excellent fishing under rather abominable conditions.

This is an important lesson. No one wants to fish in poor conditions, but the fact is that most of us must fish when we can. So, don't automatically give up when rains bring high water—remember, fish *like* water—it's we who are bothered by it. Do some scouting. Try to locate places which have slow side currents and backwaters, where fish can feed in comfort. And don't feel defeated if the water turns slightly off-color. While not pleasing to the eye, this can actually be a windfall. Trout can still see insects above them, outlined by sky light. What they may not see so readily is you.

While in this vein, let's talk about current speed and its effect on trout behavior. While trout can live happily in even the most rapid sections of rivers, there must be refuge from the currents—again, the structure principle. When trout rise, they abandon their structure, at least to some extent. Therefore, one of the major influences on how readily trout rise is the relative ease with which they can leave their holding lies and gain access to the surface.

## SLOW WATER

Much has been written about the free-rising trout of the Pennsylvania spring creeks, the Montana spring creeks and the Henry's Fork of the Snake. Despite the geographic differences, these streams have one thing in common: gentle currents. It takes little effort for a trout to pick an insect from the surface and return to its lie. Therefore, the effort/energy ratio is favorable to surface feeding. This, coupled with the abundance of insect life in these rivers, makes them prime dry-fly fisheries.

I hope you will have ample opportunity to observe rising trout in a slow pool early on in your angling career, because it is a revelation. The slower the current and less defined the structure, the more free-form the behavior of the fish. Given any appreciable surface food, they will tend to rise readily. They take their food in a leisurely yet efficient manner—after all, it's not racing past them to be gone down stream in an instant. They often drift with the current, eyeballing a morsel as they rise to intercept it—and why not? It's no effort for the fish to swim back upstream to its original position. That morsel, of course, could be someone's dry fly. Thus, our offerings get scrutinized more and more closely as current speed diminishes, in terms of both appearance and behavior. It can make for challenging fishing.

In very slow waters, trout may be inclined to move to one side or the other for a mouthful of food, and may even cruise a bit. This depends on the peculiarities of the pool. If there are definite feeding lanes, where insects are channeled in prescribed paths, the trout will take positions in those lanes. Lacking that, they may move around at will, picking away opportunistically at the insects drifting above. This makes it both easier and harder for the angler, because while fish may be actively feeding in an area, it can be difficult to pick out a distinct line of drift that will carry the fly to a trout's feeding station. This phenomenon is carried to the ultimate in lake and pond fishing, where things are reversed—instead of the fly coming to the fish, the fish must move to the fly. Thus, surface-feeding trout in still water are always on the move, and the game becomes one of trying to anticipate where a particular fish would like to take its next mouthful.

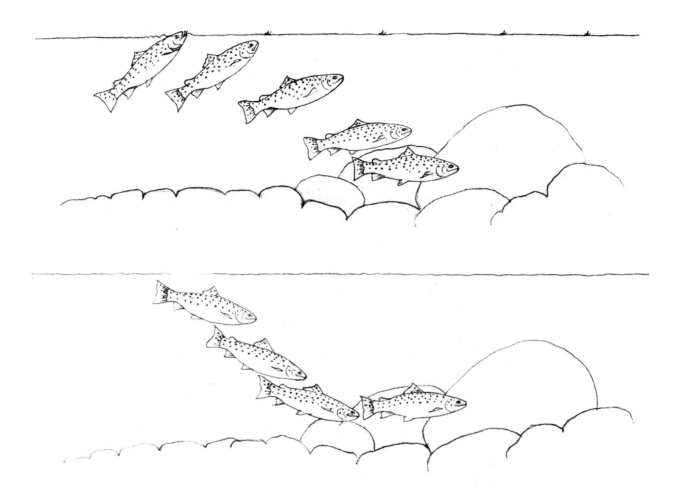

*Typical behavior of a trout surface-feeding in slow water. Notice the drift-back as the trout rises to take the fly, then returns to the original look-out position.*

Another characteristic of slow-water trout is that they tend to hang closer to the surface for extended periods. This again is caused by the minimal amount of energy expended in doing so. As long as there is sufficient inducement in the form of food, the fish will stay just beneath the surface, chancing an attack from above, feasting on the easy banquet. The rise forms tend to be gentle and energy-efficient, particularly when the prevalent insect is small. Larger flies and those which create a disturbance on the surface can induce awesome rises, however.

The leisurely feeding pace of slow-water trout imposes certain disciplines on the angler. You generally must use a longer leader and finer tippet. Delivery must be delicate—a fly line slapping onto the surface of a quiet pool is detectable for quite a distance. Most important, the presentation must be managed carefully to obtain a long, drag-free drift.

That last point is really critical. One of the most common mistakes in fishing to rising trout in a slow pool is to present the fly too close above the rise form. This is an awful temptation. We see the rise and immediately put a fly a few feet above it, forgetful of the fact that the fish may have drifted quite a distance with that insect before taking it, and is now in the process of returning to its feeding station upstream, where the process started.

Under the circumstances it is necessary to deliver your fly well upstream of a rise form—8, 10, 12 feet, perhaps even more. Ideally, it's always best to locate the trout's true feeding station, the spot at which it lies in wait for its food—this establishes a target. The task becomes one of managing the drift, so that the fish becomes a believer. Even the slightest drag spells defeat—hence the long, fine tippet, cast with some slack. This takes practice, so the beginner shouldn't be too discouraged if early encounters with slow-pool trout are unproductive.

Keep in mind the concept of the drag-free float, and be aware that mini-drag does exist. Sometimes a drift which appears perfect to us is actually dragging a bit out where the trout lie. Not only will this put the fish off, it can actually cause missed strikes. How? Consider this—when rising to take a fly, a trout automatically sets up a collision course whereby that fly will be intercepted at a certain precise location. At the last moment, the trout must take its eye off the fly—in other words, there is a little blind spot where the fish's mouth is located. The trout takes the fly by sucking it in with a bit of water, which is expelled through the gills. In slow water, especially with small flies, this sucking action is very gentle. Thus, a fly attached to a straight leader may actually be held back from entering the trout's mouth. This accounts for many of those exasperating false rises we experience. What a pity! Everything went well enough that the trout took, and thanks to imperceptible drag, there is no reward for the angler.

One of the most critical points of technique in fishing slower waters is fishing out your cast. It's always a temptation to abort a presentation when it's not going exactly according to plan, or when a trout rises temptingly within easy casting range. Resist that temptation. Do not start a retrieve or rip a fly off the surface when it's in the target zone—this puts fish down about as quickly and surely as anything I can think of. Fish out the drift as best you can, then make whatever adjustments are required on the next presentation. This is good advice for faster-water fishing also.

Slow pools often appear to lack structure, but this can be deceptive. Remember, it doesn't take much to protect a trout from slow currents.

Remember also that current flow is significantly slower near the bottom. Thus, small rocks and little hollows in the streambed become trout lies. Deep-cut banks also offer excellent protection, and make especially good holds when feeding lanes are closed.

The heads of pools, where faster currents enter, may literally scream "Trout!" at the angler, and certainly these places offer potential. However, do not ignore the lower sections of pools. Often, pools are so configured that a large protective pocket is formed near the tail. This is particularly true in cases where the bottom slopes upward rather abruptly—a bathtub effect, more or less. This creates a hydraulic cushion in that area, offering refuge to trout. These spots can be quite productive in early season, when cold water makes the trout somewhat lethargic, and comfort becomes a prime consideration.

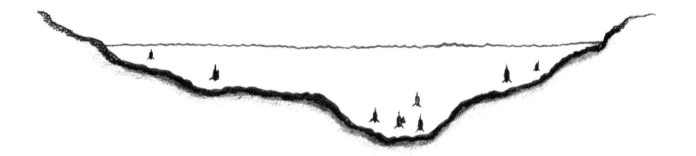

*Cross section of a typical slow pool, looking downstream. Trout are deployed in classic holding lies.*

Fortunately, trout are found in a great diversity of water types, so we don't have to constantly cope with the disciplines imposed by still pools. Let's now examine some other types of habitat and see how we might deal with the fish that live there.

## FASTER CURRENTS, BROKEN WATER

In between pools we find a practically infinite variety of faster currents. Some sections are fairly deep and have many readable holding spots. Others are shallow and not so promising, or at least not obviously so. These are commonly called riffles. They are characterized by fast, shallower water running over rather small rocks and stones. Structure is generally minimal, and protection from both current and predation is scarce. Thus, we generally wouldn't expect to find good-sized trout in a thin riffle. Typically, the population consists of smaller trout which are denied the more optimal locations occupied by their larger relatives.

There are exceptions, however. I vividly recall sitting with my friend Russell George on his patio, which overlooks a riffle between two rather large pools on the Beaverkill. Russell was complaining about the increasing number of ospreys in the area, and the amount of trout they were consuming. I observed, without much in the way of statistical backup, that the ospreys were probably killing a lot more suckers and chubs than trout, thus doing us anglers a favor. I had barely finished delivering that gem of wisdom when an osprey swooped down and picked a trout out of the riffle, neat as you please. It was a nice one—a brown of at least 12 inches, maybe 13. Russell just sort of smiled at me. I suppose I could have said that the next twenty fish that osprey caught would be suckers, but elected to keep my mouth shut instead.

What was that sizable trout doing in thin water, exposed to its natural enemies? Closer examination of the riffle, when we waded across to fish the pool below, revealed more structure than we had thought existed, so our read wasn't very accurate. However, I believe a more compelling motivation for the trout was the great array of insect life in that section of stream. A little rock rolling turned up scores of nymphs, some of which were stonefly nymphs of considerable size. Such inducements will cause hungry trout to take chances.

A great many species of aquatic insects must spend their nymphal lives in faster currents, because of the need for oxygenation. Thus, excellent hatches often originate in riffles, and also heavy spinner falls, as the insects instinctively deposit their eggs in the most appropriate habitat. This sort of activity will bring trout up into faster currents—the abundant food supply makes the effort worthwhile.

Regardless of how much food is present, the trout must still deal with the realities of the situation. Rises will be quick and lethally efficient, for there's no drifting with a prospective bite in this sort of environment. Decisions must be made almost instantaneously, or the opportunity is lost. This, coupled with the diffusion of the currents, makes the fish easier to fool. Leaders and lines are somewhat camouflaged, so a shorter leader with a stouter tippet is called for. Sometimes you can get away with a little drag, although it is still something to be avoided. Flies can be rougher and less precise, as floatability and behavior outweigh close imitation in order of importance. And the trout is less apt to be alarmed by anglers, as the rushing water masks our images and covers the vibrations caused by our footfalls.

As mentioned, trout can't hold languidly beneath the surface of a riffle, checking out the passing insects. When a hatch or spinner fall occurs and the trout move up to feed, you will notice that very specific feeding stations are assumed. The fish use the streambed and small deflections in the bottom as refuge, from whence they can accelerate upward through the shallow water, grab an insect and return. Therefore, the feeding station and the rise form are at the same spot, or very close to it. Presentations many feet above the target are neither necessary nor desirable, and drifts can be relatively short.

It should be apparent at this point that riffle or moving-water fishing is easier than slow-water fishing. Generally speaking, this is true, and I always try to introduce newcomers to the sport in such settings. However, high-movement water is not a panacea—there aren't many of those. Conditions must exist which will lure trout into this type of water, and proper technique must be followed, in order to effect convincing presentations—the water can't do it all.

Another type of water, one which more or less typifies many trout streams, is called pocket water. It is essentially infinite in its variety. Typically, it is characterized by visible and obvious structure—boulders, bends, all sorts of deflections. Of course, there is usually a great deal of less obvious structure also. This does not escape the eye of the experienced reader of water.

Broken water frequently represents the best habitat in a stream, especially for larger fish. I think of places like the Box Canyon on the Henry's Fork, the no-kill stretch of the Madison, the Wilmington Notch section of New York's Ausable, the Cornwall area of the Housatonic and many others. They all have a common attribute: the presence of excellent cover and prime feeding runs in very close proximity to one another. Trout are not commuters by choice, and the closer they can live to where they eat, the better they like it.

Readable as it is, broken or pocket water is not always easy to fish. Often the very structure which enables us to identify potential holds and lies makes it difficult to present a fly to the trout which occupy them. The swirling currents will wreck the drift of a fly almost instantly, be it wet, dry or whatever. The angler is faced with the challenge of planning and executing an approach and a presentation or sequence of presentations which will obscure his or her presence while enabling the fly to be shown to the fish in a realistic and convincing manner.

## WORKING WITH STREAM STRUCTURE

By way of illustration, let's survey a typical stretch of broken water and see how we might attempt to solve the problems it presents. The stream is good-sized, large enough to allow upstream or downstream methodology, or cross-stream fishing, as one chooses. The current is strong but wadable. There are many large rocks and boulders which deflect the current and create pockets. Some protrude above the water; others are slightly under the surface, identifiable by the swirls and boils they cause in the current. No trout are rising; however, we know they are present, and we can see numerous spots where they might lie.

You must now decide on a method. In the absence of insect activity and rising trout, a nymph or wet fly might be a wise choice—which is not to say a trout won't come to a dry fly in such a situation. So, the choice is yours.

The next decision is one of approach. Should you fish upstream or down? Which side of the river sets you up best for the type of fishing you intend to do? Where should you get into the water? What course should you follow, in order to maximize opportunities to present to the fish while minimizing the possibility of frightening them?

Conditions influence these decisions. You will want to consider the position of the sun, this being particularly critical on bright days. Try to keep it somewhere behind or to the side of you, or at the very least not glaring in your face, obscuring your vision and lighting you up like a billboard. True, it's poor practice to cast a moving shadow over trout, but from a wading position, that's unlikely to happen.

If there is a significant amount of wind, you will want to decide how best to position yourself. Sometimes, wind is the single most critical factor in how you decide to fish a piece of water. For example, if a strong wind is blowing directly downstream, you probably won't want to fish an upstream dry fly into its teeth. Does that mean you can't fish dry? Hardly. Some of my most successful dry-fly fishing is done downstream, using the variant casts described in Chapter III.

Almost invariably, you will want the wind at your back, if it is possible to set things up that way. Thus, the wind carries the forward cast while foreshortening the back cast, where there is usually less room. An exception is when a heavily weighted fly is being used. This greatly alters the aerodynamics, and casting becomes more a matter of launching a weighted object. Here, I actually prefer to cast into a wind, because I don't want my back cast ruined. I once nearly lost an eye when a powerful gust of wind stacked my back cast. The leader hit me in back of the head, wrapping twice around my hat, and the huge stonefly nymph I was using smacked me squarely in the left eye. If it had struck hook-first, I'd have become an instant cyclops.

Let's say you've taken all of this into account and have decided to fish downstream with a wet fly. Walk up the bank, keeping well back so as to avoid spooking fish, and decide where you want to start firing for effect. Then pick a point of entry where you can wade into position to make presentations to your first target area while disturbing things as little as possible. And while fishing that spot, think about where you want to go from there, and how best to move with stealth.

The large rocks in the model pool obviously provide shelter for trout, and your task is to put the fly to the fish in a natural manner. The idea is to use the currents, allowing them to carry the fly as they will, for trout instinctively position themselves so as to take advantage of the current's

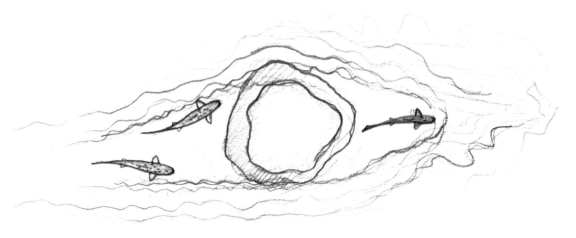

HOLDING "POCKETS" ROCK

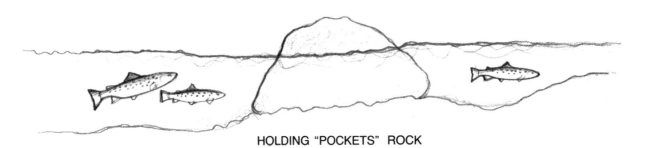

HOLDING "POCKETS" ROCK

*Top view and side view of "pockets" behind and in front of a boulder, with trout holding in typical positions.*

flow. Let's assume your first point of opportunity consists of a large boulder lying just under the surface, so that water flows over its top. This is an ideal setup; there will be a pocket in front of the rock, that hydraulic cushion mentioned earlier, and a large pocket in back of the rock, created by deflection. Simply cast your fly into the current approaching the frontal pocket, using a casting technique which creates a little slack—the S cast perhaps. The current will wash your wet fly into the pocket.

Having done what you can with the frontal pocket, you will next want to present to fish holding below the rock. The technique is very similar. Simply lengthen your line a little and cast slightly beyond the frontal pocket. Allow the current to swing the fly into the slack water below the rock, where the eddies will drift it about, as they would a natural. Pockets downstream of rocks can be quite large, so fish the entire pocket, front to rear.

If you were fishing dry, the tactics would have been very similar. The idea is still to get the fly to the trout in a natural-appearing manner, which in the case of a dry fly means a drag-free or detached-looking float. Again, you would use a slack-cast technique—the stop cast perhaps—to offset the effects of the current.

Now let's move downstream a little to the next good-looking target. This happens to be another large rock; however, it protrudes above the surface. The technique for fishing the frontal pocket is the same as before. However, a different tactic is required for the rear pocket, as the line and leader will not pass over the rock, as was the case with the subsurface one.

There are several possible solutions here, and the specific configuration will more or less dictate how best to proceed. You might be able to cast upstream of the rock, and as the far currents swing the fly into the pocket, gently flip the line or leader over the rock, so that the fly is carried into the target area. Or you might cast directly over the rock, allowing the current to slide the line off on the downstream side. Or perhaps the configuration is such that you can cast below the rock and across, so that the far current washes the fly into the pocket. You might even use all three techniques, in order to cover the pocket thoroughly.

While moving downstream, you will want to be reading the water constantly, looking for potential and thinking about how to exploit it. Sometimes two or more target areas can be covered from one location by extending the drift or innovating with the cast. This is good, provided a credible presentation can be made. However, don't attempt to cover an area unless you are sure you can execute convincing presentations from where you are positioned. It is poor practice to show the fish a bad presentation—it really turns them off for subsequent attempts. Keep in mind that your best chance at drawing a strike is usually the first time the trout sees the fly. So don't waste any casts, and make your first presentation to a spot an effective one.

Further downstream, you might encounter a stretch with faster current in midstream dropping off to eddies and slow water on one or both sides. There may well be excellent potential here—insects carried by the main current may wriggle or wash into the slower water, where trout are waiting to take them. I like to think of that line where the current drops off as a seam, with the trout positioned just to the slack side, where they can take advantage of the food supply in relative comfort.

Since real insects drift out of the faster currents and into the seam, or slow water, we want our counterfeits to behave likewise. Thus, we cast into the main current and follow the drift with the rod, mending and manipulating the line on the water so that when the fly falls off into the seam, it is not being dragged unnaturally. Once the fly drifts into the slow water or side eddies, we might raise the rod or retrieve a little line,

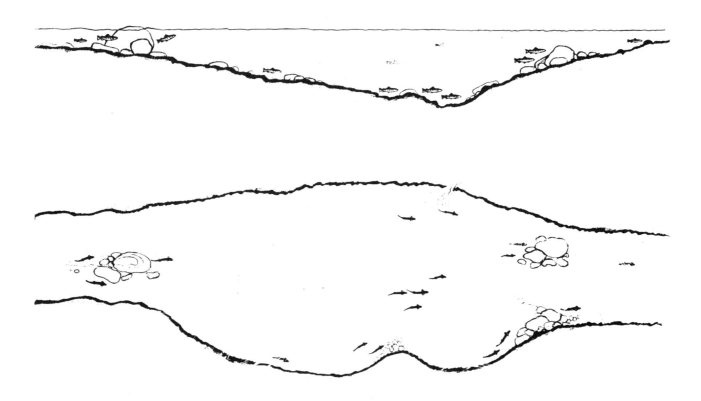

*Top view and side view of pool with varied structure. Trout in typical holding positions.*

swimming the fly, perhaps twitching it a bit, creating an illusion of aliveness.

Seams are excellent places to look for rising trout, as floating insects are often carried there by the currents. Quite often, the rises in a seam are subtle and difficult to see. The trout can take the fly with minimal effort, coming from the slack side, and the swirling currents cover the minute disturbances in the surface.

When fishing to a seam with a dry fly, it is essential to keep the line from dragging the fly. While it may be possible in some cases to accomplish this with casts across the main current and a lot of mending and tricky stuff, the recommended tactic is to get below the rising fish and cast directly upstream. Thus, the line follows the seam, or the slow water to the side of it, and travels at the same drift speed as the fly. When casting upstream over fish, be careful to cover the rise with the leader only—trout don't care for fly lines being dropped onto their backs. Usually, a prolonged float is not required in such situations, so that only the front portion of the leader need be cast over the fish.

It is also quite feasible to present a dry fly directly downstream to trout feeding in a seam. You simply execute a stop cast, allowing the line, leader and fly to drop to the water with some slack. The fly is then allowed to float right down the seam, with the leader and line following. Usually, sufficient drift duration is achieved merely by allowing the cast to flow along while extending the rod downstream. If a longer float is required, you can shake a little more line out onto the water.

Perhaps there is a deep-cut bank somewhere along our stretch of river. Such spots can be most challenging, for they are rarely easy to fish and frequently hold larger trout. On slower pools, it may be possible to fish cross-stream, employing the slack-cast, mending and line management techniques previously mentioned. However, your best bet is usually to approach from downstream, fishing the spot as you would a seam. The discipline is the same, which is to position the line and leader in the same line of drift the fly will follow, so that everything travels at the same speed and a natural float is obtained.

Suppose you had chosen to fish this piece of water upstream, starting from the lower end—how would the technique differ? If the choice is a wet fly or nymph, upstream fishing generally works best if the fly or leader is weighted. This allows the angler to use the stop cast and variations of it to deliver the fly to where the fish are. With a weighted fly, the stop cast tends to kick over, so that the fly is popped assertively into the target area.

Here again, you are concerned with not "lining" the fish. The idea is to cast the fly above the spot you consider to be the prime target, so that the current brings it back toward you, and to the waiting trout. A fairly long leader may be required, in order to cast far enough above a fish to get the desired drift, but without lining it. Also, the noncasting hand will be very busy retrieving the slack line created by the downstream drift.

The amount of weight used is relative to the situation—the speed of the current, the depth of the water, the amount of turbulence. In gentle currents, it may be negligible; in fact, it is sometimes feasible to fish a subsurface fly upstream with no more weight than the heavier-wire hook on which the fly was tied. In any event, don't use more weight than you have to—it complicates casting and causes the fly to behave unnaturally. It is desirable to get the fly down to the bottom, or nearly so, because that's where trout expect to see drifting insects. However, it doesn't take much to sink a fly which is drifting back toward you, because it is not being influenced by the leader, or at least very little.

When a slack-line, dead-drift method such as the one just described is used, it is important to be alert for strikes. Often, they will be amazingly gentle, and more sensed than felt. Sometimes there is nothing other than a subtle interruption of the line or leader's drift to indicate a take. For this reason, it's essential to use the noncasting hand effectively, so as to take up unwanted slack and stay in touch with the fly. Some type of strike indicator may be helpful here, particularly when a long leader is being used, and the line isn't able to do double-duty as a strike indicator.

The upstream dry fly is, of course, a classic technique, so much so that in certain traditional clubs on British chalk streams, downstream fishing is not allowed. The principle is the same as for upstream nymph or wet-fly fishing, which is to eliminate drag by having the line, leader and fly all traveling at the same speed. However, we are far more concerned with what the surface currents are doing. The subsurface fly sinks, and is less influenced by these phenomena. The floating dry fly is very much at their mercy, and so are the line and leader.

The most effective means for dealing with those infernal and seemingly endless swirls and boils that wreck our presentations is (1) to make full utilization of slack-casting and line-management techniques, and (2) to position yourself in such a manner as to minimize the effects of cross-currents and the like. This may include moving closer to the fish, or to where you think a fish might be. That is one of the advantages of upstream fishing—it is possible to approach fish more closely from behind. How closely depends on the particular situation, and is something you learn from experience. After having put down a number of rising trout, you begin to develop a feel for what these fish will tolerate.

By now, you have probably deduced that the eternal enemy of the angler is the presence of line and leader on the water. It is a necessary evil. The less line that is on the water, the fewer the line-management problems the angler must cope with. This is why it is best never to cast farther than you have to. It is also why I prefer a long rod—it helps me keep the line up off the water.

We could go on talking about structure and water types indefinitely, because of the infinite variety and uniqueness that exists within the angling environment. But a detailed description of all the stretches of water I've fished would be totally impractical—it would take another complete volume just to cover the major ones. What I've attempted to do in this chapter is to acquaint the reader with the basic techniques which form the foundation of effective fly-fishing. You can now spend the rest of your life refining them and adapting them to the nuances of the streams you encounter.

## SUNLIGHT AND SHADE

There are other tremendously important factors besides structure and current flow. One of these is sunlight, or lack of it. While trout are frequently motivated to come out and feed in bright sunlight, they really don't like it at all. The scientific community calls this proclivity for shunning light a "negative phototropism." I'll settle for dislike of light.

When one considers that the trout's most effective defense against predation is inconspicuousness, the tendency to shun light comes as no surprise. Other creatures of the stream appear to share this tendency. The best hatches of insects take place in mornings and evenings, when failing light makes the bugs at least somewhat less of a mark for every bird in the area. Dark, cloudy days also bring forth bountiful emergences—we see this in early season with our midday and afternoon hatches. True, some spring sunshine is needed to raise water temperatures. Even so, my most memorable experiences with the Hendrickson and other early-season flies have been on cloudy days.

The importance of this entire matter was underscored in the summer of 1985, when I finally was able to spend a prolonged vacation in the Rockies. Montana truly lives up to its nickname, Big Sky Country, and the adjoining states are similar. The sun is very bright, the skies often cloudless. Early-summer and mid-summer days seem interminable, as the sun inches downward toward the horizon. Many of the rivers are totally exposed to sunlight, as they run through wide valleys and flat plateaus— the Madison and the Railroad Ranch section of the Henry's Fork are prime examples.

While aware of the light/shadow phenomenon for many years, I have never seen it demonstrated so dramatically as during that summer. Generally, there would be morning activity, before the sun got too high—there's that angle-of-light-rays principle in practice. In midmorning, everything would suddenly slow down, and fishing would be very spotty throughout the main part of the day. Evening would bring increased activity, as the sun slowly sank and light became less intense. The best fishing, especially on the Madison, usually came just before dark, as the fish literally tore up the surface, gorging on late-evening insects.

In order to make the best use of my time and optimize my fishing opportunities, I began to scout out places which offered protection from the sun, such as the Madison Canyon and the Box Canyon on the Henry's Fork. There, I could at least work on fish that didn't feel as though they were in a television studio. I also learned to keep an eye on the weather. Frontal movements which brought cloud cover were Godsends. I recall several days on the Madison when the clouds rolled in, and in a matter of minutes there was insect activity and feeding fish. It was almost magical.

I did another thing that summer which really paid dividends. I located pools on various rivers which were well shaded at one end of the day or another. These I designated as morning pools and evening pools. I used them to extend the fishable hours of the day, simply by way of having shade later in the morning or earlier in the evening. The evening pools were particularly valuable, that being when the better hatches and spinner falls occurred. There were several spots where in mid-August the fishing would start at 7:00, while in the exposed stretches nearby, nothing happened until the last gasp, just as darkness fell. What a difference that made!

This is a practice I would strongly recommend to all fly-fishers who seriously want to improve their results. Learn the rivers you fish. Map the exterior structure—the pools and runs that are protected by bluffs, mountains, stands of trees or whatever, from either morning or evening sun. Use this information when planning your fishing day—it can make an enormous difference.

If clouds bring rain, as they often do, don't be dismayed—put on your rain jacket and have some fun. As stated earlier, we are the ones who don't like water—fish love it! Rain can help in several ways. It can bring down the temperature of a stream during warm weather, and raise the water levels to provide better cover. It can keep insects on the water where trout can get at them before they take off. And it helps us hide from the fish by distorting the window through which they see. Ever drive a car in a rainstorm when the wipers weren't working? That's about what it's like for the trout.

## TEMPERATURE

Having mentioned temperature, let's discuss that highly critical factor. There are temperature levels at which trout feel most comfortable and function best. Browns and rainbows are happiest when water temperatures are in the low-to-mid-60s range. Rainbows generally can tolerate slightly higher temperatures than browns, particularly in fast, broken currents which are better oxygenated. Brook trout like it 5 or 6 degrees cooler. Temperatures start to become lethal for browns and rainbows when 80 degrees Fahrenheit is exceeded, and above 75 degrees Fahrenheit for brookies.

When temperatures are optimal, fishing is generally at its peak. The trout's metabolism is at its highest level, and food is processed rapidly. The fish feel their best, and feed voraciously. Coupled with major insect activity, these periods of optimum temperature produce the fishing we talk about and think about all winter.

However, it would be a terrible mistake to think only in terms of prime time regarding temperature, especially low temperature. Trout are quite adaptable, and can survive amazingly well in lower-than-optimum temperatures for long periods, albeit with somewhat altered behaviorisms and biological functions. This extends the range of trout habitat to northern and high-elevation waters which never reach 60 degrees Fahrenheit, or even come close. It also accounts for the phenomenal success of certain "tail-race" fisheries, which are supported by extremely cold water from deep reservoirs, released through watergates at the bases of dams.

Trout will feed in colder temperatures, a fact I discovered many years ago when I bait fished. I have caught trout in waters as cold as 40 degrees Fahrenheit, and even a degree or two lower—it isn't very pleasant, but it can be done. One of the things I learned was that smaller baits worked better than large ones in cold water—little worms, tiny minnows, perhaps a couple of salmon eggs. At the time, I could not have explained this. Now I am aware that it has to do with the fish's reduced metabolism.

Cold-water habits of trout are characterized by several notable phenomena. They tend to hole up in quieter pools and more protected pockets, not relishing having to cope with currents. Feeding periods become progressively shorter with decreasing temperature. Feeding times run toward midday and afternoon, when what sun there is has its greatest effect. Food is taken in smaller bites, and is digested slowly.

Cold fish tend to be lethargic and do not move enthusiastically toward food. The angler who would be successful in cold water must compensate for this. Usually, it is the dedicated nymph fisherman who prevails here, slow-drifting small, dark flies along the bottom, working the water carefully with precise, repetitive presentations.

It is interesting to consider that much of the world's great trout habitat lies in cold, even frigid regions. For example, the gigantic rainbows of Alaska's Bristol Bay–Iliaska area spend their entire lives in waters which never reach 60 degrees Fahrenheit, and most of the year are much colder. What, then, accounts for their size? There are several factors. Perhaps the most important one is that they are allowed to stay alive a long time. Thus, while growth rate is slow, the fish live to be very old—an important consideration, as trout continue to grow virtually until the day they die. Food supply is extremely abundant, so that during the summer months when conditions are at their best, the fish can feed voraciously and grow a great deal in a very short period of time. Without having access to ecological data, I would also suspect the alkalinity of the water is quite high, which contributes to the welfare of the trout and the organisms in their food chain.

I also believe—and I emphasize the term "believe"—that trout adapt to colder temperatures over a period of generations. All creatures have evolved, and continue to evolve, ourselves included. In a constant environment, evolution is slow, as there is little pressure to adapt. Changing conditions cause the process to accelerate. Species which cannot adapt do poorly, and may perhaps perish, witness the brook trout of the northeast. I think it quite possible that given excellent habitat in other respects, trout can thrive at colder-than-optimal temperatures. The Alaskan rainbow phenomenon would tend to support this theory, as those trout have everything in their favor except temperature. To say they are of a superior strain is too simplistic—what accounts for the evolution of that strain? I have to believe habitat is the answer, cold waters notwithstanding. Can you imagine what those trout would be like if optimal temperatures prevailed over a long growing season? They reach 20 pounds and more as it is.

## TAIL-RACE FISHERIES

As I mentioned, cold-water tail-race fisheries exist below many impoundments. In some cases, this was not trout habitat originally, which lends some support to the argument that dams aren't all bad. As a generalization I wouldn't agree with that. They are *almost* all bad, and are managed badly. Still, there is no denying the quality of tail-race fisheries in such unlikely places as Arkansas, Tennessee and Georgia. As a by-product, these dams have created fabulous trout fisheries where none existed be-fore.

Tail-race fisheries are characterized by fluctuations in water levels, particularly where hydroelectric power generation is involved. Some are managed on a regular-release basis, and it is very important to be aware of the schedule. Not only will this optimize angling opportunities, but it will help keep you from getting into dangerous predicaments when waters are on the rise.

Fishing below a dam doesn't have to be dangerous; however, the potential is there, and tragedies have occurred. Thus, it is essential that you be aware, alert and mobile. Do not push your luck or indulge in any foolhardy behavior. When waters begin to rise, get to a safe place, even if that means leaving the river. Don't hesitate—waters can rise quickly, stranding the imprudent wader. As soon as you detect rising water levels, move.

As for fishing tactics below an impoundment, the same disciplines exist as for any trout river. However, conditions may be dramatically different from those on undammed rivers in the same area, because of the lower temperatures caused by the release of very cold water from the bottom of a reservoir, via gates in the base of a dam. Thus, an artificially cold habitat is established. This can be very supportive of trout, provided temperatures aren't too extreme—I've encountered that situation—and fluctuations aren't too sudden or drastic. Unfortunately, we see a lot of the latter.

Where releases are constant and temperatures are consistently cold, insect activity can be altered considerably. Emergences tend to come later in the year, when summer temperatures mitigate those of the frigid wa-ters. There is a particular river I fish which is part of the New York City water supply system that is noted for having consistently cold releases. As a consequence, we get a bountiful hatch of Ephemerella dorothea in July and August. Under normal conditions, this emergence would occur from late May to mid-June. Thus, it is often necessary to relearn the hatching cycles. The diurnal cycles also vary, as the insects take advantage of mid-day and afternoon temperatures. As a result, early-season conditions are simulated, whereby peak activity occurs throughout the warmer portion of the day, even in summer.

The big problem with tail-race fisheries is fluctuation. At this writ-ing, no amount of reasonable bargaining has been sufficient to convince the people who control water releases that trout habitat should be of any concern. No matter what the purpose of the impoundment—irrigation, power generation, domestic water supply—they do as they please. Often, this produces alternate flood-drought-flood-drought fluctuations and extreme variations in temperatures within very short time periods. This is harmful to trout habitat, and in severe cases can cause massive fish kills, particularly when an artificial drought is created.

Be that as it may, tail-race trout fishing can still be terrific. The main thing is to know your river intimately, for they vary greatly one from the other. You may have to play the high-tide, low-tide game, picking your times and places. Probably you will notice that fish redeploy as water conditions change, just as they would with seasonal variations in a normal river, but much more quickly. Rising and ebbing flows alter holding lies and feeding lanes—this the angler must adjust to. Lower water tends to concentrate the trout and the drift of food, and unless it is too low, this should be the best time to fish.

## SPAWNING MIGRATION

Another factor which can dramatically affect fishing potential is the spawning activity of the trout resident in the fishery. This is particularly true where a reservoir, lake or even the sea lies downstream. Trout tend to be migratory, some strains extremely so. As spawning time approaches, larger fish which have abandoned the river for the more abundant food supply below return to mate, providing the angler with a chance at fish not available throughout the season.

Perhaps the most dramatic example of the potential of a migratory fishery is the Great Lakes salmon-steelhead resource. After years of study and habitat assessment, federal and state fish management departments cooperated in a stocking program whereby steelhead trout and two species of Pacific salmon—king and coho—were introduced in selected areas of the Great Lakes. The results are legendary. Given an enormous food supply for which there was little competition, the fish grew rapidly to great size. A marvelous lake fishery was created for those who enjoy trolling and boat fishing. In addition, many streams now host generous runs of fish seeking to spawn, thereby offering the fly rodder a chance at really enormous game fish.

Despite the great migrations, natural reproduction is insignificant, and repopulation is achieved almost entirely by stocking. The returning fish are prevented from reaching prime spawning areas in the streams by impoundments and natural barriers, besides which they are not native to these watersheds in the first place. This is a blessing. Many of the Great Lakes feeder rivers have excellent trout fisheries upstream, and these could easily be ruined by an onslaught of enormous strangers.

The Pacific salmon offer some potential for fly-rod sport, but they are nothing compared to the steelhead. The salmon cannot feed, and are already in the process of dying when they enter the rivers—they actually deteriorate before your very eyes. The steelhead have no such fatal biological cycle, and will take various flies quite readily. Egg patterns, such as the Glo-bug, are most effective, as these fish become extremely egg-concious at spawning time. Certain western steelhead patterns also produce well, particularly the Skunk. In some streams, these fish will take nymphs readily, as their ability to feed does not stop during the spawning period, as with salmon. Look for steelhead in the Great Lakes streams from mid-fall throughout the winter and into very early spring.

The steelhead do tend to be somewhat leader-shy, so you can't use an excessively heavy tippet, great as the temptation to do so might be. Generally 3X and 4X tippets are required, depending on water conditions and the size and type of fly being fished. Sometimes 2X will work, when the water is a bit high or off-color. Even with the improved strength of modern leader material, it is no mean feat to land a 15- or 20-pound steelhead on 3X or 4X, and you can expect to lose a lot of the fish you hook. Just be sure your tippet material is fresh, and tie your knots with the greatest of care.

There are also angling opportunities created by spawning runs of a more normal type. Any stream that feeds a cold-water lake or reservoir where suitable habitat for large fish exists can be expected to have a migratory run of some sort. When this occurs depends primarily on the species of trout. Rainbows are primarily spring spawners; brown and brook trout are fall spawners. However, I have noticed that rainbows may also run up into the streams in the fall, tagging along with the browns. I have caught many nice rainbows in the Rocky Mountain rivers during fall brown-trout runs, though it was obvious from their appearance that they were nowhere near ready to spawn themselves.

While open seasons have been extended to allow autumn fishing on many rivers, quite a number are closed in early fall, so that spawning fish are not disturbed. This is a particularly important management policy in the east and northeast, where self-sustaining brown and brook trout populations exist. Nothing compares to the quality of wild trout, and we want to do all we can to ensure and enhance propagation. So even where fall fishing is allowed, be very gentle with these fish. Take particular care in handling and releasing ripe fish, so as not to cause them to spill their precious cargo prematurely.

When the subject of sea-run trout fishing arises, we tend to think of the incomparable steelhead rivers of the Pacific northwest, or perhaps the anadromous brown trout of the British Isles and Scandinavia. However, there is sea-run fishing to be found elsewhere, including such unlikely places as Long Island, Cape Cod, the New England coastal estuaries and certain Canadian streams. In recent years there has been sufficient recognition of the potential of this sport fishery that some tidal rivers are being specially managed. Certain streams now receive supplemental stockings of brown trout with the express intent that these fish become anadromous and run to the sea. The expectation, of course, is that they will come back to the stream to spawn. Brook trout will also become anadromous, given an opportunity, although I am not aware of any fisheries management programs involving migratory brook trout.

In the northeast, one of the best sources of information about migratory trout fishing are the state conservation departments. As I stated, they are becoming interested in the potential of these resources, as the popularity of the sport increases and fishing pressures mount. For that matter, the fish and game departments possess a wealth of information on all sorts of fishing opportunities, and can often provide maps at very reasonable prices. Don't hesitate to call—they are invariably polite and helpful.

## STREAMER FISHING

Writing about spawning runs and migratory trout got me thinking about streamer flies. I purposely did not cover streamer-fly fishing in this discussion of water types and presentation techniques, because I wanted to concentrate on dry-fly, wet-fly and nymph fishing, those being the bread-and-butter methodologies. But streamer fishing can be a tremendously effective and exciting method for those who practice it with a modicum of skill, so let us wrap up this chapter with a brief treatment of the subject.

Streamer fishing is a bit different. With drys, wets and nymphs, we are attempting to imitate insects in various forms, or in certain cases, small crustaceans that look and behave somewhat like insects. With streamers, we are seeking to imitate—or at least convey an impression of—small fish. Sometimes we do this with rather bizarre-looking fly rod lures which look about as much like a fish as Vincent van Gogh's *Starry Night* resembles the view of the heavens through the telescope at Mount Palomar. However, the fish don't look at it that way. They draw no distinction between imitator and attractor patterns, only between what they do and don't want to eat or attack.

I feel that in streamer-fly fishing, presentation is more important than pattern much of the time. Yes, there are realistic-type streamers which work super-well in the right situation—but only when presented with some artfulness. You could throw a dry fly onto the water with nothing attached, and in all likelihood a fish would take it—in fact, more readily than one tied to the end of a leader. Such is not the case with a streamer. It would just tumble meaninglessly down the river. It is the streamer's connection to the leader—and ultimately to the angler—which inbues it with a sense of purpose and credibility.

There are so many streamers and ways to fish them that it would require a major book to treat the subject in any depth. However, there are a few common denominators and basic techniques which will at least allow the beginner to get into the game. One of these is the concept of action. Small fish are constantly moving, sometimes vigorously, other times just enough to maintain position. When presenting a streamer fly, I strive to keep it swimming and in a life-suggestive attitude. Generally, the fly should be facing upstream, although there are situations when a cross-stream retrieve is effective.

The type of retrieve and how much action should be imparted is a matter of judgment and a function of water type. In fast, diffused water, it is often sufficient to merely guide the streamer into the pockets and lies, imparting little swimming movements and managing the cast so as to keep the fly in a lifelike attitude in the water. In slow currents, it is usually necessary to work the fly a good deal more, because the water isn't doing it for you.

This was really brought home to me during one of my Montana excursions. I had the privilege of fishing with Jack Gartside, a super fly tyer and highly innovative angler. We had miserable weather in September, which got the fish moving up out of the lakes into the feeder streams somewhat earlier than normal. Jack took me to several of his favorite haunts—large, slow-gliding pools where fish running upstream could hold in comfort. The drill was to cast across to the far bank and retrieve the streamer with long, rhythmic strokes. The retrieve was fast, yet between each stroke there was a slight pause. Jack's theory—and I believe it was totally validated by our success—was that the minute pauses convinced the trout that the fly could be had without undue effort, and gave them an opportunity to strike.

The pattern we used much of the time was Jack's original Soft-Hackled Streamer, which is made primarily out of marabou plumes, tied in a unique manner. This fly has unbelievable action. Wooly Buggers and sculpin patterns were also effective. The flies were slightly weighted, so that they would ride just beneath the surface, or in lieu of that, one split shot was added above the first leader knot. We used floating lines, so that we could mend the cast easily and keep the fly from nosing downstream.

This was exciting fishing. The trout were sizable and in a rather territorial mood, as they tend to be during a migratory run. Whether they were that intent on eating what they took to be a small fish or were simply reacting to the intrusion, I can't say—some of each perhaps. In any case, the strikes were jarring, with huge boils on the surface, because the flies only sank a few inches.

That's one way to fish a streamer. It won't work all the time—nothing does. There are situations where you will want to fish your fly deeper, getting it down to the trout, rather than trying to make them come to it. This is somewhat like fishing a sunken nymph, except that movement, rather than dead drift, is the objective. How much action? It's impossible to say precisely. Tease the fly around in likely-looking holding spots, working the structure of the stream, and experiment with more or less animation. Usually, the fish will let you know what they like.

When streamer fishing, I adjust my leader in two ways: I make it shorter overall and use a substantial tippet. The heavier the fly, the shorter and stouter the leader. For those excursions with Jack Gartside, I used 2X Dai-Riki most of the time, with an overall leader length of 7 to 8 feet. Dai-Riki in 2X diameter tests around 10 pounds, yet it is still sufficiently flexible to allow the fly plenty of action. The thing to remember is that with streamers you will be casting out of the target area, then using the current to position the fly as desired. It is this supervised interaction between the fly and the water that brings streamers to life and makes them enticing to the fish.

Choice of fly very much depends on the situation. If there is a natural forage fish present, one the trout are known to like, it would be wise to imitate it. Sculpins are abundant in waters across the country, so patterns which simulate this small member of the catfish family are generally effective, particularly the Muddler Minnow. There are still a lot of dace and shiners around, which can be imitated with various patterns, such as the Black-Nosed Dace. In waters where a lot of natural reproduction takes place, trout tend to be a bit cannibalistic, and a pattern which looks like the young of the predominant species—brown, brook, rainbow, whatever—can be highly productive. The message here is that there definitely is an imitative school of streamer fishing, where the game is to choose a pattern which looks natural and try to make it behave that way.

When fishing with imitative streamers, I generally prefer smaller sizes, so that I'm not asking the trout to take a stomachful in one gulp. This is relative, of course—in Alaska we often fish gigantic streamers which imitate salmon smolt—and there are rainbows big enough to pop them down like a jelly bean. On a hard-fished eastern river, it is advisable to keep in mind the size of the trout one might expect to encounter, and be a bit conservative—it is usually better to go a size smaller, when in doubt.

There is also the attractor school—that's what Gartside and I were doing with those surrealsitic creations in the episode described above. These methods work better on excitable, less sophisticated fish, like those spawners out west. Here, we are concerned with action, color, contrast. Larger flies often work well, particularly in big-trout country. Softer materials which breathe and pulsate in the water are favored—materials like marabou, rabbit fur and Flashabou, a recently introduced synthetic which shows great promise.

Reluctantly, I will conclude this chapter, resisting the temptation to ramble on ad infinitum. Fishing lore is best communicated in parable, à la Isaac Walton, and I would very much enjoy writing a Vade Mecum based on my misspent and overprivileged life on the streams. Perhaps, someday, I shall. Meanwhile, it is my hope that you will successfully build on the foundation provided herein, and enjoy the experience immensely.

# CHAPTER X _____

# *Getting Fish On, In and Off*

The reward for choosing the right fly and presenting it skillfully is a strike from Friend Trout. Then you may engage in the ancient and pleasurable ritual of hooking, playing, landing and almost always releasing the fish. This chapter sets forth a few basic guidelines for doing that.

We often fish for smaller trout these days, conditions being what they are. We can get into bad habits because of this, as modest-sized fish can be successfully handled with considerable nonchalance. Then comes that unexpected strike from a big fish, and we blow it with a spastic reaction or ill-conceived tactic, denying ourselves that jubilant moment when we hold up a large trout for all to see before returning it to the river.

It was a number of years ago, but I still vividly recall an incident on one of my favorite Catskill streams. There had been a recent stocking, and I was entertaining myself educating a pod of hatchery graduates that had been dumped unceremoniously off a bridge a few days before. They were hungry and desperate, and I had a hookup on almost every cast. I would then skid the little fellow across the water, quickly extract the de-barbed hook and send him off a bit more worldly-wise.

Eventually I became bored and moved down to a deeper section near the tail of the pool, suppressing a fleeting thought about changing my tippet and refreshing my knots. A few casts later I drew a strike and hauled back nonchalantly. To my great amazement, a huge rainbow trout exploded into the air, did a two-and-one-half somersault with full twist and surged off angrily downstream. One shake of the head and my Zug

Bug became his, an unwelcome souvenir of a close encounter, which in time would rust out or be rubbed loose against the streambed.

As my heartbeat subsided, the realization that I had screwed up on a trophy-sized trout came home to me, utterly and painfully—a rare opportunity gone. Furious and frustrated, I screamed a few expletives in the general direction of the departed fish, to the great amusement of two teenage girls who were watching unnoticed from the bridge. Truly, this was one of the low points of my angling career.

The first step in the process of bringing a trout to net is to engage the hook securely in its jaw. This becomes progressively easier the sharper the hook. Please do yourself a favor and carry a hook hone in your vest—and use it! Keep those points as sharp as possible—it makes a tremendous difference. As you fish, check the hook point frequently. Do not fail to do so after contact with the streambed or with a rock or tree limb on the back cast. Points can be blunted or broken off very easily by these casual encounters, particularly with delicate dry-fly hooks.

Another factor that has a great bearing on success is the health of your tippet and the two critical knots which connect it to the fly and the rest of the leader. Learn to tie these knots properly, as their breaking strength is a direct function of their configuration. Retie them frequently, certainly after a spirited set-to with a strong fish. Use knots which are most appropriate for the task at hand, as described in Chapter V.

Keep in mind that leader material is somewhat resilient, and knots will tend to loosen a bit just sitting. Thus, you should check the leader knots and snug them up or retie them after taking a lunch break or when starting out in the morning. And give some thought to the type of water and size of fly being used. Don't try to fish a large, weighted streamer with the 5X tippet you used during the hatch the night before—you're begging for trouble.

Much has been said about the proper technique for striking a fish. Of course, this is very much relative to the situation and the nature of the fish itself. On television we often see the violent and repetitive yanks required to effectively engage a large saltwater fly in the bony jaws of a tarpon, but that's neither necessary nor desirable on a trout stream. Here, the main ingredients in a successful strike are attentiveness and deftness. We want to react very quickly, countering the fish's take, but smoothly, and with no more force than is required to get the job done.

Except when fishing streamers, salmon flies or such, there is usually a bit of slack between ourselves and the fly, that being the artifice used to manage a drag-free presentation. When a take is seen, felt or sensed, this slack must be instantly taken up so that pressure may be exerted and engagement achieved. The first rule is, don't fish with an indiscriminate amount of slack—use only enough to obtain the desired effect. The less slack there is to deal with, the less hand and rod movement, and the quicker the hook is driven home.

The water itself can be used as an aid in hooking fish—in fact, they often hook themselves on the take, because of the moderate resistance of the water against the fly line. This resistance exists whether the line is submerged or floating on the surface. Thus, a striking technique which allows the line to remain in the water, more or less, is often more effective.

When a rod is jerked sharply upward, a little-understood reflex action is caused—the tip portion of the rod dips downward, toward the water and the fish. The more limber the rod, the more pronounced the reflex. Immediately following comes the recovery—the tip comes up, seeking to straighten. This exerts pressure on the hook, but said pressure is delayed and somewhat out of control. Thanks to graphite, this phenomenon is less drastic than it once was—those noodly-tipped fiberglass rods of yesteryear sometimes created serious problems for the angler in striking fish.

Over the years, I have sought to train myself to strike with a more lateral movement, and with some assistance from the left hand. I try to avoid that desperate upward surge, even when surprised by an unexpected take. Thus, I minimize reflexive rod action and enlist the water as an ally in helping me hook my trout.

Incidentally, there is an interesting technique which Lefty Kreh advocates and dramatically demonstrates. He shows how to strike a fish by driving the rod toward the water, rather than jerking it away. The movement is very similar to the power stroke of a roll cast. The effect is to pull the line sharply and instantly toward the angler, thus defeating rod reflex. I've tried it, and it works, though admittedly I haven't yet undertaken to change the habits of my angling lifetime. The only real problem I have with this method is that one must be in just the right position to execute it. Anyway, it's something for you to think about, and perhaps experiment with at some point.

There are times when the trout take so aggressively that any striking technique will work—it's nearly impossible to take the fly away from them. Other times, they lip the fly tentatively, and your reaction must be near perfect if engagement is to be achieved. This is particularly true in slower currents, where the trout can take an insect almost at leisure, and with minimal effort. When this is complicated by mini-drag created by little eddies on the surface, it can be maddening. The slower sections of the Henry's Fork of the Snake epitomize this condition. I've had days when strike after strike failed to as much as scratch a lip. It was as though the trout had no mouths. You can learn a great deal at such times.

Incidentally, this reminds me of an incident on the Henry's Fork which bears recounting. After trying for a half-hour, I hooked and subsequently landed a 21-inch female rainbow that had been delicately sipping small pale-olive Mayflies in a channel between the weed beds. The fish had five dry flies in its face, one of which was the size 20 Pale Morning Dun attached to my leader. The other four were diverse in nature, overdressed, and far larger than I thought a Henry's Fork fish would take at that time of year. So much for selectivity! So much for experience retention! I quickly extracted the five flies and returned the great trout to the stream, where a succession of anglers might benefit from its remarkably catholic tastes.

Very well—you are attached to one end of a fly-fishing outfit and a trout is fast to the other. How best to bring it to net? This again depends on circumstances—the size of the trout, the type of water, the strength of the terminal tackle. Small fish can be handled with a dispatch bordering on impunity—you simply let them jump or struggle a bit, and as they tire, strip them in. Landing larger trout demands skill, patience and attentiveness, often a great deal of each.

Once a fair-sized fish is hooked, I try to get it on the reel as soon as possible; that is, I dispose of the slack and play the fish with the tackle, rather than with slack line held in my left hand. There are several reasons for this, not the least of which is to avoid tangles which will prevent me from allowing the fish to take line.

Years ago there was a guest ranch on Montana's Boulder River called the Lion Head—it still exists, but is now strictly private. The ranch owned four miles of stream—prime water, which the guests fished at their pleasure. One evening there was a heavy caddis hatch, and I got a taste of what Montana fishing could be like when everything is just right. The swarm of insects brought up many of the old mossbacks that inhabited the deep pools and undercut banks, and the sight of huge dorsal fins and broad, spotted flanks set me to trembling.

I hooked two smaller trout of about 14 inches, fought them by hand, released them quickly and set to work on what appeared to be a porpoise somehow transplanted from the Florida Keys. It took, and immediately I recognized that I must get this fish on the reel. However, in my haste and excitement I had allowed some loose coils of line to accumulate around my feet. A snarl had developed, and as the powerful fish surged off, the bird's nest was drawn up against the stripper guide. For a moment, the leader held, as I pulled frantically at the tangle. Then the fish got impatient and popped the 3X tippet as though it were spiderweb. Again, that helpless, empty sensation. Another hard lesson for the eastern dude, learned after the fact, as usual.

Another reason for playing large fish from the reel is that it allows the utilization of the reel's drag system. However, this is strong medicine, to be used only at appropriate times, and with great discretion. When I'm salmon or saltwater fishing, I rely heavily on the drag to exert controlled pressure on running fish, and I select reels which are excellent in respect to the quality of that mechanism. With trout fishing, this is seldom the case. Usually, I set the drag quite light, as the main objective is that the spool should not revolve too fast and overwind. I may supplement the amount of resistance by applying a little pressure to the line with my fingers or, if the reel is an exposed-rim model, by fingering the rim.

It should be kept in mind that the tackle itself and its interaction with the water apply considerable resistance, even without employing the reel's drag mechanism. Water working against a fly line can create a great deal of pressure, particularly in fast currents, and where a lot of line is in play. Also—and this can be critical—the line passing through the guides can build up a very significant amount of friction. This is a reciprocal of the attitude at which the rod is held.

Let's elaborate on that last statement. Visualize that classic pose with the dramatically arched rod held at a severe angle to the water. The fisherman is really putting it to the fish—"giving 'em the butt," as the old-timers expressed it. Picturesque indeed, and perhaps an appropriate tactic where large game fish and heavy tackle are involved. But in a typical trout-fishing situation, this may well not be the recommended procedure, for the fish has to pull the line all the way up through the guides and over the tip before it can run line off the reel. Quite frequently enough resistance is thus caused that the trout breaks off or becomes unhooked.

One of the main tactics in playing a trout is to allow it to run off line, circumstances permitting. This is best done by pointing the rod right at the fish, so that it can take line directly off the reel, with virtually no resistance from the guides or the severe angle at the tip which exists when a rod is held high. Controlled pressure is then discreetly applied by the reel's drag and the angler himself.

It does not take a lot of heavy pressure to tire a trout, even a sizable one. I have done in many good-sized fish in short order by merely allowing them to fight against the line in the current. They don't seem to be able to keep themselves from expending energy wastefully while calculating how best to combat the situation. I've seen many rainbows literally leap themselves into exhaustion when a moderate dash downstream into a deadfall or brush pile would have almost surely have earned them freedom.

Salmon are a different story. From the day they go to sea as a smolt, they spend their time feeding heavily, building up an incredible reserve of energy against the time when they will return to fight their way upriver on the spawning run. When a salmon is hooked, that energy is marshalled for the battle—*all* of it. I will never forget that first Atlantic salmon from Iceland's Grimsa. It was only an 8-pounder, but it bent my 9-weight rod double and kept it that way for a very long time. You do not defeat a salmon by letting it exhaust itself against gentle resistance—you must virtually tip them onto their backs.

That goes for Pacific salmon as well as Atlantics, at least the species I've had experience with, which includes the sockeye and coho. I have the greatest respect for these fish when they are fresh-run from the sea, large silver salmon in particular, that being the Alaskan slang name for coho. I've yet to fish for west coast steelhead—that's on my list of must-do's—but I understand they are incredibly powerful fish also. It must be that oceanic influence—although I will say the Great Lakes transplants are no slouches—they can flat-out tear up your tackle.

Back to trout. When a good fish is hooked and a long and spirited battle is contemplated, case the area and quickly develop a game plan. You will want to keep the fish away from objects it can use to beat you—fallen trees, rock outcroppings, undercut banks, anything that might jeopardize the leader. You will also want to select a landing area, which ideally would be a calm, virtually currentless backwater or side channel, where the trout can't use the current against you. One of the most difficult places to land fish I know of is the lower Madison from McAtee Bridge downstream, because it is one big riffle. A hooked fish simply shoots out into the main current, makes a 90-degree turn and heads for Ennis Lake. There is no chance to get downstream of the fish or to keep it in the pool—there aren't any pools! You simply hang on for dear life and hope you can move the fish in near the bank before it works free, without breaking a leg in the process.

I mentioned getting downstream of a fish. This is generally desirable, as it gives the hook better purchase and influences the creature to swim against the current, in order to escape where it perceives its problem to be coming from. It is not always easy to get below a fish—sometimes, in fact, it's impossible. Use your good judgment.

It's usually much easier to land a big fish in slow, open water, as the fish has virtually no allies, and it's you against it. I have a very high success ratio in lakes and ponds. I did manage to lose my career dry-fly trout in a western spring creek last fall, however, and in a virtual lagoon. The fish had moved up into the current to intercept hatching Mayflies, and I hooked it there. It did a U-turn and cruised off downstream toward a slow pondlike area where the stream had been dammed. I was fighting a marl streambed, so by the time I got onto the bank where I could run after this animal, the fly line and 50 yards of backing were out. Still, I thought I was in control. That was before I saw the submerged fencepost, the only obstruction in the entire pool. The trout had looped my line around it and was swimming back upstream, shaking its massive head menacingly. It was enormous—around 8 pounds, I honestly believe, which is credible, as one of over 10 had been taken there the previous season. But it wasn't to be—the fish used the post as leverage and broke off. It all seemed so well rehearsed. I'm glad Bob Dodge saw that trout, as it is common knowledge that orthodontists from rural Ohio never lie.

Often, large fish are encountered which jump and tail-walk, particularly rainbow trout, Atlantic salmon and certain saltwater species. This is great fun and exciting to see, but it is also a moment fraught with peril for the leader. Fish go through some incredible gyrations in the air, shaking their heads, performing intricate gymnastic stunts and generally tearing up the neighborhood. All of this is very threatening to a taut leader. The angler must be alert and ready to give a little slack to a leaping fish, by simply lowering the tip of the rod or extending it slightly. The disciples of the Atlantic salmon call this "bowing to the fish"—and Salmo salar is certainly a fish worthy of being bowed to.

As the fish tires and is brought into the landing area, there is a tendency to relax and be prematurely jubilant. Resist that temptation, for this is a critical time. The fish probably has something left, and upon getting its first close-up view of the angler, is certain to shoot the works. You must be prepared to release line instantly and let the fish run—but it should be a controlled run, under an appropriate degree of restraint. We don't want the fish to get way out into the current again, if it can be prevented. When playing a fish from the reel, the angler has to be ready to let go of the handle instantly, so as to avoid breaking the fish off when a sudden surge occurs.

When the fish shows unmistakable signs of being played out, it is time for netting. I do hope you are carrying a net—it makes handling fish much easier on both you and them. The net needn't be large, unless you're a steelheader, or something like that. However, the net bag should be deep, to accommodate sizable trout. It is also important that the bag be of soft material. There are those who say that handling a fish in a net is harmful, in that it disturbs body slime and invites fungus. Harsh, abrasive bag materials, such as monofilament, lend credence to this position. Unfortunately, net bags are made of synthetics today, in order to eliminate rot and mildew. These are somewhat rougher on the trout than the old-fashioned kind, so we must be more gentle.

The moment at which a fish is ready for handling requires a little judgment. The idea is to tire the trout to the point that it may be handled gently yet can still be released with virtual assurance of survival. This means no heavy-handed grabbing, squeezing and wrestling two falls out of three. Usually, when a fish rolls over onto its side, it is ready—but take care. With a final lunge, a trout can wrap a leader around your leg quicker than you can play jump-rope in waders.

If the hook is debarbed and a pair of hemostats is at hand, the trout can be released quickly, and none the worse for wear. It is best to keep the fish in the water and handle it as little as possible. If you can lay your rod on the bank or tuck it under an armpit, both hands are free for the task at hand. I try to grab the bend of the hook with the hemostats, holding the net and resident trout in the water with my other hand. Usually, a quick tug disengages the hook, and the trout is left with nothing more than a pin-prick.

If it is necessary to hold or restrain the trout, do so very carefully—as I said, no wrestling. It's good practice to turn the fish over onto its back, as they seem to become disoriented and less inclined toward violent struggling. And be sure to avoid contact with the gills—they are very delicate and even slight injury can prove lethal.

Returning a trout to the stream isn't simply a matter of dumping it out of your net bag. First, you must be sure it can swim. After all, the creature has just been through a taxing battle. Often it is necessary to resuscitate the fish by holding it in the water, facing upstream in a swimming position. But don't work the trout back and forth, forcing water to pass through its gills backward. This can actually drown the creature. After a bit, its oxygen debt will be repaid, and the trout will dart off to reflect on its strange adventure in the safety of a deep pocket.

As the practice of releasing fish has become virtually universal among fly-fishers, we have become a generation of camera buffs. Certainly it's a wonderful thing to record your triumphs on film—however, it shouldn't be done at the expense of the fish's health. Trout can't be kept out of the water for long poses, so any picture taking must be done in a matter of seconds. I now carry a fully automatic self-focusing camera, which facilitates quick and easy shot taking. It also makes life easier for companions who are pressed into service as photographers.

The matter of kept fish is a highly controversial and volatile issue, and I will probably get in trouble with certain factions by even suggesting that a trout might be killed, ever. Rather than duck the issue, however, I would prefer to address it straight-on, so as to create some enlightenment. It's a bit like talking to one's children about sex.

Quite honestly, I enjoy eating a trout once in a while. It is a treat I must forgo on all but the rarest occasions, because I feel a strong commitment not to deplete the resource. Much of my close-to-home fishing is done in no-kill waters, so there is no question of thumbs-up or thumbs-down. But where it is legal to harvest a fish or two, the angler's judgment and sense of propriety are the governing factors.

Think about a particular trout resource—any one you care to name. It can support only a certain population of trout, and no more. Why? Because of the food supply—fish can't live where there's not enough to eat. Therefore, a process of attrition takes place which reduces the population to that which the resource can support. In some cases, over-predation can reduce a trout population well below that figure. The only predator capable of causing serious resource depletion is us. We humans, with our big brains and highly developed technology, are the ones who upset the natural balance.

There are waters which are so marginal they can only support trout at certain times of the year, and little or no carry-over is realized. Some of these waters are rather generously stocked by the state fish and game departments, in order to provide a recreational resource. While this isn't productive of the kind of sport that would interest a serious angler, it is still a viable program, as it expands the resource and provides opportunities for the casual angler. These are commonly referred to as put-and-take fisheries, and there is nothing wrong with killing fish there, because they will not survive anyway.

There are other waters which can support large populations of trout from a water-quality and food-supply standpoint but which have limited capacity for reproduction. Such waters are quite common today. One of the best examples I can think of is New York's Beaverkill. While there is some spawning, most of the fish originated in a hatchery. Although I am not in complete agreement with the manner in which the stocking program is conducted, I do agree with the concept.

The Beaverkill is managed as a quality fishery. There are two large no-kill sections where no bait fishing is allowed and all trout must be released. Outside of these areas, the creel limit is five per day, at this writing. Does that make sense? Apparently, the policy is reasonably compatible with the overall management objective. Many of the fish killed are fresh stockers, which have a low survival rate, even in top-quality habitat. The great number of sizable trout in the no-kill sections indicate that having the river partitioned as it is constitutes a viable policy.

The Beaverkill's main tributary is the Willowemoc Creek, a major trout stream in its own right. It differs somewhat from the Beaverkill, in that the spawning areas in the headwaters and tributaries are more productive. Still, it is managed like the Beaverkill—there is a no-kill section and a five-fish limit on the rest of the river. Does this make sense? In my opinion, no. I believe the Willowemoc could be a virtual self-sustaining fishery, and should be managed on a totally no-kill basis, except for perhaps the lower few miles near its confluence with the Beaverkill. Other than that, I don't feel that any trout should be killed in the Willowemoc, because of the spawning potential.

As you can see, there is no simple answer to the question of when and where it's okay to take a trout or two. The experienced angler who is intimately familiar with the waters he or she fishes can usually make an enlightened decision about whether a particular resource can afford to give up a few fish. As for the rest of us, we would be well advised to err on the conservative side and limit our harvest to when we are in a seldom-fished, remote watershed, a stocked pond, some place where it is obvious that overkill is not a problem.

Another thought. If you do decide to take a few eating trout, take the smaller ones. Nine to eleven inches is a nice size—they fit into a frying pan and can be cooked through without charring the outsides. Let the big ones go—they have proven resourceful enough to survive over time, and have earned the right to propagate the species.

Having made the decision to kill a fish, it becomes most important that it be properly handled. The flesh of trout is very delicate, and will not tolerate an inhospitable environment for very long. Therefore, the fish must be cleaned promptly and thoroughly and kept cool, or better yet, downright cold. See the series of illustrations for the recommended procedure in field dressing a trout.

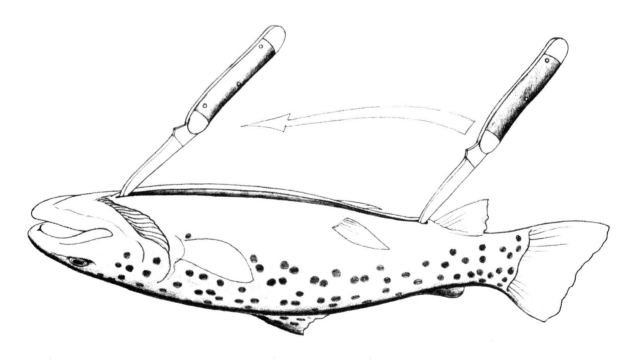

*Cleaning a trout. Begin by turning the fish belly-up and making an incision from vent to throat as shown.*

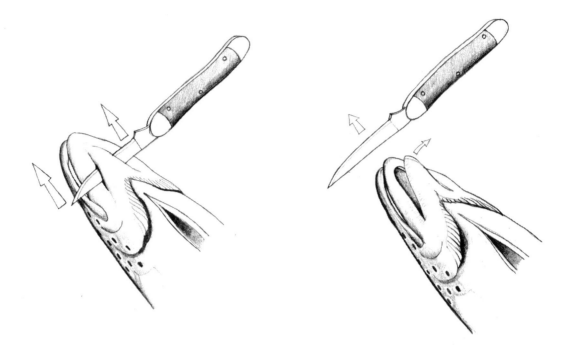

With the blade facing frontward, run the point of the knife through the trout's jaw at the base of the tongue, then cut forward, freeing the tongue.

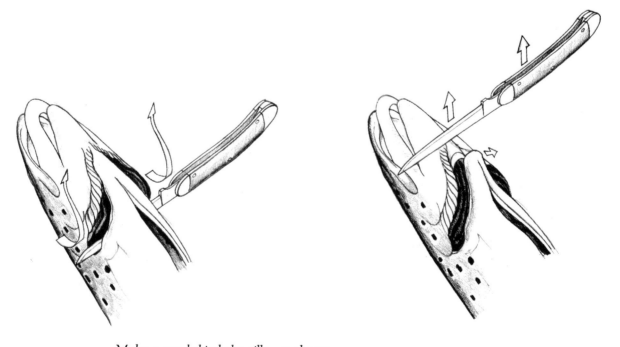

Make a cut behind the gills, as shown.

250

*Seize the tongue and pull backwards. The gills should come along, however, it may be necessary to cut them free where they join the roof of the trout's mouth, particularly on larger fish.*

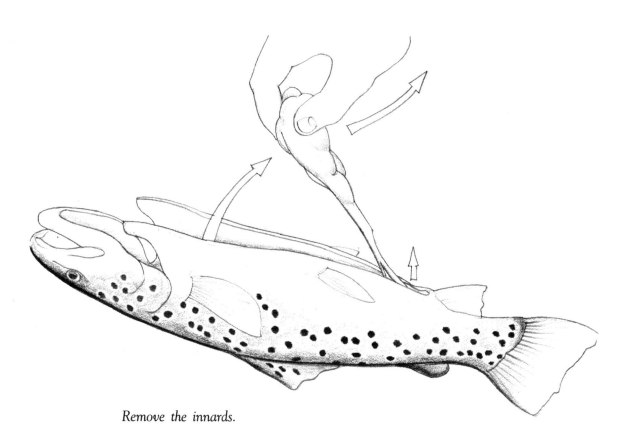

*Remove the innards.*

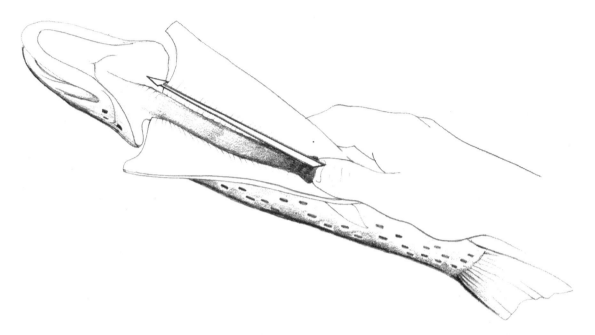

*Scrape out the blood clot along the spine with your thumb nail or the tip of a spoon, if you prefer.*

In chilly weather, trout will keep in a creel for a while—several hours, at least. The Articreel is a good model, as it utilizes the process of evaporation to keep fish cool. I always have an ice chest in the car, where I can keep food and beverages chilled. It also serves as a repository for that infrequent trout, such deposit being made as soon as possible. It's a good idea to keep some plastic bags in the car or stream bag.

Sometimes we find little isolated pockets of water where a trout can be kept alive until it's time to go home. This is an ideal situation. It is also quite feasible to cache a fish in a cool, shaded area, on a bed of moss or ferns. Sometimes a spring seepage keeps the ground almost refrigerator-cool. However, there is a security problem here, because the mink, raccoons and other creatures will be quick to make off with your catch. I've seen it happen. So hide the fish well, and try to stay fairly close by.

It was once thought that trout had to be eaten almost immediately, or they would lose their flavor. True, it's best to consume them promptly, but they will stay fresh and delicious for quite a while under refrigeration—several days, or even more. Keep them tightly wrapped in plastic, to avoid loss of moisture.

Trout can be frozen and kept for several months without incurring freezer burn, if properly wrapped. However, the best method I know of for freezing trout is in a solid block of ice. A half-gallon milk carton will hold several modest-sized trout, and makes an ideal receptacle for freezing. Trout preserved in this manner will keep indefinitely, and will taste stream-fresh when thawed. What a lovely treat around the end of January!

There are lots of fancy recipes for trout, and some are certainly delicious. However, I still prefer a pan-fried trout to any other. This is very simply done, even by non-cooks. Here's the procedure:

1. Put some flour lightly seasoned with salt and pepper in a paper shopping bag.
2. Throw in the trout, twist the tip of the bag to seal, and shake vigorously, so as to thoroughly coat the fish.
3. Remove the trout and scrape the flour out of the body cavity with your fingers.
4. In a frying pan large enough to hold the trout with heads and tails in place, heat one of the following:
   a. Strained bacon grease
   b. Clarified butter
   c. A mixture of half regular butter and half margarine
   d. The vegetable oil of your choice (peanut oil is great)

   Mixing butter and margarine has the effect of neutralizing the fat solids in the butter, producing a result similar to clarified butter. Whatever type of fat, grease or oil you choose, use enough to keep the fish well lubricated throughout the cooking process, but not so much that they are awash in it.
5. When the grease is sufficiently hot that the trout will sizzle slightly when placed in the pan, lay them in. You can test the heat by dipping in the tip of a tail.
6. Fry over medium heat until the trout are golden brown on one side, then turn and repeat. Cook thoroughly—steaks are nice when rare, but not trout. Test for doneness by inserting a dull knife along the dorsal fin and gently lifting the flesh. If it's done all the way to the backbone, dinner is ready. A 10-inch trout will take about 15 minutes, more or less, depending on the fire, the pan and the girth of the fish.

Often we are dealing with recently stocked trout, which are far more expendable than wild ones. While better feeds have improved the table qualities of these fish, they still do not have the flavor of "real" trout. Thus, I like to add a little seasoning to the flour mixture—a little dill or thyme or crushed rosemary, even a bit of garlic salt. Some of the packaged blends are quite tasty, such as Jane's Crazy Mixed-Up Salt and Laureleaf lemon-pepper marinade. Whatever turns you on.

An Indian guide once cooked trout for a group of us using a recipe that I found quite delicious, though I must admit to having had a few misgivings during the preparation. We were at a semi-wilderness fishing club in Canada, and the trout were both plentiful and large—in fact, on this particular day we hadn't taken a brookie under 2 pounds. These being well in excess of pan size, the guide prepared them as follows:

1. The trout were cleaned and cut into steaks approximately 2 inches thick.
2. In a large deep-sided pan, a mixture of half margarine and half unsalted butter was brought to high heat. Lots of the mixture was used, enough so that the steaks were slightly more than half covered when dropped in.
3. The steaks were deep-fried, first one side down, then the other. No batter, no nothing. The key is the temperature of the butter-margarine mix—it must be hot enough to sear the exterior of the fish instantly.

Here's another campfire recipe I particularly like. It works on practically any size trout, and can also be done at home, over a charcoal grill or in an oven.

1. Lay a cleaned trout on a large piece of aluminum foil.
2. Add the following: a little lemon juice, thin slices of tomato and onion or shallots, a shake of salt and pepper.
3. Fold the foil tightly around the fish and cook on a mesh grill over an open fire. Turn at the halfway mark. A 12-inch trout will take about 20 minutes.

Again, you can experiment with flavorings. A strip of bacon adds an interesting touch.

Unless limited by the size of the cooking vessel, I much prefer to cook and serve trout intact, with the heads and tails on. Not only are they classier in appearance, but they are easier to eat. There is an ingenious technique for dissecting a trout on a plate which does away with almost all of the bones. It was shown to me by Margaret Renner, who, with husband George, ran a lovely private trout club on the upper Beaverkill River for many years.

It's just the slickest way to eat a trout I've ever seen, and I can't thank Margie enough. Refer to the illustrations and captions.

Enough of the Julia Childs stuff. There is one other matter I wish to address before closing this chapter. I approach it with certain misgivings, as I wouldn't want to be misinterpreted as taking a position of advocacy. I'm talking about trophy fish for mounting.

I am not at all crazy about a lot of huge, dead fish hanging on den

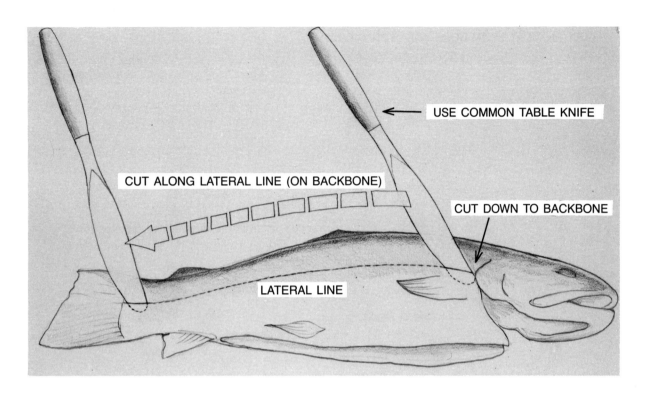

*Deboning a cooked trout. Begin by making an incision the length of the lateral line. Use a dull tipped knife and only enough force to keep the tip against the bone.*

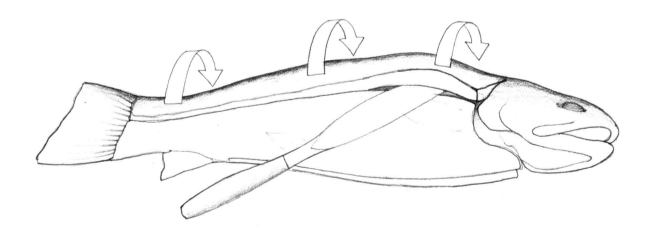

**LOOSEN MEAT FROM BONE AND "TURN" OVER**

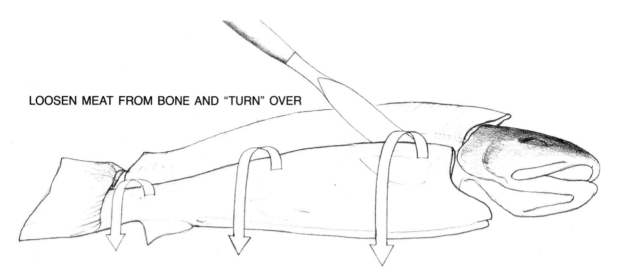

LOOSEN MEAT FROM BONE AND "TURN" OVER

*Using the knife blade as a spatula, gently separate the meat above the incision from the bones, roll it off onto the plate. Do the same with the meat below the incision, working along the rib cage.*

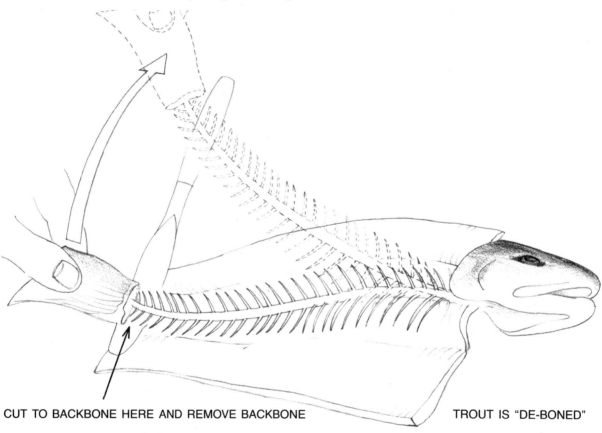

CUT TO BACKBONE HERE AND REMOVE BACKBONE          TROUT IS "DE-BONED"

*Insert the knife blade under the spinal bone, thus holding the meat against the plate. Pick up the tail and gently lift out the trout's entire skeleton. The meat is now virtually bone free.*

256

walls, although I certainly can appreciate a first-class job of taxidermy as much as anyone. Like the ancient Greeks said, "All things in moderation." I would only hope that anyone who wants a trophy makes it a point to take it from a resource which can withstand some discreet harvesting. As mentioned earlier, the more responsible Alaskan outfitters have put a stop to the killing of rainbow trout because it takes so long for them to grow to large size. The outfitters in Labrador's Minipi region allow one trophy brook trout per person per visit. That's the way it has to be if fishing quality is to be maintained. Here are some important tips for preserving a trophy, as related to me by an excellent taxidermist:

1. Carry a camera and immediately take some color pictures of the fish, using a high-integrity film, such as Kodachrome. Thus, the taxidermist can capture the individuality of the particular fish.
2. If you are near refrigeration facilities, don't field dress the fish. Wrap it immediately in cloth or absorbent paper and keep it wet. Prepare it for freezing by rewrapping in cheesecloth or freezer paper and over-wrapping with plastic material. Wrap very tightly, and freeze it solid. When it's time to take the fish to the taxidermist, deliver it still frozen.
3. If you don't have access to a freezer, follow this procedure: field dress the fish by deciding what side will go against the wall and removing the innards through an incision in that side. Carefully cut out the gills. Wrap with wet newspaper or toweling and keep the fish as cool as possible. Unless the taxidermist is immediately accessible, follow the freezing process as soon as facilities are available.

Top taxidermists are rare, expensive and very busy. It may take as long as two years or more before your mount is completed. Be patient, do not compromise, and pay the going rate for first-class work. I've seen some very beautiful fish reduced to hideous caricatures by well-intentioned but unskilled amateurs, and that is nothing short of a crime.

# Equipment Maintenance, Care and Rx

You will derive far more pleasure from your fly-fishing equipment, and also avoid unnecessary hassles and expenditures, if you devote a little time and effort to maintenance. This requires no major commitment—in fact, it is really a pleasant off-season activity which will help fill those winter days, until you get hooked on fly tying.

In addition to preventive maintenance, we will touch on a few fixes for problems which are commonly encountered on the stream. A little first-aid training in this area can save a pleasant day and keep it from becoming a misfortune.

## RODS

Graphite and glass rods require little maintenance; however, there are a few important considerations:

1. Check the guides for wear. Worn guides will quickly eat up a fly line. Have them replaced as soon as they show any signs of wear.
2. Check the windings which secure the guides in place. Today's polymers do a great job of protecting windings, but nothing lasts forever.

3. Lubricate the ferrules with a piece of paraffin or storm candle, as mentioned in Chapter I.

4. If you have a bamboo or older glass rod with metal ferrules, keep them clean. Acetone does a fine job. Rub it onto the male ferrules with a piece of cloth, then use a cotton swab to clean the female ferrule. If you wish, you may lubricate metal ferrules with a thin coating of very light-viscosity oil. Do not use steel wool under any circumstances. If you have a recalcitrant ferrule, take it to an experienced rod mechanic.

5. If ferrules do stick, follow the procedures described in Chapter I for unjoining them.

6. Be sure your rod is dry before putting it away in its bag and tube. This is absolutely critical with bamboo rods and any rod which has bronzed guides.

7. Don't expose rods to heat. I once knew someone who destroyed two rods by carring them in the trunk of a car which had a faulty exhaust system.

8. Be very careful of rods around automobiles—car doors and tailgates are potentially lethal. Watch out in boats and canoes also—I had a rod broken while floating the Box Canyon. It was a spare I had brought along, just in case. It should have been kept in a rod tube.

9. Exercise caution when walking through thick woods and brush. Actually, it's best to dismantle the rod for longer walks, but failing that, at least carry the rod butt-end first.

Should you opt for a bamboo rod, some additional care and maintenance procedures are in order, as follows:

1. It is best to store the rod with the sections standing on end in a rod rack. If you must store it in its bag and tube, be sure it is kept away from moisture and leave the cap off the tube.

2. Avoid contact with insect repellents and solvents—they will eat the finish.

3. If a ferrule is loose or won't seat fully, get the problem fixed before fishing the rod.

4. Don't use supplemental weight or heavily weighted flies with a bamboo rod.

5. Don't overline the rod—use the AFTMA-recommended line weight. Also, don't fish with old, worn-out lines, as they are probably full of cracks and will absorb water, which greatly increases their weight.

6. When engaged in a long battle with a heavy fish, turn the rod over now and then, so that it is flexed in the opposite direction. This will help avoid putting a set in the tip.

**7.** If the rod has two tip sections, use them alternately and equally.

In my vest I carry several items which can be real life-savers when a minor emergency arises:

**1.** Ferrule cement—for reaffixing a loose tip guide.
**2.** Butane lighter—for melting the ferrule cement.
**3.** Narrow plastic tape—for securing a guide which is losing its windings.

In my car bag, I carry a small selection of guides in a pill bottle, for emergency replacement, using the plastic tape. Included are several tip guides of various sizes. Thus, if I or a companion should break a few inches off the tip of a rod, a slightly larger tip guide can be put on with the ferrule cement, and the rod can be used temporarily. I also carry a couple of pieces of surgical tubing which can be used as grips when un-joining rods with stuck ferrules.

Incidentally, loose ferrules on graphite or glass rods can be snugged up with a very thin application of automobile belt dressing. I doubt this would work very well on metal ferrules, with their critical tolerances, although it might suffice as a stop-gap measure.

There may come a time when you will want to clean the cork grip of a rod, as they become soiled eventually from being held by fishy hands. A solvent will do the job, but care must be taken to limit contact to only the cork, as it may damage rod windings and finishes. The grip can be cleaned up further by the judicious application of extremely fine-grit sandpaper, but don't get carried away—you don't want to alter the shape and size of the grip.

## REELS

Fly reels, particularly the single-action type, are so simply constructed that a good one, given adequate care, should last an angling lifetime and more. Very little is required in the way of maintenance.

To protect the finish, the reel should be kept in some sort of case—a leather bag, or perhaps one of the handy neoprene cases Simms puts out, which can be put on while the reel is attached to the rod. As with rods, dry off the reel before putting it away.

At least once a year, give your reels a thorough cleaning and lubrication. Remove the line and backing, also the spool. Then wash both the spool and reel proper in gasoline or a similar solvent, getting at all the little recesses and crannies where residue accumulates.

Put a pea-sized dab of Teflon grease, gun grease or Vaseline in the mouth of the cylinder where the spindle goes, then replace the spool and crank it for a moment to distribute the grease. Remove any excess with a paper towel. Coat the reel and spool with a light spraying of WD4O, and wipe off the excess. Incidentally, don't use oil in place of grease on a reel; it's too runny. The exception is if it becomes necessary to lubricate the handle assembly.

If you have any complex reels with sophisticated drag systems and/or multiplying gears, it's important to understand their idiosyncrasies before taking them apart and cleaning them. Take advantage of any manufacturer's literature, and don't hesitate to write or call for assistance. Some shops have an employee who is a reel maven, and those persons can be most helpful. If by some rare chance you should come by a Bogdan reel, maintenance information should be obtained either from Stan Bogdan himself—at this writing he lives near Nashua, New Hampshire—or from Bill Hunter, in care of Hunter's Angling Supplies, New Boston, N.H. 03070.

If a reel or spool is dropped in a sandy or gravely area, there's an excellent chance it will pick up some particulants. Should this occur, wipe out the reel and spool thoroughly with a tissue or whatever is handy. If any catching or grinding persists when the handle is turned, further cleaning is mandated. Don't use a reel with any sand particles in it—they are very hard and can score the metal.

Reels are held together by a number of small machine screws. It is wise to tighten these periodically, as a precautionary measure. Don't overlook the ones which hold the mounting shoe to the reel proper. If a screw tends to loosen repeatedly, put some screw-lock or a small drop of shellac in the socket.

It is possible that the line guide on a reel may become worn and grooved, just like guides on a rod. This also will eat a fly line. Inspect the line guide periodically, and replace the part at the first indication of wear. Most are held in place by one or two screws.

## LINES AND LEADERS

As I stated earlier, today's synthetic fly lines are far more durable and maintenance-free than the old silks, but they are not indestructible, and some basic TLC will ensure good performance and long life.

1. If you should get hung up on a tree or someplace, don't yank hard on the line, as it will stretch and cause cracks to develop in the finish. Work it free gently.
2. Do not use a petroleum or solvent-based dressing on a line—it will interact with the plastic.

3. Do not expose the line to excessive heat—for example, don't leave a reel on the dashboard or rear deck of a car, where the sun will beat on it.

4. Closely related to the preceding item, don't expose the line to direct sunlight unnecessarily.

5. Keep insect repellents away from fly lines.

6. Keep your fly line out from underfoot. Don't walk on it against a boat deck or stream bottom.

7. If you must use a good line for practice casting, do it on water or grass—don't cast it onto a parking lot or gym floor.

Keep your fly lines clean. One of the main reasons a new line floats best is that it hasn't had the chance to pick up any extraneous material. Floating lines collect residue as they are fished, especially if some sticky silicone floatant is applied—which is why I don't approve of them. Lines can be cleaned quickly and easily with Bon Ami or dish soap and warm water.

Vinyl upholstery and car-top cleaners also do a great job on fly lines. Amway is one of the best, much as I hate to admit it. Besides cleaning the line, it creates a slick coating which allows the line to shoot through the guides more easily. It is best to apply such a cleaner the day before and polish thoroughly. If the line is fished too soon after the cleaner is applied, it will wash off quickly.

Floating lines have a certain amount of memory, and tend to come off the reel in tight coils after periods of nonuse. These may be quickly removed by gently stretching the line with your hands. The key word is "gently"—remember that lines will crack if they are overstretched.

Modern lines will tolerate being left on the reel over the off-season, but it isn't the best practice. If you care about your lines, remove them from the reel spools and clean them, as described. Then store them in large coils held in place with four twisted pipe-cleaners or baggie ties, evenly spaced. Be sure to attach labels that identify the weight and type of line—for example, DT6F. If the leader is removed, have some means of identifying the end of the line you wish to reattach to the backing the following season, especially if the line isn't a double-taper. If you have whipped a loop into the end of the line, that's identification enough.

As for leaders, the only part I try to save is the butt section, which is needle-knotted to the line. I inspect the knot and the line adjacent to it for wear, and if any is in evidence, the butt is replaced. I tie my own leaders, so I simply add the required sections to the butt. If you use store-bought leaders, they can be retained, provided they are in good condition. However, the tippets should be clipped off and replaced before going astream the next season.

## WADERS

Some types of waders require more care than others, because of the material used in their construction. Pure rubber and rubberized-canvas models are particularly critical because they degenerate in direct sunlight or in subfreezing temperatures. To be on the safe side, it is best to treat all waders with the tender loving care required of the two types just mentioned, for quality wading gear is one of the most critical investments the angler makes.

It is recommended that all waders be hung up to dry after use, both inside and out. Even if the waders are perfectly watertight, they accumulate moisture from perspiration, especially in warmer weather. It's a lot more pleasant and considerably easier to slip on a dry pair of waders the next morning, rather than clammy ones.

Stocking-foot waders can be turned inside-out, once the outsides are dry. For that matter, boot-foot waders can be treated likewise, except for the feet. However, I prefer to hang boot-foot waders, either upside-down from boot hangers or right-side-up by the suspender connectors. Don't hang them by the suspenders proper, or the stretch will be dissipated. They seem to dry faster and air out better when hung right-side-up.

I wouldn't recommend storing any wader in freezing temperatures, but whatever you do, don't subject rubber or rubberized canvas to such temperatures. Extreme cold causes rubber to crack, and your first journey astream the following season will be a very wet one.

It's a good idea to carry patching material in the fishing vest. What kind depends on the type of wader. In the case of rubber and rubberized canvas, there are many substances that will readily adhere to them, such as Pliobond, Barge Cement and the stick-patching stuff that is heated with a flame and daubed on. The latter is great for quick patching. So is duct tape, which sticks to rubber very well indeed. Naturally, the surface must be dry for any of these to work.

Life gets more complicated with waders constructed of the various synthetics which continue to come into the marketplace. I will give you an example. In the late 1970s I did some field testing for Red Ball, who were coming out with a new ultra-light stocking-foot wader. Some time after the test was over and I had sent in my observations, I sprung a leak. I tried to patch it with the quick field-patch stick stuff, but it wouldn't hold, so I resorted to slow but usually dependable Barge. It wouldn't hold either. Intrigued, I kept applying cements until one worked, which, to my amazement, was Pliobond, which doesn't hold on many synthetics. Since that time, Red Ball has changed the composition, and Pliobond works no longer. Now one must use the patching tape put out by the manufacturer.

Of course, there may be another adhesive that will stick to whatever the Red Ball waders are made of, but I haven't yet found it.

Understand that I'm not bad-mouthing Red Ball—in fact, I like and use their product. Certainly we can expect the wader companies to continue to utilize new fabrics in an effort to create better products. I do feel they should be very explicit about what adhesives can be used to repair their waders, however, because leaks in waders are in the same category as taxes—you can't avoid them indefinitely.

Neoprene waders are patchable, using a substance called Aquaseal. It actually interacts with the material and the patch becomes stronger than the area around it, like a weld. I have recently been informed that Aquaseal works on other types of waders, including the Red Ball. I'll pass that along, although I haven't had a chance to try it out. The same source tells me Goop also sticks to Neoprene and is particularly good for sealing leaky seams. Incidentally, Goop and Shoegoo are very similar, and I think either would do the job.

Synthetics have also complicated the process of putting felt soles on waders and wading shoes. Back in the days when everything was rubber or leather, Barge Cement was the answer. With synthetics, it's problematical. Acting on a tip I picked up in a magazine, I tried using PVC pipe cement for gluing felt to a pair of vinyl-soled wading shoes. It didn't hold. I wish I could be of more help to you in this area, but the several manufacturers I contacted were disinclined to give specifics about adhesives.

This much I can say—if you want to refelt a wading shoe or boot foot over worn felt, Barge is in a class by itself. The following procedure can also be used on rubber and leather, as stated:

1. Clean and rough up the surface, using a wood rasp or very coarse sandpaper. If you are felting rubber boot feet which have raised ribs or cleats, cut them off with a knife.
2. Cut the new felt soles and heels to shape and label them "left" and "right."
3. Put a thorough and generous layer of Barge Cement on both surfaces and let it dry for 24 hours at room temperature.
4. Put another layer of Barge on both surfaces and let it get very tacky, which will take 20 or 30 minutes. Then carefully position the felts onto the soles. Get them exactly right the first time—you will not be able to make an adjustment.
5. Pound the daylights out of both soles and heels with a heavy stick, like a sawed-off broom handle. Beat on each surface for a couple of minutes. It is helpful to insert shoe trees before doing this.
6. Bind the two feet with strips of rubber cut from an old inner tube,

then tape the strips in place and let dry for a least 24 hours at room temperature.

Replacement felts are sold in fishing shops, sometimes in kit form, with a tube of Barge included. The problem is, there's only about half enough Barge for the job. Barge can be obtained at shoe repair shops and places that supply these shops. It comes in various quantities. Don't buy an overly large container, as it doesn't store all that well after being opened. If you must store some excess, keep it in the refrigerator and rub some Vaseline around the threads where the cap goes, so that it can be opened some day without a pipe wrench.

If you wish to create a metallic surface while refelting, this can be done by driving some aluminum rivets through the replacement felts and spreading them by striking them with a hammer against a hard surface, such as a concrete sidewalk. Use a hand drill to put holes in the felts, creating a pattern which distributes rivets around the edges and middle portions of both the heels and main soles. Then proceed with the Barge process—it also sticks to metal. If aluminum rivets aren't available, aluminum or galvanized nails will work quite well—the ones with the big flat heads. Drive them through the replacement felts inside to out, then cut them off with wire cutters so that they protrude a bit, like the studs on a snow tire. It is best do do this between the first and second applications of Barge.

## FLIES

Because I am a fly tyer, I admit to a degree of laxity in caring for the flies in my stream boxes. This is due to sloth, not ignorance, and I expect to improve my habits at some point, when I begin to tire of those long nights at the vise. At any rate, here are the procedures I suggest for storing flies over the winter months.

Dry flies need the most TLC. Ones which have been used can be restored to near-new condition by placing them in a sieve and holding them over a jet of steam. Store them in a cardboard or wooden box, turned up on their noses to save the hackles. You might also want to inspect the heads and if they appear to need protection apply a drop of cement with a needle.

Other types of flies may not require steaming; however, it's a good idea to sort them out and neaten them up a bit. Then lay them out in cardboard or wooden boxes also. Why do I specify wood or cardboard? So that moth repellent can be added without fear of it melting plastic, which some types will do.

At some point during the winter, it is advisable to inventory your fly collection and think about what needs to be tied or purchased for the following season. Fly tyers greatly appreciate lots of advance notice. When sorting, keep a hook hone nearby, and touch up those points which were dulled over the previous year.

## FISHING VEST

By the end of an active season, your fishing vest is generally in need of a good washing. Remove anything that's pinned onto the garment, and empty the pockets. Wash the vest on a gentle cycle and hang dry, or take it to a dry cleaner.

Velcro is becoming increasingly popular for securing pockets, but most vests still have some zippers also. A little Teflon grease or naval jelly will keep these in smooth working order. It's a good idea to check the stitching which attaches the zippers to the vest, as these tend to come undone with time and use.

## TOOLS, IMPLEMENTS AND GADGETS

Off-season affords ample opportunity to sort through the various items carried in the vest or car bag and put them in first-class condition for the next season. Is that nail-clipper getting dull? Replace it or sharpen it. Also sharpen your knife, and apply a coating of rust inhibitor. Put a drop of light oil on the metal hinges of your flyboxes.

Inventory your tippet material, and be honest with yourself about its age. I don't recommend keeping fine-diameter tippet material longer than a year or so, fine meaning 3X and smaller. This is not a good place for false economy—leader material doesn't cost much and is very critical, as we have learned.

Inventory the other items in your arsenal also. Be sure you have enough wader patch, lip balm, sunblock, fly floatant, small sinkers and whatever. Think about how you might want to supplement or improve your setup. Did the lack of some implement cause problems last season—a hook hone, or perhaps a bodkin for picking out knots and clearing hook eyes? Put it on your winter shopping list.

Try to keep your fishing gear in one area, as far as that is possible. As the new season approaches, check to see that you have what you need and know where everything is. The night before your first trip is no time for a scavenger hunt, and a little organization can save a lot of aggravation.

# CHAPTER XII _____

# Love It
# or Lose It

Up to this point, the purpose of this book has been to provide an orientation which will enable the reader to fly-fish with competence, and thus enjoy the great pleasures this pastime offers. However, none of this has any value or application if there are no trout, and perhaps no water pure enough for trout to inhabit.

Does this sound far-fetched? Consider that over 85 percent of all waters once inhabited by trout have been ruined by acts of man—pollution, impoundments, channelization, and so on. That leaves less than 15 percent for the growing multitudes of anglers, a figure to keep in mind when wondering why you seldom have a pool to yourself.

Sounds ominous, doesn't it? Even hopeless perhaps? Well, it's *not* hopeless—in fact, there are reasons for optimism. All it takes is a strong enough commitment and resolve on our part to see to it that no more trout water is destroyed and that all that is salvageable is reclaimed. Fortunately, we live in a society which has a legal mechanism for achieving things of this type.

Yes, this sounds political—and it definitely is. Did you actually think that in trout fishing you had discovered a source of pure joy, untouchable by the financially insatiable developers who are squeezing the juice out of the world, and the political animals they try to put into office to foster their interests? No way. We have evolved a social attitude which exalts money totally out of perspective to all else. When everything has a price tag, anything becomes expendable, including trout streams. Even the completely valid and totally documented arguments pertaining to human needs for pure water cut no ice.

Consider the case of New York City. Nearly two centuries ago, this burgeoning young metropolis had reached a point where its needs—or wants—for water exceeded the output of its aquifer. So, the city politicians rolled out their checkbooks and began buying up rivers. Those residents of then-rural Westchester and Putnam counties who lost their farms, homesteads and businesses were out of luck—the political machine had enough clout to simply take what it wanted.

By the turn of the twentieth century, the magnificent Croton River system and all of its tributaries were reduced to nothing more than a series of slowly eutrophying artificial lakes—but still more water was needed. So, the ever-thirsty metropolis looked farther north, to the Catskills. One by one, the legendary trout rivers met their fate—the Rondout, the Neversink, the Esopus, the Schoharie, both branches of the Delaware—all were dammed, and their precious flows diverted into a municipal water-supply system so wasteful and inefficient that much of the water is lost to leakage and misuse.

With the angling renaissance of the 1960s and the coincident environmental movement, many people became concerned about this situation. Attempts were made to negotiate with New York City on such matters as regulating flows from dams, repair of distribution facilities and control of water use. They laughed at us—arrogantly, sardonically laughed. It became immediately apparent that no scientifically valid, socially responsible program was acceptable to the city's political establishment—all they cared about was maintaining the status quo.

So that's the sort of thing we are up against. I singled out New York as an example, but they aren't the only villains—far from it! At all levels municipal, state and federal—bureaucracies are grinding away at all of our natural resources, water in particular. For many decades the Army Corps of Engineers has spearheaded civil projects of vast proportions whereby rivers are dammed indiscriminately, with no consideration of the consequences. A bunch of human beavers in uniform run amok. How can this happen—what is the military doing mucking around in civil programs? Who authorized such a boondoggle? Congress, that's who—the folks who represent you. How many of you feel the rubber-stamping of these pork-barrel projects is in your best interest, or that of the country? I don't recall having had an opportunity to vote on any of that stuff.

One of the most controversial projects in recent history was the Hell's Canyon dam on the south fork of the Teton River, a blue-ribbon trout stream. The Army Corps of Engineers blessed the project and gave it a clean bill of health geologically. Opposition came from environmental groups, notably Trout Unlimited, which invested considerable funds in legal and scientific counsel. Their expert witness, an internationally recognized Ph.D. geologist, delivered a convincing documentary of the geological instability of the area and the impracticality of constructing an earthen dam, as proposed. This testimony was ignored, and the project was completed. Within a matter of months, earth tremors caused the dam to give way. The ensuing flood did many millions of dollars' worth of damage and killed nine people. To my knowledge, the feds never even said they were sorry.

These reckless projects can be defeated by intelligent and organized efforts, as has happened many times in recent years. Usually, it can be proven that the project isn't practical in terms of its intended function, and is fiscally unsound. The Tock's Island dam proposal on the lower Delaware River was defeated when the Corps of Engineers was unable to document the many millions of dollars' worth of recreational benefits they claimed. Actually, there would have been a negative recreational effect, and even worse, the annihilation of the great Delaware River shad run, which produces millions in food fish annually.

I could go on indefinitely, citing case after case, but I hope I've already made my point, which is simply that anglers must fight to protect the delicate environment in which our sport exists. This implies a code of personal ethics and conduct—things like returning fish to the water unharmed—and also a commitment to the support of worthy organizations which represent our interests.

Can such organizations be effective? Absolutely! Consider the case of the National Rifle Association. I don't care whether or not you hunt or what your attitudes are toward gun control. The fact is that the NRA is a political miracle—a monument to citizen involvement in the political process. Today, the membership numbers approximately three million, the great majority of whom are of voting age. They cover an extremely broad demographic spectrum, and are diverse in many respects. However, they all agree on one issue, and that is the continuance of the right to own firearms, as provided in the Constitution.

Three million people in one organization, united on a single issue, scares the daylights out of even the most skeptical of politicians. Can you imagine what we fisherpersons of the world could do if we were tightly organized? There are far more fisherpeople than hunters, and we could make three million look like a small number. However, despite diligent efforts, this hasn't happened. Fisherpeople seem to be much less inclined toward effective political action, perhaps because there is no such clearly defined central issue as the right to possess arms.

I contend that there is—or should be—such an issue, and that issue is water, the essential element which supports both fish life and human life. If we could effectively dramatize the threat to all waters, including the pristine and vulnerable waters which comprise trout habitat, we would very quickly establish a broad political base. We would find allies in nonfishing groups, such as mothers who are worried about the water their kids drink and forestry people who see vast woodlands being decimated by acid rain. Equally important, we would make it inescapably obvious to the political sector that fishing is a major industry, both recreationally and commercially, and that fisherpeople represent an enormous constituency.

I urge you to affiliate with a fishing organization—several, in fact. In my opinion, the most important is Trout Unlimited. TU is a national organization committed to the protection and enhancement of the cold-water fishery. It is geographically structured—a national organization which includes a number of paid professional employees, state councils which formulate statewide policies and projects, and individual chapters which represent regions and watersheds. If you live in trout country, there is almost certainly a Trout Unlimited chapter in your area. In fact, there may be one nearby even in an urban area—for example, New York City and metropolitan Long Island have TU chapters.

Trout Unlimited is not a method-oriented organization—that is, they do not exclude persons because of the way they choose to fish. However, it is undeniable that TU consists mainly of fly-fishers, for the simple reason that to date they have been the only ones who care enough to get involved. This is lamentable, as the bait- and spin-fishing practitioners need clean, unspoiled water for their sport just as much as we fly rodders do for ours. It bothers me to think of the thousands of local rod and gun clubs in the trout-supporting regions of the country who spend their efforts beating up on the fisheries-management people of their state to stock more trout when what they really should be saying is, "Hey, let's clean things up."

Currently, a campaign is underway to attract more non-fly-fishers to Trout Unlimited. This has caused some controversy, as the old guard who formed and have long supported TU don't feel too charitably disposed toward these people, who have been indifferent and often hostile to TU's efforts over the years. I hope this can be resolved, so that we can all work together. My position is, "Let's save the resource. Then we can sit down and have the world's biggest fight over how to fish it."

I wrote a letter to the editor of TU's magazine, *Trout,* expressing my views. It was meant to be conciliatory while putting the spin and bait fishers on notice that if they want credibility as conservationist-environmentalists, they need to stop the gross overkill and nonsporting practices in which they currently engage. The letter may never be published in *Trout,* but I include it here, because I feel it strikes to the heart of the issue.

Clifton Park, New York
January 2, 1986

The Editor
Trout Magazine
Box 6225
Bend, OR 97708

Dear Editor:

I read with high interest and considerable amusement the letters, pro and con, pertaining to the great fly-fishing vs. bait-fishing conflict. Isn't it amazing how vitriolic the repartee can get over this long-standing and seemingly unresolvable issue!

More than three decades ago I began my trout-fishing career using spinning tackle and any bait or lure I thought the fish would take. I killed them all, or at least, all that met legal specifications. I and my family ate them and enjoyed them, without guilt.

Now I fish with a vast arsenal of expensive and sophisticated fly tackle. I can tie just about any type of fly one might care to name, including the intimidating fully dressed Atlantic Salmon patterns. I spend large sums to chase after trout and salmon, frequenting the "glory holes" of the angling world. And I have authored three very successful books on fly-fishing and tying, plus numerous articles. A metamorphosis, by any measurement.

I'm a long-time member of TU, along with many other organizations which are engaged in the "save-the-salmonid" wars. I've done a fair amount of work for these groups, TU more so than the others, and I still do, time and personal resources allowing. I have no intention of quitting TU because it has become politic to invite the zip-gunners and worm-washers into the fold. However, I feel compelled to make a few comments.

While habitat preservation and restoral is quite obviously the prime issue, resource management runs a very strong second. In fact, where habitat is still in good condition, I believe resource management *is* the major issue, and I refer specifically to control of fish "harvest" and allowed methodology.

I spent two months in the Rockies last summer, and witnessed a great deal of appalling conduct regarding trout. Some of this was within the law—for example, killing a limit at any opportunity. Some was not, such as cheating on special regulations. I saw Cutthroat trout killed at Buffalo Ford on the Yellowstone, which is against federal regulations. I made a guy release a fish there, risking a smack in the jaw, something age and infirmity leaves me ill equipped to protect against.

With few exceptions, all of this plundering was done by spin fishermen and fisherwomen. Incidentally, I cannot agree that treble-hooked lures are no more injurious than single-hooked ones. You can cite all the statistics you want. We who are out there watching the action know differently. I am not a total no-kill purist. I will "harvest"—yes, that translates to "kill"—a trout or two for the dinner table, on infrequent occasions, when I am positive the resource will not be harmed by my doing so. I even took a few in the Catskills last spring, with discretion, but I won't be doing that again, because it sets a bad example—I've become rather visible these days, thanks to the books. Also, after the drought-induced fish kills of 1985, we don't have any expendable trout in those watersheds.

I guess where I come out is that while I would certainly welcome an alliance with the bait and spin fisherpeople, my personal experience indicates that their rank and file behave in a manner which is diametrically opposed to the concepts of sportsmanship, the principles of resource management and the policies and goals of Trout Unlimited. I offer a challenge to this faction: clean up your act. Stop using tackle and methods which cause high mortality in released fish. Stop stuffing the creels and coolers. Show me by word and deed that you are ready to join with the legions of fly-fisherpeople, who've been fighting the battle these many years, as stewards of the cold-water fisheries. Do these things, and you're OK with me.

Dick Talleur
Clifton Park, New York

So please join Trout Unlimited. It costs so little—basic dues are $15.00 a year at this writing, for which you get an excellent quarterly magazine and other benefits. If you can help by contributing time and talent, so much the better, but at least join, so you may be counted. In many respects, political activism is very much a numbers game. Contact a local chapter, or write TU National as follows:

Trout Unlimited
501 Church Street N-E
Vienna, VA 22180

There are other excellent organizations, some national, others regional and local. One which I hold in particularly high esteem is the Theodore Gordon Flyfishers of New York City. While essentially involved in protecting the trout resources of New York State, TGF has members all over the USA and even in other countries.

TGF started out in the mid-1960s as the New York City chapter of Trout Unlimited. A breach occurred over TGF's use of the term "Flyfishers" in their name—there's that method thing again. While TU was nearly 100 percent fly-fisherpeople, the policy was that embracing a particular methodology was not to be a condition of membership. For a number of years, relations between the two organizations were somewhat strained, but that has been resolved, and they now cooperate closely.

The Gordons have taken advantage of the enormous talent base which exists in the greater New York City area, and are an extremely active and effective organization. They are also a fun group, conducting many informative and enjoyable activities related to fly-fishing and publishing a fine newsletter and an occasional magazine called *Random Casts*. Since many of my readers are certain to be located in TGF's home area—simple statistics ensure that—I will provide the address for obtaining membership information:

Theodore Gordon Flyfishers
P.O. Box 978
Murray Hill Station
New York, NY 10156-0603

I want to mention another fine organization which I'm sure will interest you. This is FFF—the Federation of Fly-Fishers. It is composed of individual members and affiliated clubs throughout the country. Joining FFF is an excellent way to get to know other fly-fishers and learn more about the sport. The organization publishes a most interesting quarterly magazine called *The Fly-Fisher*, and sponsors regional and national conclaves where you can meet the most prominent names and greatest talents in fly-fishing. While not specifically an activist organization, FFF certainly has its head on straight about the issues that concern us all. For membership information, write to:

Federation of Fly-Fishers
Box 1088
West Yellowstone, MT 59758

I really hope that you learn to care enough about fly-fishing that you will become a member of these organizations and perhaps others which serve your particular region or area of interest. The movement sorely needs new talent and a larger base of support. And in addition to making a contribution to a vital cause, you will meet a lot of nice people who will help you with your fishing.

We must not be politically intimidated. When the so-called environmental movement really got going in the late 1960s and early 1970s, we naively thought that all we had to do was communicate our message, with incontrovertible proof about the effects of pollution and so on. But that's not quite the way it works. Industries which felt threatened mobilized against us. Socioeconomic groups turned on us in the erroneous, almost paranoid belief that environmental controls would cost jobs, and we began to see bumper stickers along the lines of "Save a Job—Eat an Environmentalist." There was a lot of dissention and conflict within our own ranks. Those who fished by other than fly-fishing methods thought we were out to get them. And we learned that the Audubon Society, great an organization as it is, does not look kindly on people who tie feathers onto hooks.

The backlash effect culminated with the first Ronald Reagan administration. President Reagan appointed James Watt, a known environmental obstructionist, as Secretary of the Interior. This man was diametrically opposed to the very principles and legalities appurtaining to his position. Such schemes as selling off the national parks to oil and lumber interests were actively pursued. Fortunately, the political process prevailed, and top officials within the Department of the Interior were caught in some major acts of malfeasance. Heads rolled, and one person actually did a little time. This turned out Watt's light, and Reagan "accepted" his resignation before the start of his campaign for reelection.

At this particular point in history we have a federal administration that scares people into supporting it by telling them there are only two issues that matter—economics and foreign affairs. I think this is deplorable. Certainly those issues are important—but they are not the *only* ones. I refuse to believe that maintaining a strong defense and sound economy means we must live with acid rain and dam up free-flowing rivers, and I resent any government to which I pay taxes branding me and millions of other legitimately concerned citizens unpatriotic, by insinuation.

So, as I said, let's not be politically intimidated. We have as much right to protect that which is important to us as do the various industrial and political interests with whom we find ourselves in confrontation. I don't believe the United States Army should have the right to condemn rivers, or that a municipality should have the power to appropriate and abuse the water resources of a vast region, with no accounting. I hope you feel likewise and join the march.

# CHAPTER  XIII _____

# *The Essence*

In the preceding chapters I have sought to communicate the fundamentals of fly-fishing tactics and technology. But fly-fishing goes far beyond mere technology, and I'd like to share some of the pleasures, aesthetics and spirituality with you also.

To myself and many others, fly-fishing is a life-style, an ethic and a frame of reference which creates a unique perspective in our lives. It profoundly influences how I plan other activities and how I structure my time. I think about when my favorite rivers should be prime, and try to schedule my work and personal responsibilities around these times. I'm always inquiring about restaurants that serve late enough that one can get a good meal after the evening spinner fall, and I make it a point to know about the all-night diners where a quick coffee and pastry can be had en route to a rendezvous with an early-morning hatch.

My mental VCR switches on and runs the endless, ever-expanding mind tape of my angling experiences, sometimes sharp and clear, other times a déjà vu. I can see rainbow trout tumbling in midair over the Esopus, the Madison, the Henry's Fork or a high-mountain lake. I can see a pair of brook trout, resplendent in spawning colors, hovering in ecstasy over a gravel bed, as we lie flat on our bellies, watching. A huge salmon leaps again and again at the Laxafoss on Iceland's Grimsa, somehow overcoming this seemingly insurmountable barrier for the privilege of making love in a rockpile many kilometers upstream.

The tape runs a scene from the late 1960s, that era of the flower-child, when a lovely young woman unabashedly skinny-dipped in the pool I was fishing. Sophisticated as I thought I was, I found myself feeling awkward and self-concious as she sunbathed on a large boulder and asked how the fishing was. I didn't leave, however. I am still touched by the innocence of that interlude, and lament that such a thing could never happen in today's social climate.

I am treated to a replay of my old friend Dudley Soper, eking out a living in his cluttered rod shop. Dud was one of the great characters of fly-fishing, and I doubt there will be another like him. There were times when Dud reminded me of Patrick McManus' indomitable Rancid Crab-tree, but there was so much more to the man. He was a virtual chame-leon, able to adapt to the urbanities of a luncheon at the New York Angler's Club as well as the earthy ribaldry of a rural cracker-barrel session. He wrote beautiful poetry and told very funny off-color jokes, but never in bad taste, for Dud was a gentleman. I see his tall, angular frame poised in the tail of a still pool like a great blue heron. Then the rhythmic cast, and a sparsely dressed parachute pattern falls above a rise, gentle as thistledown on a dewy lawn. I miss Dudley and so do a lot of people.

The tape switches to June 1955. I've been fly-fishing for about six weeks, sandwiching it in between worming and minnow fishing. I've caught some small stuff, and am already beginning to think of myself as a quasi-expert. It's early morning, and I'm fishing under a bridge, with fog still lying thick in the ravine. I'm having trouble with the drag on my $4.95 reel, and am fiddling with it, my cast of wet flies washing in the current downstream.

A large trout leaps, and I wonder why. An instant later, I find out—it has taken one of my flies! I play the fish in a state midway between ecstasy and terror—I can't bear the thought of losing this fish. By some miracle, I don't, and at last it is lying spent in my net. Sixteen and a half inches of glistening, golden brown trout—and a fat one at that. Now I *know* I'm an expert. By noon, that unfortunate trout has been in and out of my creel so many times the red spots are worn off.

Next is a scene from the late 1960s. A special no-kill section has been established on one of our blue-ribbon eastern rivers, and we fly-fishers have all become self-righteous, self-appointed game wardens, even though many of us are only recently reformed. I wade around a bend, and there is a man with a spinning rod, launching a night-crawler that looks as though it had starred on "Wild Kingdom."

"Hey! You can't fish with live bait here," I shout. Without a word, he turns and plunges a hand into his bait pail. "What are you doing now?" I ask. "Strangling my worms," comes the wry retort.

It is a long and pleasing tape, and I hope to keep adding to it for many years to come. Of all the pseudo-tapes in my mental library—run-ning marathons, shooting grouse, swishing perimeter jump shots, friends and lovers—the fishing tape is my overwhelming favorite, because it strikes at the essence of my most intense experiences and truest feelings.

To me, fly-fishing is becoming proficient at, but never totally mastering, a game of such dimension that no one person can know it all. It is a succession of successes punctuated by failures. One must be willing to risk failure in this sport, for learning and growth occur only when a person's reach exceeds his or her grasp.

Fly-fishing is about rivers, places, fish, books, tackle, flies and people. It is a Garrison rod—there were less than a thousand of them, and each a consummate masterpiece. It is Ernie Lussier's art work, or Stidham's, Pleissner's, Shaldach's, Abbott's, even Winslow Homer's. It is literature—no sport has been so marvelously chronicled and documented. Skues, Halford, Francis and the other immortal Britishers. The early Americans—Theodore Gordon, George LaBranche, Ed Hewitt, and later Preston Jennings, Ray Bergman and Art Flick. The writers of the American fly-fishing renaissance—Ernest Schwiebert, Bob Boyle, Larry Solomon, Lefty Kreh, Dave Whitlock, Lee Wulff, Charlie Brooks, Charlie Fox, Len Wright, Swisher and Richards, Caucci and Nastasi. The fly-tying writers—Paul Jorgenson, Chauncey Lively, Eric Leiser, Joe Bates. Writers who expand the dimensions of angling—Nick Lyons, Arnold Gingrich, Roderick Haig-Brown.

Fly-fishing is watching Bob Dodge catch a big rainbow on his very first fly that I had showed him how to tie that afternoon. It is being onstream with Russell George, my musician friend who plays in such company as Dizzy Gillespie, Ray Charles, Frank Sinatra, Mel Torme and many other giants. I always smile when I think of Russell hooking a nice brown on a Dun Variant I had tied him and improvising a Sinatra-esque refrain: "I-so-ny-chia does it every time."

Fly-fishing is about handicapped people loving the sport so much they are able to compensate for their afflictions and join in the fun. There was a man who fished the Battenkill for years—his first name was Al, I forgot the last. He was paralyzed on the entire right side of his body from a war injury. Somehow, he mastered fly-fishing, using an automatic fly reel and lots of unique moves. He taught himself to tie flies, using his mouth as a second hand. Now there is a program in Colorado where blind people are being successfully taught to tie flies. Incredible. These are things I think about when minor aches and pains intrude on my pleasure.

There is so much more I could say about what fly-fishing amounts to in my life—but better yet, I hope that what I've written in this volume will put you onstream with confidence and competence, that you may begin to build your own mind-tape library. I wish you the very best of angling success and pleasure.

# BIBLIOGRAPHY

The following books were used as reference:

| | Title | Author | Publisher |
|---|---|---|---|
| 1. | Tying and Fishing Terrestrials | Gerald Almy | Stackpole Books Box 1831 Harrisburg, PA 17105 |
| 2. | Hatches II | Al Caucci, Bob Nastasi | Winchester Press 220 Old New Brunswick Rd Piscataway, NJ 08854 |
| 3. | Art Flick's New Streamside Guide | Art Flick | Winchester Press (See #2) |
| 4. | The Trout and the Fly | John Goddard, Brian Clarke | Winchester Press Nick Lyons Books (See #2) |
| 5. | The Compleat Brown Trout | Cecil E. Heacox | Winchester Press (See #2) |
| 6. | Fly-Casting with Lefty Kreh | Lefty Kreh | J. B. Lippincott Co. Philadelphia and New York |
| 7. | Practical Fishing Knots | Lefty Kreh, Mark Sosin | Winchester Press (See #2) |
| 8. | Stoneflies for the Angler | Eric Leiser, Robert H. Boyle | Alfred A. Knopf New York City |
| 9. | The Caddis and the Angler | Larry Solomon, Eric Leiser | Stackpole Books (See #1) |
| 10. | What the Trout Said | Datus C. Proper | Alfred A. Knopf New York City |
| 11. | Nymphs | Ernest G. Schwiebert | Winchester Press (See #2) |
| 12. | Trout | Ernest G. Schwiebert | Winchester Press (See #2) |
| 13. | Selective Trout | Doug Swisher, Carl Richards | Winchester Press Nick Lyons Books (See #2) |
| 14. | Videotape: All New Flycasting Techniques | Lefty Kreh | Outdoor Safaris International 1221 West Coast Hwy. Newport Beach, CA 92663 |

# Index

(Page numbers in *italics* indicate illustrations)